THE MOVIE LOVER'S TOUR OF
TEXAS

THE MOVIE LOVER'S TOUR OF

TEXAS

REEL-LIFE RAMBLES THROUGH THE LONE STAR STATE

VEVA VONLER

TAYLOR TRADE PUBLISHING

Lanham • New York • Dallas • Boulder • Toronto • Oxford

Published by Taylor Trade Publishing
An imprint of The Rowman & Littlefield Publishing Group, Inc.
4501 Forbes Boulevard, Suite 200, Lanham, Maryland 20706

Distributed by NATIONAL BOOK NETWORK

Library of Congress Cataloging-in-Publication Data
Vonler, Veva.
The movie lover's tour of Texas : reel-life rambles through the Lone Star State /
Veva Vonler.—1st Taylor Trade Publishing ed.
        p.   cm.
Includes index.
ISBN 1-58979-242-4 (pbk. : alk. paper)
1. Motion picture locations—Texas—Guidebooks.   2. Motion picture industry—
Texas—Guidebooks.   3. Texas—Tours.   4. Texas—Description and travel.
5. Texas—In motion pictures.   I. Title.
PN1995.67.T4V66 2005
384'.8'64—dc22
2005008692

To June Edwards Donowho,
who, even before I was born,
took me to the movies in Ranger, Texas

And to my leading men,
Bob and Kevin Huffaker
and Zach

I think a film made in 1923 or 1936 or 1975 tells you
more about the country and the city it was made in
than some of the history books.
MARTIN SCORSESE, 2003

She asked me, baby, what's so great?
How come you're always going on
About the Lone Star State?
LYLE LOVETT, WILLIS ALAN RAMSEY,
and ALISON ROGERS,
"That's Right, You're Not from Texas"

Contents

Acknowledgments

M Y SINCERE THANKS go to Anne L. Cook and Brent Dollar of the Texas Department of Transportation, who graciously and efficiently provided the TxDOT maps and photographs for this book. I am also grateful to Tom Copeland, Director, and Carol Pirie, Assistant Director, of the Texas Film Commission, who patiently responded to question after question. Dozens of other friendly Texans, too many to list here, answered queries; but especially helpful were Rick Ferguson, Executive Director of the Houston Film Commission; Shelly Hargrove, of the Georgetown Convention and Visitors Bureau; Kimbra Peirce, of the Uvalde Convention and Visitors Bureau; and Troyanne Bush, of the Bastrop Chamber of Commerce. Dan Eggleston, Jerry Cotton, and Gordon Smith were also most generous in sharing their knowledge of Texas films and suggesting additional resources. And, finally, I want especially to thank the two people who made sure I persevered in this book-writing adventure: Janet Harris for her unfailing encouragement and editorial expertise, and my husband, Bob Huffaker, for his love and fantastic cooking skills.

Foreword

I'M A VERY LUCKY MAN. For twenty-two years, my job at the Texas Film Commission has been to sell Texas to film-makers. Added to the fact that Texas pretty much sells itself, it's been a lively way to make a living.

In the never-ending search for film locations, I've photographed Texas from windmill platforms, small planes (including one with an open cockpit), helicopters, Humvees, hunting buggies, and bucket trucks. I've worked with ranchers, Texas Rangers, actors, directors, immigration officials, screenwriters, judges, boll weevil inspectors, and folks that seemed to be some combination of all of the above.

Like Coca-Cola, Levi's, and Lucchese, Texas is a brand known all over the world, by its name, its reputation, even its shape. Since the earliest days of the film industry, Texas has been prime real estate for the movies. Sure, there's the stereotypical Texas that Hollywood perpetuated for years; sometimes they even got it right, but many of those films weren't even made in Texas at all. On the other hand, Texas locations have doubled on film for Morocco, Baghdad, San Francisco, Afghanistan, Nevada, Utah, Bolivia, and quite a few more, so I figure we've won a lot more than we've lost.

From Canadian to Brownsville, from El Paso to Port Arthur, Texans have seen on-location filmmaking up close, and enjoyed the fruits of the film dollars that get spent in the process. It never ceases to delight me to visit a film set that's shooting in one of our small towns. It's a welcome windfall, bringing with it community pride, involvement, and, oh yeah, those dollars I mentioned earlier. Just ask the people in Eagle Pass, Sanderson, Smithville, or Marfa, to name a few—they'll tell you how exciting it can be to see your hometown on the big screen.

Now, with this book, you can enjoy an insider's look at Texas movies. At the very least, I hope it inspires you to stick around at the end of movies and watch the credits. You might be surprised at how often Texas shows up in the "Special Thanks to . . ." section. Even better, pack up this book and hit the highway for a Texas road trip. Even after all these years, there's still nothing I'd rather do.

TOM COPELAND, director,
Texas Film Commission
January 2005

Preface

Movies with a Lone Star State of Mind: Lights! Camera! Travel!

ESS PARKER SWINGS his rifle in a fierce last effort to defend the Alamo in *Davy Crockett, King of the Wild Frontier*. John Wayne sets out to drive his herd of longhorns to Missouri in *Red River*. James Dean laughs triumphantly in *Giant* as he is drenched with black gold from his gushing oil well.

Gun battles. Cattle. Oil. These images probably spring to mind when you think of Texas movies. But in some of the thousands of productions filmed here since the earliest days of the movie industry, you will encounter less stereotypical aspects of the state. *The Movie Lover's Tour of Texas* guides you region by region with recommended films that convey the diversity in the landscape, in the people, and in the history of Texas.

You can visit the Gulf Coast with Ed Harris and Amy Madigan aboard shrimp boats in *Alamo Bay*. You can slog among the moss-draped cypress trees of Caddo Lake with Powers Boothe in *Southern Comfort*. You can admire the upscale neighborhood of Shirley MacLaine in *Terms of Endearment* and then compare it to the inner-city streets of *Jason's Lyric*, each film offering a starkly different view of Houston. You can visit the glorious Big Bend with Willie Nelson in *Barbarosa*, or maybe you'd rather join Kevin Costner and his band of new college grads on their *Fandango* road trip through West Texas.

In short, *The Movie Lover's Tour of Texas* invites you to travel around the state without leaving home. All you need for the Reel-Life Tours is a VCR or DVD player. But just in case you choose to hit the road, *The Movie Lover's Tour* also suggests itineraries that will take you to filming locations as well as to other movie-related sites. Each Real-Life Tour and each Travelogue points you toward intriguing destinations such as the actual "last picture show" in Archer City, a couple of North Texas banks that Bonnie and Clyde really held up, and the dance hall where John Travolta performed his heavenly dancing as the title character in *Michael*.

Whether you decide to travel through Texas for "reel" with your remote control or for "real" with your steering wheel, *The Movie Lover's Tour of Texas* offers numerous points of departure for exploring each of these seven tourism regions of the Lone Star State: the vast Panhandle Plains, the vibrant Big Bend Country, the dusty South Texas Plains, the sparkling Gulf Coast, the forested Piney Woods, the laid-back Hill Country, and the centrally located Prairies and Lakes, where characteristics from the other six all converge.

You've only to load the DVD, rewind the tape, or fill up the gas tank, and you're ready for the adventures that await you in *The Movie Lover's Tour of Texas*. So—in the words of at least one of the Texas characters we've all met in the movies—"Let's hit the trail, pardner!"

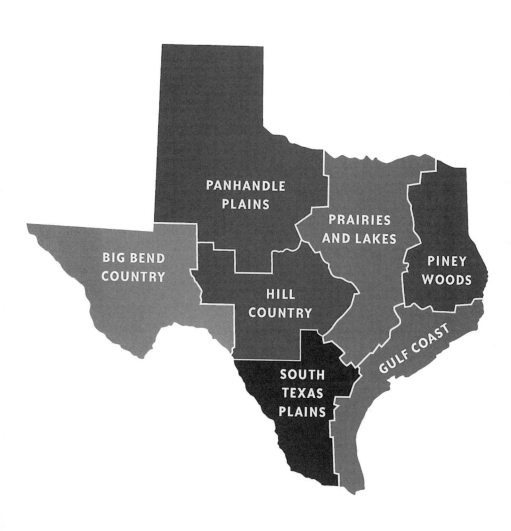

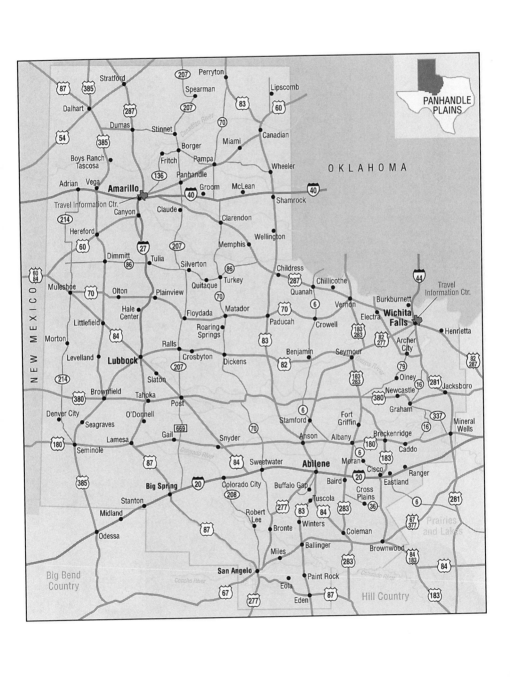

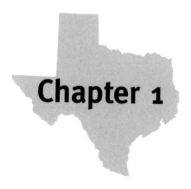

Chapter 1

Panhandle Plains

Only in Texas do you ever see a sunset like that.
Vincent D'Onofrio in *The Whole Wide World*

ESTABLISHING SHOTS

The Region on the Map

"THE PANHANDLE," for most Texans, refers to only a part of this region, that part on the map that juts up with New Mexico on its west and Oklahoma to the north and east. Its south edge is more or less defined by Highway 86 as it runs through Tulia and Estelline and then connects with Highway 287 to Childress. Below that line you'll find the Texas High Plains to the west and the Lower Plains to the east, separated by the Caprock Escarpment. The "Caprock" is a name used by Texans to denote the High Plains area of the Panhandle, but you will sometimes hear the High Plains referred to as the "Llano," a reference to the Spanish explorers' name for this southernmost tip of America's Great Plains: the Llano Estacado.

The regional cities that provide starting points for movie lover's tours are Amarillo, Big Spring, Abilene, and Wichita Falls. At both Amarillo and Wichita Falls, you will find an official Texas Travel Information Center, where you can pick up free maps, brochures, and friendly advice.

The Region Onscreen and Off

The past seems to haunt this section of Texas more than any other, perhaps because of the loneliness of the vast skies and dusty plains stretching down into the Big Bend Country. Despite a few good-sized cities and towns, these plains mostly lack the modern urban distractions that drown out the whispers of history. And those whispers can be melancholy indeed, recalling glories of long-gone oil booms and ranching empires as well as the often bloody travails of pioneering farmers, of soldiers manning frontier forts, of cowboys broiling in summer and freezing in winter. West Texas, the term most Texans use in referring to the combined regions of the Panhandle Plains and Big Bend Country, is today dotted with more than its share of shuttered buildings and deserted main streets.

Early in its development, the movie industry recognized in West Texas a romance and grandeur that was ideally suited to the screen. The makers of classic western movies found a ready-made set of wide open spaces dressed with tumbleweeds, spectacular sunsets, and cactus, which then became synonymous with Texas itself for viewers who did not realize that these movies dealt with only part of the state's landscape.

Of course, similarly sweeping vistas are found in other states as well, and many a movie has claimed to depict Texas when it was actually shot elsewhere, even such classics as *Duel in the Sun*, *The Searchers*, and *Red River*. In fact, *Texas Tex* (1908), possibly the first fictional movie ever made with a Texas setting, was not even filmed in the United States, but rather in Denmark. If loyal Texans are offended by these departures from authenticity, they probably should remind themselves that Texas has often served as a stand-in for other locales, such as Kansas in *Leap of Faith*, Africa in *Ace*

Ventura: Nature Calls, and Iraq in *Courage Under Fire*, to mention only a very few.

The Panhandle Plains region encompasses the stomping grounds of Charles Goodnight and Oliver Loving, the original cattle drivers who blazed a trail into New Mexico. When Loving died a premature death there in 1867, Goodnight honored his friend's request to be buried in Texas, transporting his body by buckboard to Weatherford's Greenwood Cemetery. If that trip sounds familiar, you've probably seen or read *Lonesome Dove*, which draws on some of these men's adventures.

Goodnight placed his permanent brand on the Panhandle in 1876, when he and John Adair founded the JA Ranch by driving into the magnificent Palo Duro Canyon 1,800 head of cattle, a herd that eventually increased to 100,000. Although the partnership lasted only a little over a decade, the JA Ranch continues in operation today, along with numerous others that sprang up following Goodnight's lead. Then in 1883 the Ogallala aquifer was tapped for irrigation, and soon farms became as numerous as ranches. Those early farming days in the Panhandle serve as the setting for the 1978 film *Days of Heaven*, although the movie's spectacular scenery is not that of Texas, but rather of Alberta, Canada, where Texas native Terrence Malick shot the movie.

Not only did Charles Goodnight inspire much of the lore we associate with the movie cowboy, but he also decided in 1916 at age eighty to make a movie himself. Apparently wishing to leave a record of the West as he knew it, he filmed real cowboys—not gunfighters—and real Indians who were not necessarily hostile to the whites. He even staged a buffalo hunt featuring Kiowa Indians killing the buffalo as their ancestors had. The film, called *Old Texas*, was shown to groups in Colorado and New York, but it was not viewed widely. Perhaps Goodnight's insistence on accuracy kept his film out of competition with the more romantic accounts in the Hollywood-produced westerns. The imagination of the public had already been captured by what T. H. Watkins calls "predigested folk drama, very simple stories acted out very simply to prove very simple things. You've got your good guys; you've got your bad guys."

REEL-LIFE AND REAL-LIFE TOURS
Feature Presentations:
Panhandle Plains in a Starring Role

The Wind (1927)
Lillian Gish, Lars Hanson, and Dorothy Cumming
Directed by Victor Sjostrom

Reel-Life Tour

Although not filmed in Texas, *The Wind* offers a realistic, if rather disturbing, view of life on the Texas frontier of the 1880s and is also worth watching as one of the last great silent films ever made. The filming locations in the Mojave Desert are very similar to the West Texas plains around Sweetwater, where the story is set. Based on Dorothy Scarborough's novel of the same name, the film effectively visualizes the setting the author described as a place where "there was nothing to break the sweep of the wind across the treeless prairies."

Lillian Gish plays Letty, a sheltered young woman from Virginia, who tries to adjust to the hostile landscape and the inhospitable home of her cousin Cora. For the sake of survival, Letty marries one of the half-civilized cowboys. While he is away most of the time working, she becomes increasingly desperate as a result of her solitude, accompanied only by the unceasing howls of the wind. The titles underscore her misery: "Wind Sand Wind Sand Yesterday Tomorrow Forever." MGM ordered a happier ending than the one Scarborough wrote in her novel; but even so, Letty is still left with the grim fate of the frontier wife, like that of her cousin Cora, who in one memorable scene carves up a steer's carcass hanging in her living room.

The force of nature that threatened Lillian Gish with madness in *The Wind* is demonstrated at Lubbock's American Wind Power Center. Courtesy of Kevin Stillman/TxDOT

Real-Life Tour: Sweetwater

Needless to say, today's women of Sweetwater, Texas, do not suffer the physical and societal hardships that oppressed Letty and Cora. In fact, the city's Chamber of Commerce indignantly called *The Wind* libelous when Scarborough published it in 1925. Perhaps the book and the movie exaggerated the horrors women faced on the frontier. You may want to visit the Pioneer City-County Museum to judge for yourself by viewing photographs and exhibits detailing early settlers in the region. You may also consider attending the popular Rattlesnake Roundup that Sweetwater sponsors each March, when prizes are awarded for largest and smallest snakes captured, and the climactic event is a rattlesnake-eating contest.

The Sundowners (1950)
Robert Preston, Robert Sterling, John Barrymore Jr.,
and Jack Elam
Directed by George Templeton

Reel-Life Tour

The Sundowners, not to be confused with the 1960 movie of the same name about Australian sheepherders, follows the typical B-western pattern, emphasizing horses and gunplay. It was filmed on location around Amarillo and the gorgeous Palo Duro Canyon, and features Robert Preston playing Kid Wichita, a gunslinger who confronts the no-good cattle rustlers threatening his brothers' livelihood.

The opening credits of The Sundowners acknowledge the filming locations, even giving the names of specific ranches and their owners—Newton Harrell, John Currie, and Hugh Currie—along with graphics of their cattle brands. For anyone old enough to remember the Saturday morning "kiddie shows," those opening credits rolling over a garishly colored sunset-with-windmill scene accompanied with swelling background music can easily arouse nostalgic recollections of popcorn, jujubes, and bubble gum, creating the proper frame of mind to enjoy the story.

The Sundowners realistically chronicles frontier family dynamics and the still emerging rule of law in the Panhandle. The father of the feckless sheriff is a kind of Goodnight-like fellow who mourns his son's character flaws as much as his death. The only married couple we meet offers a grim portrait of a loveless union in which the wife, like Letty in The Wind, apparently sees marriage as necessary to a woman's survival on the frontier.

The Technicolor shots of Palo Duro Canyon are especially beautiful, as are the many scenes of cowboys roping and herding and shooting at each other among the wildly dramatic and colorful rock formations. Other shots of the flat plains under blue skies suggest the vast majesty of the Panhandle Plains. Even the sardonic character of Kid Wichita acknowledges the landscape's awesomeness by jokingly claiming to be the creator of the canyon, saying on one occasion, "You see that rock over there? I had more trouble with that rock than I had diggin' the rest of this here canyon." *The Sundowners* is fun to watch just for the scenery, but it also offers an interesting story and respectable acting.

Real-Life Tour: Palo Duro Canyon

Palo Duro Canyon, the second-largest canyon in the United States, is all the more breathtaking because after you have driven through apparently endless monotonous plains, you suddenly come upon an unheralded slash in the earth and look down at a riot of colors, shapes, and textures. With depths up to eight hundred feet, the canyon has spawned eye-catching rock formations, such as the Sad Monkey and the Devil's Slide. One called the Lighthouse is probably the one Kid Wichita claims to have placed there in *The Sundowners*.

A small part of the canyon, located about fifteen miles southeast of Amarillo, was designated Palo Duro Canyon State Park in 1933. The park's eight-mile drive to the canyon floor provides awe-inspiring views and a chance to follow the route used by Charles Goodnight when he drove his 1,800 head of cattle into the canyon in 1876 to establish the first ranch in the Panhandle.

The Whole Wide World (1996)
Renée Zellweger, Vincent D'Onofrio, and Ann Wedgeworth
Directed by Dan Ireland

Reel-Life Tour

The Whole Wide World takes us into twentieth-century Texas, the 1930s to be exact, and it features authentic characterizations, automobiles, and architecture. The story is based on Novalyne Price's memoir of her relationship with Robert E. Howard, the creator of such pulp icons as Conan the Barbarian and Red Sonya. Set in the southeastern area of the Panhandle Plains, in and around the towns of Cross Plains and Brownwood, the movie details a touching almost love affair between two young people, each struggling to find a coherent view of reality and a voice to describe it.

Zellweger plays Novalyne, a bright aspiring teacher and a writer of *True Confessions* stories such as "I Gave My Daughter Movie Fame." The movie opens with a lovely shot of vacant summer fields and blue sky and a Model T stirring up the dust. Novalyne's voice-over announces: "I met Robert Howard today," and she departs from her grandmother's typical front porch to go for the first of many drives she will share with Robert, played by D'Onofrio. They immediately begin discussing their favorite writers, and in the unlikely setting of a West Texas back road, they delightedly quote the likes of H. L. Mencken.

Despite her attraction to Robert, Novalyne moves on to devote herself to becoming a teacher rather than a writer; but, as her memoir affirms, she never forgot the tormented young man who sparked her own youthful imagination. The movie that memoir inspired offers a fascinating view of small-town life on the southeastern edge of West Texas in the 1930s.

Real-Life Tour: Cross Plains, Brownwood

The Whole Wide World was shot in Texas, but not in the Panhandle Plains, where the story takes place. The movie was filmed in a much greener region, around Austin, amid prairies rather than plains; but anyone interested in the subject of this film would surely want to make a pilgrimage to Cross Plains, where the Robert E. Howard House has been restored to the way it looked when Howard lived there with his family from 1919 till his death in 1936. Also, the Cross Plains Public Library features first editions of many of Howard's books along with some of his original manuscripts.

About thirty miles south of Cross Plains is Brownwood, where Novalyne Price studied at Daniel Baker College, later incorporated into Howard Payne University, and where Robert Howard is buried near his mother in the historic Greenleaf Cemetery.

The Stars Fell on Henrietta (1995)
Robert Duvall, Aidan Quinn, and Frances Fisher
Directed by James Keach

Reel-Life Tour

Like *The Whole Wide World*, another movie that lacked wide distribution, *The Stars Fell on Henrietta* is worth searching out for its view of life on the Texas plains during the Great Depression. Its main characters are ordinary farm people instead of radical, intellectual seekers like Novalyne and Robert; their primary concerns are economic rather than literary. Aidan Quinn and Frances Fisher play Don and Cora Day, who are trying to make a go of a small cotton farm on the outskirts of Henrietta, Texas. Into their semi-desperate lives comes Mr. Cox, played by Robert Duvall in one of his patented lovably eccentric roles, who claims to be able to hear oil under the ground. Because the Days are about to lose their farm to the bank in Henrietta, Don is susceptible to the promise of riches inherent in Cox's assurances that a huge pool of oil exists under the property. But Cora is more than skeptical and kicks Don out of the house when he brings home drilling equipment.

The film is loaded with period details and characters who epitomize the spirit of these plains during the 1930s. The very way in which Mr. Cox meets the Days is a case in point. Don observes Mr. Cox and his cat, Matilda, sitting by the side of the road and stops to see if he needs any help. Cox replies in the negative, and Don drives on home; but a short time later, when a horrible dust storm strikes, Don ventures out to bring Cox and cat into the safety of the farmhouse. This is just one of many examples in the film of everyday decent folks looking out for one another. Of course, there are bad guys also. One of the worst is the owner of a Greek restaurant where Cox works briefly as dishwasher. He is obviously one of those "foreigners" from back East and exploits the locals shamelessly as employees while he simultaneously fawns over anyone he thinks has money.

Duvall's touching yet humorous Mr. Cox is one of several Texas characters he's brought to vivid life on the screen. His importance to the state's movie industry was recognized by the Texas Film Hall of Fame in 2004, when he was presented with official papers making him an honorary Texan. In keeping with the tenor of Duvall's performance, *The Stars Fell on Henrietta* manages to be a feel-good movie without tipping over into sentimentality. The Panhandle Plains region is realistically portrayed with the Depression-era dust storms swirling around hardworking people trying to eke out a living on depleted soil while they watch the oil derricks sprout and gush riches for the fortunate few.

Real-Life Tour: Henrietta, Abilene, Anson

The real Henrietta is located on State Highway 287 about twenty miles southeast of Wichita Falls, and while no significant evidence of the Oil Boom remains in town, you can drive west on Highway 82 about twenty-eight miles to Nocona, then go north about seven miles until you find yourself in the middle of the North Field: acres and acres of pumping oil wells as far as the eye can see, still productive almost a century after oil was first struck here in 1912. However, *The Stars Fell on Henrietta* was not filmed in Henrietta. As often happens, the actual place was deemed inappropriate, and much of the film was shot farther west, in various locations around the Panhandle Plains towns of Abilene and Anson. The oil boom town itself was recreated in the Prairies and Lakes town of Bartlett.

Double Feature:
The Last Picture Show (1971) and *Texasville* (1990)
Timothy Bottoms, Jeff Bridges, Cloris Leachman,
and Cybill Shepherd
Directed by Peter Bogdanovich

Reel-Life Tour

These two movies offer interesting snapshots of a small Pan-handle Plains town, first as it was in 1951 and then as it was thirty years later. The town is Archer City, renamed "Anarene" for the films, and most of the same characters—played by the same actors—appear in both movies. *The Last Picture Show*, a multi-Oscar-winning classic, presents a grimly realistic account of frustrated lives. Fortunately for the producers, most viewers recognized the lovely artistry of the movie despite the unlovely surface of its setting. The mournfulness of the story is undeniable, and the local folks were rather upset by the scandalous behavior of the movie people both onscreen and off, but *The Last Picture Show* offers a true-to-life picture of one of many dying West Texas towns in the mid-twentieth century. The music heard on the soundtrack coming from pickup radios and jukeboxes is the same music that played in 1951; the interactions of townspeople are completely believable, whether they're grousing about the failures of the high school football team or sharing tales of economic woe. Thanks to excellent coaching, the actors for the most part get the accent right, too, although in at least one scene Timothy Bottoms says "somethang" rather than the real Texas pronunciation, "somethin'."

For a wealth of background information on the production of *The Last Picture Show*, see the filmed reminiscences of the director and several of the actors which accompany the DVD version of the movie. And for even more juicy tales, look up the February 1999 issue of *Texas Monthly* magazine and read Don Graham's cover story, "The Making of *The Last Picture Show*: Jeff Bridges, Cybill Shepherd, and Others Remember the Filming of a Texas Classic." In this article, Bogdanovich recounts, for example, how he decided to make the film in Archer City. And he and other participants describe how their shared off-camera dramas served to enhance the passions shown on the screen.

Texasville did not enjoy the critical acclaim that greeted *The Last Picture Show*, but taken on its own terms, it is an entertaining follow-up. Some Archer City residents who deplored the first movie's unflattering portrayal had perhaps been mollified by its great commercial and artistic success, for nineteen years later most of them enthusiastically welcomed the filming of the sequel. It didn't hurt, of course, that several of the cast members, mostly unknown in 1970, had subsequently become Big Stars and lent Hollywood glamour to the shoot.

The high school seniors of *The Last Picture Show* have reached middle age in *Texasville*. Duane (Bridges) is now an oil company owner facing the specter of financial ruin in the declining economy of 1984. Sonny (Bottoms), who still seems dazed by his teenage traumas, is mayor of Anarene and trying to manage the planning of a centennial celebration for the town. Much slapstick humor ensues, but the end of the film finds Jacy (Shepherd) joining her old mates in an affectionate, if rueful, acknowledgment of their past and future foolishnesses. Annie Potts plays Duane's sharp-tongued wife, Karla, who is a welcome addition to the original cast even if she does mispronounce the name of Bowie, confusing the rock star's name with that of the North Texas town.

Real-Life Tour: Archer City, Wichita Falls, Olney

Archer City is the town Larry McMurtry wrote about in his novels, even though he called it Thalia, so it was an unusual convergence with reality that Peter Bogdanovich decided to film his movies there. Archer City hasn't changed a great deal since *The Last Picture Show*, although several of the buildings are no longer standing. The pool hall, for example, was torn down in the 1970s. But you'll recognize the square, the Dairy Queen just south of town, and, of course, the Royal Theatre.

Sadly, the Royal had burned to the ground in 1965, so the interior movie theater scenes in *The Last Picture Show* were filmed inside the West Tex theater down the road from Archer City in Olney. Unfortunately, that theater has disappeared, replaced on Olney's Main Street with a gazebo and courtyard. The shell of the Royal shows up in *Texasville* when the confused Sonny imagines he is watching a movie there, but today the theater has been reconstructed and serves as a venue for live music, plays, and films.

Wichita Falls is the "big city" where the Anarene characters go for shopping and entertainment. The swimming-pool scene in *The Last Picture Show* was shot there, as were some scenes in *Texasville*.

Hud (1962)
Paul Newman, Melvyn Douglas, Patricia Neal, and
Brandon de Wilde
Directed by Martin Ritt

Reel-Life Tour

Hud offers Paul Newman at his antihero, gorgeous, sexy best playing a reprehensible skunk. In another black-and-white film based on a Larry McMurtry novel, Newman *is*, as the posters declare, the title character, a crude and unscrupulous young Texan who works on the small ranch of his disapproving father, Homer Banning, played by Oscar-winning Melvyn Douglas. The film's director, Martin Ritt, has expressed surprise that the audience favors the rascal Hud over the moralizing old man, but McMurtry understands the appeal. He points out in his 1968 book of essays called *In a Narrow Grave* that Hud's portrayal suggests the archetypal "Westerner which movies themselves have helped create." He even goes so far as to identify Hud as Charles Goodnight's descendant, facing the disintegration of the old ways and values. "If the Old Man were

Hud's age today," McMurtry says, "what would he do? . . . If [he] were ranching now the frustration it would entail might cause him to waste his force in the same ways Hud wastes his. And Hud, given a frontier, might become a Charles Goodnight."

The movie opens with titles over an expansive shot of a straight, straight highway running through barren, absolutely flat land. Music from the transistor radio in his shirt pocket accompanies Lonnie—played by Brandon de Wilde, the now grown-up kid from *Shane*—as he wanders through the early-morning streets of Thalia looking for his uncle Hud. The wind is blowing smartly, as is usual in the Panhandle, when Lonnie spots Hud's Cadillac convertible in front of a married woman's house.

Lonnie is summoning Hud to the ranch because of a mysteriously dead cow. Ultimately the death turns out to have been caused by hoof-and-mouth disease, and Homer must destroy his entire herd. The scene where the cattle are rounded up and shot is truly horrifying, but its crisp black-and-white cinematography invites an interesting comparison with the Technicolor version of cowboys using exactly the same methods to herd cattle around Palo Duro Canyon in *The Sundowners*.

The conflict between Hud and his father becomes more heated. Not only does Homer deplore Hud's general behavior, but he is appalled at Hud's suggestion that he should have sold the cattle to unsuspecting buyers before the disease was confirmed. Hud, who wants to drill for oil, tries to have his father declared incompetent so he can gain control, and he shows no compassion even when his father dies of a heart attack.

At the end of the movie, Hud is indeed in charge of the ranch. The sensitive Lonnie can't deal with the demands of a ranch that has lost its cattle, so he leaves. Hud will turn it into an oil field if possible; if not, he will keep fighting some other way to come out on top.

When the movie came out in 1963, it caught the imagination of many young Texas males, such as Joe Buck in *Midnight Cowboy*, who hangs a *Hud* movie poster in his New York hotel room. Aside from the magnetism of Newman's performance, the authenticity of the movie impressed Texans. There are plenty of familiar details. In another Oscar-winning role, Patricia Neal as the housekeeper believably carries out her domestic duties, preparing typical meals in the kitchen, serving ice cream from a freezer, and eating it while sitting on the front porch to catch the cool night air. The interactions of townspeople in the little café and in the movie theater all look and sound right. No doubt many of the extras were inhabitants of Claude, where the movie was shot; the high school boys wear jackets with C's on them.

Visually, *Hud* evokes the harsh but magnificent beauty of the Panhandle Plains; the power of the landscape is a real presence, thanks to the marvelous cinematography of James Wong Howe. You see the bright, wide-open country, not the claustrophobic, desiccated town of *The Last Picture Show*. But the sense of time passing and inevitable loss permeates both movies.

Real-Life Tour: Claude, Palo Duro Canyon

The crossroads of US 287 and FM 1151 are easy to recognize near the little town of Claude, about thirty miles southeast of Amarillo; and the town itself looks much as it did when *Hud* was filmed there decades ago. The movie's ranch house was only a mile or so outside of Claude, but the cattle-working scenes were filmed near the edge of Palo Duro Canyon. Larry McMurtry expressed his approval of the location this way: "There was a certain fitness in having a film which was in some sense about the end of ranching filmed so near the place where Old Man Goodnight had established the first Panhandle ranch . . . the great JA . . . whose present headquarters are only a few miles from where *Hud* was filmed."

You might enjoy reading McMurtry's entire essay, "Here's HUD in Your Eye," which is the first one in his 1968 book called *In a Narrow Grave: Essays on Texas*. It includes hilarious and irreverent observations on the interactions between the Hollywood folk and the locals during the filming of *Hud*.

Documentary/Short: *Growin' a Beard* (2003)
Scott McAfee and Roy Wardlow
Directed by Mike Woolfe

Reel-Life Tour

Growin' a Beard is a thirty-minute film that takes you to the Panhandle town of Shamrock. As its name suggests, the town is proud of its Irish roots, having developed from the 1890s post office in the dugout home of an Irish sheep rancher. The movie documents the biggest annual event in Shamrock—St. Patrick's Day. To be more precise, it documents the preparations of some of the townspeople for that yearly extravaganza—men growing competitive beards.

These men, in anticipation of the beard-judging contest, stop shaving after New Year's Day, and the filmmaker follows their progress as they nurture their facial hair into the required Donegal, a particular style of Irish beard usually associated with leprechauns. The five men discuss their efforts and display their progress as the weeks pass, with the film tracing their story through the final judging at the St. Patrick's Day celebration. In the process, the viewer is introduced to life in this particular small town. Although there is humor in the very seriousness of the contestants' dedication to the competition, the filmmaker treats the townspeople with respect and does not reach for laughs at the expense of his subjects. A certain amateurishness adds to the charm of the film. For example, when a wandering cat is allowed to interrupt an interview, you have the feeling you are watching a genuine slice of life.

Growin' a Beard provides just a brief view of a little piece of the Panhandle Plains, but the DVD offers a couple of bonuses for the movie lover's vicarious tour. First of all, there is a featurette on the premiere of the film in Shamrock, giving more glimpses into the town. Photographs from the 1939 St. Patrick's Day parade, one year after its inception as an annual event, are of historical interest. And Mike Woolfe also includes another short he made called

The 72 Oz. Steak, which documents one man's attempt to eat the four-and-a-half-pound steak dinner at Amarillo's Big Texan restaurant. The full name of the establishment is the Big Texan Steak Ranch and Opry, and for decades it has offered this meal free to anyone who can polish it off in one hour. A fictionalized attempt is enacted by Billy Bob Thornton in the movie *Waking Up in Reno.*

Real-Life Tour: Shamrock

Since 1938, Shamrock has celebrated St. Patrick's Day on the weekend nearest March 17, with tons of Irish food, fun, and festivities, including a parade, the crowning of Miss Irish Rose, and, of course, the beard contest. If you miss this two-day event, you can still view a fragment of the genuine Blarney Stone from County Cork, Ireland, in Shamrock's Elmore Park and pay a visit to the Pioneer West Museum, housed in the former Reynolds Hotel, a typical drummer's hotel of the 1920s. Shamrock also claims the "tallest water in Texas," in reference to its 50,000-gallon tank that reaches 181 feet into the sky.

Grand Champion (2004)
Jacob Fisher, Joey Lauren Adams, and Emma Roberts
Directed by Barry Tubb

Reel-Life Tour

Texas native Barry Tubb wrote and directed this film, which he has called his "love letter to Texas." Intended to be a wholesome film for the entire family, *Grand Champion* recounts the adventures of some children who abscond with a champion steer named Hokey before he can become barbecue. Joey Lauren Adams plays a single mother whose young son, Buddy, played by Jacob Fisher, has raised the steer and then is horrified when he learns what the buyer is planning to do with Hokey. Bruce Willis as the buyer is only one of a slew of cameo players, including Julia Roberts, whose niece Emma Roberts plays Buddy's sister. (Anyone in the market for romance should note that it was on location in Texas for this film that Julia and future hubby, cinematographer Danny Moder, heated up their romance.) Other cameos include numerous Texas music luminaries such as George Strait, Joe Ely, Robert Earl Keen, and Natalie Maines.

In addition to the authenticity brought to the film by these Lone Star State personalities and by the creative oversight of loyal native son Tubb, an extensive visual tour of West Texas locales rewards the viewer of *Grand Champion*.

Real-Life Tour: Snyder

Barry Tubb's hometown, Snyder, provides many of the locations for *Grand Champion*, including the Scurry County Coliseum, the Travis gym, and Tubb's grandfather's house. On the Coliseum grounds you can visit Heritage Village, made up of restored historic structures. The Scurry County Museum is worth a visit to review the city's history as an oil town and as the home of famed buffalo hunter J. Wright Mooar. The rare albino buffalo he brought down in the 1870s is celebrated with a white buffalo sculpture on the city square. Also on the square is the restored Ritz Theater, now home to live performances rather than the movies it was built to screen.

Short Takes: Panhandle Plains in a Supporting Role

The Buddy Holly Story (1978)
Gary Busey, Charles Martin Smith, Don Stroud,
and Maria Richwine
Directed by Steve Rash

Not filmed in Texas, *The Buddy Holly Story* used a much-too-lush-looking stand-in for Lubbock, but it is still an excellent biographical movie with an outstanding performance by Gary Busey in the title role of the Panhandle Plains singer/songwriter. If you are a fan of the singer, you will want to visit Lubbock's Buddy Holly

Center and pay homage to the Buddy Holly Statue and Walk of Fame, which pays tribute to other Texas natives who have distinguished themselves in the entertainment industry. You might also want to take in some live music at the nearby Cactus Theater, a restored 1930s movie house.

Leap of Faith (1992)
Steve Martin, Debra Winger, Lolita Davidovich, and Liam Neeson
Directed by Richard Pearce

Leap of Faith may have offended some locals because of its cynical take on tent-revival evangelists and because it is supposed to take place in fictional Rustwater, Kansas, not Texas; but it nevertheless offers a cinematic tour of the Texas High Plains countryside and downtown Plainview, where several scenes were shot in the Quick Lunch Diner and on the surrounding streets of Seventh and Broadway. Memories of the filming linger in photos on the diner walls and in the still visible Rustwater Bengals logo painted by the film crew on the nearby water tower. In addition to visiting these filming locations, movie lovers will also want to check out the two 1920s movie palaces on Broadway: the Granada and the renovated Fair Theater.

Leap of Faith's revival tent was fabricated in Groom, a few miles east of Amarillo, where other scenes were shot, including the appearance of school buses labeled "Groom ISD." Perhaps the film's producers were drawn to Groom in part because of its famous landmark, the Cross of Our Lord Jesus Christ, which towers over the flat prairie. It stands 190 feet tall at the intersection of I-40 and FM295 and is visible from almost twenty miles away.

Cast Away (2000)
Tom Hanks, Helen Hunt, and Wilson the Volleyball
Directed by Robert Zemeckis

OK, you don't associate Texas with islands in the middle of the ocean, but this Tom Hanks vehicle does include some great shots

of a lonely Panhandle crossroads—remember those four highways stretching way out there to the horizon? Those scenes near
the end of the movie, when Tom is searching for his former fi-
ancée, were filmed near the town of Canadian, more specifically
on the Arrington Ranch, a fifth-generation working beef cattle
and guest ranch.

Midnight Cowboy (1969)
Jon Voight, Dustin Hoffman, Sylvia Miles, and Brenda Vaccaro
Directed by John Schlesinger

If you haven't seen this movie in a while, you may have forgot-
ten how much footage there is of Joe Buck's life in Texas before he
left for New York City. The opening scenes, starting with the credits, show off the streets of Big Spring in the 1960s. The first shot is
of a completely white background which, as the camera pulls
back, turns out to be the sunlit screen of the Big Tex Drive-In. Joe
Buck is then seen in his Big Spring Motel room, and as the credits
roll, he leaves the room to stride through the streets to Miller's
Restaurant. On the way he passes the Rio movie theater, its marquee
announcing John Wayne's *The Alamo* with unevenly spaced let-
ters. He boards a bus to New York, and you watch with him the
desolate countryside as it passes outside the windows. The other
passengers are typical West Texas folks, including an old cow-
hand chewing tobacco. Joe Buck's transistor radio picks up a faith
healer's rant, and he observes "Jesus Saves" lettered on a rooftop
along the highway, triggering the first of many flashbacks to his
lonely youth, filmed around the town of Stanton. The Millhollon
Place, built around 1906, shows up in these flashbacks along with
Moss Creek Lake for the baptism scene. Jon Voight speaks with a
believable Texas accent as Joe Buck, and his character remains ag-
gressively "Texan" in Manhattan. He hangs a poster of Paul Newman as Hud in his hotel room and uses expressions like "gonna
snatch you baldheaded," a familiar threat to misbehaving West
Texas kids.

Hangar 18 (1980)
Darren McGavin, Robert Vaughn, and Gary Collins
Directed by James L. Conway

Although the residents of Big Spring enjoyed the excitement created by the shooting of *Midnight Cowboy* in their hometown, they—along with most Texans probably—were rather shocked when they saw the finished movie, which was a bit risqué for the times. And they were still talking about it more than ten years later when the next movie crew came to town. *Hanger 18* is infinitely inferior to *Midnight Cowboy*, but at least it presumably did not outrage anyone's morals. A sci-fi story based on the Roswell, New Mexico, legends of alien landings, this movie features scenery around Big Spring and shots of the former Webb Air Force Base, which had been closed in 1977 and converted to a prison. Downtown scenes were filmed in Midland.

Melody Ranch (1940)
Gene Autry and Bob Wills
Directed by Joseph Santley

Melody Ranch is not really a Texas movie; in fact, it's hard to know what state has the greatest claim to it. Gene Autry, a Texas native in real life, plays an Arizona native returning to his hometown in this film, which was shot in California. The movie lover's tour claims it because it features a true Texas icon, playing himself: Bob Wills, who turned up in numerous shorts and feature-length movies during the 1940s. Known as Bob Wills and His Texas Playboys, his band popularized a style of music called Texas swing, which continues to be a big part of the Texas music scene today. The town of Turkey, in the Panhandle, celebrates this native son with its annual Bob Wills Reunion in April, with a monument at the end of Main Street, and with the Bob Wills Museum showcasing memorabilia such as fiddles, boots, and hats. Turkey also is home to a restored movie theater, the Gem, built in 1928 and worth a visit.

Indiana Jones and the Last Crusade (1989)
Harrison Ford, Sean Connery, and Denholm Elliott
Directed by Steven Spielberg

The final scene of *Indiana Jones and the Last Crusade*, with its riding-off-into-the-sunset image, was filmed on the Figure 3 Ranch, about a thirty-minute drive southeast of Amarillo. Although the movie pretends that the spectacular view is in the Middle East, it is actually near Palo Duro Canyon. Moreover, you can go there to sample some authentic Old West atmosphere if you choose to experience the Figure 3's Cowboy Morning, which includes a wagon ride from the ranch to the canyon's rim, where breakfast is prepared using a campfire and chuck wagon. Alternatively, you can opt for Cowboy Evening, a steak dinner similarly presented. Either adventure can be a dream come true for a fan of movie cattle drives.

Cadillac Ranch (1996)
Suzy Amis, Renée Humphrey, Caroleen Feeney,
and Christopher Lloyd
Directed by Lisa Gottlieb

Like *The Whole Wide World*, the movie *Cadillac Ranch*, with its setting in the Panhandle Plains, was actually filmed down around Austin. It recounts the adventures of three sisters who, despite years of animosity, join forces to hunt for a stash of money hidden by their deceased father. If you have seen it, or even if you haven't, you'll probably want to make a run out west of Amarillo on I-40 to see the real title subject: ten Cadillacs half-buried, with their back bumpers sticking up, reportedly, at the same angle as Cheops' pyramids. Dubbed by its creator as "avant garde art," Cadillac Ranch is located on the south side of the I-40 between exits 60 and 62 and is said to represent the "golden age of automobiles," from 1949 through 1963.

PANHANDLE PLAINS TRAVELOGUES
Scouting the Locations

Planning driving tours in the Panhandle Plains can be a challenge; you'll quickly discover that it's difficult to plan a trip without at least one or two double-backs. Texans are used to driving long distances, but other folks may be dismayed at how far it can be between restaurants and gas stations. We're not exactly talking the Sahara here, but you will probably want to carry water and snacks with you when you set out to explore. Especially during spring and summer, you need also to be aware of the vicious storms that can be upon you with amazing suddenness, unleashing buckets of rain and enormous hailstones. In the winter you ought to carry a blanket or two in case of car trouble between towns. The landscape can be stark, to say the least, but many people have been enchanted by its luminous grandeur, which you can experience by driving some movie-related routes.

Amarillo ➤ Groom ➤ Shamrock ➤ Canadian ➤ Pampa ➤ Amarillo (240 miles)

The unofficial "Capital of the Panhandle," Amarillo is a good place to begin your exploration of the Panhandle Plains. You can pick up maps and brochures at the Texas Travel Information Center, located on I-40 East, as well as at the downtown Amarillo Visitor Information Center on Buchanan Street. You're sure to find friendly folks at both locations, perhaps even some fellow movie lovers who will suggest local sites to visit. If you're hungry—really hungry—you may want to stop first at the Big Texan Steak House, located at 7701 I-40E and featured in the DVD bonus materials for *Growin' a Beard* as well as in *Waking Up in Reno*, a movie with no other reason to be mentioned here. Then you can continue east on I-40 to Groom and visit areas filmed in *Leap of Faith*. The Bible Belt flavor of that movie is borne out when you catch sight of the gigantic Cross of Our Lord Jesus Christ, which stands near I-40 just west of Groom. A related site to visit is the Blessed Mary Restaurant, where you pay what you wish for your food and the proceeds are all given to charities.

At Shamrock, after checking out the Irish connections and meeting the friendly inhabitants like those in *Growin' a Beard*, you have a good reason to get off the interstate and travel north on Texas Highway 83 about fifty miles to Canadian, where you will encounter a terrain vastly different from that generally associated with the Panhandle, a terrain of many hills and valleys and enough trees along the banks of the Canadian River to have inspired an annual Fall Foliage Festival. The scenes from *Cast Away*, however, featured a crossroads stretching across the flattest of plains as far as the eye can see in every direction. To visit that location, head for the Arrington Ranch House Lodge on US 60, where you can see the two-story house featured in the film. You can even stay there if you like, since it is a B and B. The town of Canadian has its own attractions, including a wonderful old building that opened in 1909 as a vaudeville house called The Pastime Theatre. Renamed The Queen, it provided a venue for silent films in the 1920s and then was finally dubbed The Palace Theatre for the showing of the first talking film in 1932. It was completely restored and reopened as a first-run theater in 1998, the only theater in the Panhandle with a THX sound system. In case you will be starting your Texas touring here, you will be glad to know that a new visitor center is under construction by the Texas Department of Transportation and may be open for business by the time you reach Canadian.

Leaving Canadian and heading southwest on US 60, you'll see the land rise and then flatten out again toward Pampa, whose name appropriately echoes the South American Spanish term for a grassy plain, as in the *pampas* of Argentina. If you have time, you might want to visit Pampa's White Deer Land Museum, celebrating early ranching days in a 1916 building. Travel about fifty miles farther down US 60 and you'll be back at Amarillo, where this trip began.

Amarillo ➤ Claude ➤ Quitaque ➤ Turkey ➤ Canyon (195 miles)

This itinerary makes a great big loop that could lead you back into Amarillo, if you are making that your headquarters. But you might consider ending the day in or around Canyon, where you can start the next morning in the vicinity of Palo Duro Canyon State Park.

From Amarillo, take Highway 287 southeast to Claude, where you will probably recognize the downtown area from *Hud*, particularly the intersection of US 287 with FM 1151. Note the water tower, which Larry McMurtry was bemused to see emblazoned with the name of *Hud's* fictional Thalia during the early 1960s filming. Claude also provided backdrops for *The Sundowners* in 1950 as well as for a TV movie called *Sunshine Christmas* in 1977.

Leaving Claude going south on State Highway 207 will set you on a course for some truly breathtaking scenery as you approach the rim of Palo Duro Canyon. After miles of flat agricultural lushness, the highway suddenly plunges into the spectacular southern reaches of the canyon, actually taking you down into the canyon and up the other side, where a rest stop provides a spectacular view and a perfect place for a picnic. Continuing south on 207 will bring you to another drop, into the gorgeous Tule Canyon, seven hundred feet deep and half a mile wide, with its beautiful Lake Mackenzie sparkling right next to the highway.

When you reach Highway 86, turn east toward Silverton and follow 86 to the tiny town of Quitaque. Here you can choose to take FM 1065 north to the Caprock Canyons State Park, where you may catch sight of some shaggy buffalo, the actual descendants of the last wild survivors that Charles Goodnight determinedly saved in the late 1800s and included in his film *Old Texas*. If you want to pay tribute to Bob Wills, the King of Western Swing and star of *Melody Ranch*, stay on 86 for another ten miles to his hometown of Turkey, where you can also admire the restored Gem Theatre. Then you may either backtrack through Quitaque to Silverton or enjoy looping around via Highway 70 to 256 and then back to Silverton, taking 86 from there on to its intersection with I-27, which goes north to Amarillo.

You will definitely want to take 217 east to the small college town of Canyon, home to West Texas A&M University, with its excellent Panhandle-Plains Historical Museum. Beyond Canyon about twelve miles on 217 is the entrance to Palo Duro Canyon State Park, with its magnificent multicolored rock cliffs and formations that play such a large role in *The Sundowners*. During the summer *Texas Legacies*, a musical extravaganza, is presented against the awesome backdrop of the canyon walls. The park's many other attractions include a replica of the shack Charles Goodnight used when he was developing his ranch there. At the park's Visitor Center, you can even purchase a copy of his 1916 film *Old Texas*. The Figure 3 Ranch, located east of the park, offers its famous Cowboy Breakfast on the rim of the canyon and provides access to the location of the final scenes in *Indiana Jones and the Last Crusade*.

Amarillo ➤ Plainview ➤ Lubbock ➤ Post ➤ Snyder ➤ Big Spring (255 miles)

Leaving Palo Duro Canyon, you bid farewell to the spectacular locations of *The Sundowners* and *Old Texas* as you head south on I-27. You will pass through Happy, which of course is *not* where *Happy, Texas* was filmed; so although a visit to "The Town without a Frown" might well be a pleasant diversion, you needn't look for movie sites there. Continue on down to Plainview, however, and *Leap of Faith* fans will be richly rewarded. A quick bite at the Quick Lunch can be followed by a stroll through the downtown to admire the old movie theater façades and other historic buildings that provided a readymade set for the Steve Martin film.

Head for Lubbock by continuing south on I-27 out of Plainview. Slightly larger than Amarillo, Lubbock is the major city of the

Panhandle's South Plains. Its main claim to fame for movie lovers is probably the association with favorite son Buddy Holly, but its Ranching Heritage Center will appeal to fans of western movies. Authentic structures such as a bunkhouse, dugout, blacksmith shop, and ranch homes have been moved to this sixteen-acre site and restored according to their specific time periods, which range from the 1700s through the 1900s.

Take US 84 south from Lubbock for some spectacular views of the contrast between the High Plains and the Lower Plains. As you cross the majestic Caprock, you encounter the tidy little town of Post, its north and west sides marked by looming steep cliffs and colorful canyons. Post was developed in the early 1900s by cereal king C. W. Post, who envisioned a perfect farming community. Among its many restored historical buildings is the Garza Theater, one of the earliest West Texas venues for silent movies.

About forty-five miles farther south on US 84 you will arrive at Snyder, where you may recognize sites from *Grand Champion*, including the Scurry County Coliseum grounds, where you can also visit the Heritage Village. The Scurry County Museum documents the city's past as an oil town and as the home of famed buffalo hunter J. Wright Mooar. A white buffalo sculpture on the town's square celebrates the rare albino Mooar brought down nearby in the 1870s. Also on the square is the restored Ritz Theater, now the home of live performances rather than movies.

From Snyder, this itinerary chooses a less-traveled road, Highway 350, southwestward to Big Spring. This trek will take you through rural areas and let you hop up on the Caprock again. Then the road descends into the valley where Big Spring is situated, and you can compare its current downtown with the one Joe Buck strutted across in *Midnight Cowboy*. One of the locations for *Hangar 18*, the former Webb AFB, is home to Hangar 25 Air Museum, housed in a restored 1942 hangar where World War II bombardiers were trained. The museum features various aircraft and aeronautical exhibits and artifacts, but no Roswellian aliens as suggested in *Hangar 18*.

Big Spring ➤ Stanton ➤ Sweetwater ➤ Anson ➤ Abilene (180 miles)

It's back to the Interstate from Big Spring for a quick hop west to Stanton if you'd like to see the Millhollon House, which was featured in *Midnight Cowboy*, and then retrace the miles to Big Spring and on to Sweetwater, a speedy sixty-six miles or so east on I-20. Here you can see the modern incarnation of the lonely vastness that Lillian Gish encountered in *The Wind*. The city has come a long way from the dugout that served as a store for buffalo hunters in 1877. And rather interesting to note, in light of the hostility to women portrayed in *The Wind*, is the fact that Sweetwater's Avenger Field was a training site for women pilots during World War II. Movie lovers will want to visit the Texas Theater at 114 East Broadway Avenue, which has been in daily operation since its opening in 1935, billed as "one of the very few show houses in West Texas built exclusively for talking pictures."

If you feel like wandering around some of the back roads that Kevin Costner supposedly travels in *A Perfect World*, take FM 126 north through Noodle to US 180, which you can then take east to Anson. Besides providing locations for *The Stars Fell on Henrietta*, Anson boasts an Opera House, built in 1907, that was once known as the "fanciest" venue between Fort Worth and El Paso for silent and talking pictures. As you head toward Abilene, south on US 83/277, you may see the remains of the Pepper Tree Diner, constructed for the 1983 film *Independence Day*. No, not THAT *Independence Day*, but rather a little-known film starring Kathleen Quinlan and David Keith that was shot in Anson.

Springing from a tent town beside the railroad in 1880, Abilene was inspired by its location on the Western and Dodge cattle trail to borrow its name from the Kansas trail drive destination. Today it is a vibrant and spacious city of educational institutions and many cultural amenities. The Paramount Theatre, listed on the National Register of Historic Places, is a must-see for movie lovers. Fully restored to its 1930s art deco beauty, it boasts two grand staircases,

The elegant Paramount Theatre in Abilene restored to its 1930 grandeur.
Courtesy of Michael A. Murphy/TxDOT

arched columns, handblown glass chandeliers, and a velvet-blue ceiling with glittering stars and floating clouds. In 1963, James Stewart and Sandra Dee appeared here for the premiere of *Take Her, She's Mine*, and Stewart delighted the crowd by playing "The Eyes of Texas" on an accordion.

Abilene → Cross Plains → Brownwood → Wichita Falls (250 miles)

Following Highway 36 south out of Abilene will bring you to Cross Plains, which probably earned its name as the site of multiple crossroads for military and stage coach travel prior to the Civil War. A marker in Treadaway Park notes that both Robert E. Lee and Ulysses S. Grant camped here beside Turkey Creek. But the main interest for the movie lover is the connection with Robert E. Howard, portrayed by Vincent D'Onofrio in *The Whole Wide World*. Howard lived in Cross Plains from 1919 till his death in 1936. The restored Howard House, listed on the National Register of Historic Places, is located on Highway 36 and can be visited on a limited basis. You can obtain information at the Cross Plains Public Library, which is open weekday afternoons and owns a large number of Howard's books, copies of *Weird Tales* magazines, and original manuscripts.

The Whole Wide World fans will probably want to take Highway 279 south out of Cross Plains to Brownwood, where Howard is buried in Greenleaf Cemetery. Although the movie was filmed in Central Texas, the story it tells took place in this area of West Texas. Novalyne went to school in Brownwood at Daniel Baker College, which was later absorbed into Howard Payne University.

This itinerary includes a rather long drive of at least 175 miles from Brownwood to Wichita Falls, the starting point for the next suggested itinerary. If you have time to follow some of these winding country roads, you'll experience the flavor of the Lower Plains towns with no big-city sprawl to distract you. A fairly economical route would be to take US 183 north out of Brownwood to Cisco, where you can view the Hilton Museum, housed in the building that Conrad Hilton purchased in 1919 to have a place to sleep and that became the first hotel in the Hilton chain. From Cisco, in the interest of speed, you might want to take I-20 east for a while, but if time permits, drop in on the Roaring Ranger Museum, housed in the old train depot in Ranger, a town that saw one of the most spectacular oil booms in history. Also just off I-20 is the ghost town of Thurber, with its fascinating history of coal mining, unionized citizenry, and multinational population.

About fifty-six miles east of Cisco, you can take US 281 north, which leads all the way to Wichita Falls, with interesting towns such as Mineral Wells and Jacksboro along the way.

Wichita Falls ➤ Archer City ➤ Henrietta ➤ Nocona ➤ Spanish Fort (105 miles)

This itinerary can be shorter or longer, depending upon how much you want to explore this area. *The Last Picture Show* is, of course, the focus of the movie lover's tour in this region, along with its younger sibling *Texasville*. To visit the major location for those films, take Highway 79 south from Wichita Falls to Archer City, where you will recognize the downtown buildings and the Royal Theater. Fans of *The Stars Fell on Henrietta* will probably want to visit the real Henrietta, which lies just a few miles east of Wichita Falls on US 82. Then about thirty miles farther east you will come to Nocona, a town that will be of interest to *Red River* fans, since it is very near one of the major crossings of the Chisholm Trail. Nocona was the last settlement before the Trail entered Indian Territory, and it celebrates that history each July with its Chisholm Trail Rodeo and Parade. If you follow FM 103 north out of Nocona, you will encounter the tiny village of Spanish Fort, with an amazing history of its own as the location of a large eighteenth-century Taovaya Indian city. About three miles west of Spanish Fort is the Red River Crossing, where hundreds of thousands of longhorns forded the river on their way to Abilene, Kansas, between 1860 and 1885.

PANHANDLE PLAINS CAST AND CREDITS

Some notable movie folk who were born or grew up in the Panhandle Plains:

Powers Boothe, actor, born in Snyder
Darlene Cates, actress, born in Borger
Cyd Charisse, actress, born in Amarillo
Barry Corbin, actor, born in Lamesa
Mac Davis, actor, born in Lubbock
Danny Elfman, composer/actor/producer, born in Amarillo
Lee Horsley, actor, born in Muleshoe
Carolyn Jones, actress, born in Amarillo
Larry McMurtry, screenwriter, born in Wichita Falls
Barry Tubb, actor/screenwriter/director, born in Snyder

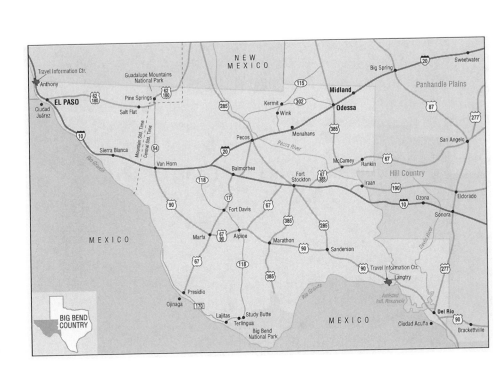

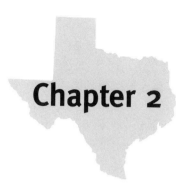

Chapter 2

Big Bend Country

Sure is pretty country. I wouldn't mind owning a ranch out here.
Eddie Mills in *Dancer, Texas Pop. 81*

ESTABLISHING SHOTS
The Region on the Map

THE MOST WIDE-OPEN SPACES of all may be found in the Big Bend Country of Texas. This observation can be confirmed by a glance at the highway map. This wing-shaped region south and west of the Panhandle Plains features the convergence of Interstates 20 and 10 near its center, with I-10 continuing westward to the New Mexico border; but otherwise you see only those thin blue highways connecting a few scattered tiny towns. The cities perch on the edges, with El Paso at the northwestern tip, Midland/Odessa on the northeastern edge, and Del Rio at the southern extreme. And at the southernmost point sprawls the magnificent Big Bend National Park.

In between are unique towns, several mountain ranges, and landscapes that abruptly change from mind-numbing monotony to breathtaking variety and back again. This is the perfect place for those who love to travel by automobile. Commercial flights touch down only in those cities on the edges, which are many miles apart and many miles from the heart of the region—many lonesome miles. Big Bend Country boasts the largest county in Texas, Brewster, which is almost as large as the states of Connecticut and Rhode Island combined, yet is home to fewer than ten thousand souls. Once you leave the interstate, you may drive for an hour or so without meeting another vehicle. But when you do meet one, the driver will probably lift a hand in a leisurely greeting.

Movie lover's itineraries start from El Paso, Marfa, and Alpine. Official Texas Travel Information Centers are located in Anthony, on I-10 at the New Mexico state line, and in the Judge Roy Bean Visitor Center at Langtry, northwest of Del Rio on Highway 90.

The Region Onscreen and Off

Although the Big Bend Country has much in common with the desolate areas of the Panhandle Plains, especially in serving as the backdrop for many a classic western movie, its major distinction arises from its proximity to Mexico. Geographically most of it is part of the huge Chihuahuan Desert, which stretches up from central Mexico and extends into southern New Mexico. Another name for the region, Trans-Pecos Texas, was inspired by the meandering river running diagonally across it from New Mexico to the Rio Grande.

Perhaps because of its isolation, it has retained the frontier spirit of the Wild West, expressed by the live-and-let-live independence of its self-reliant inhabitants who live far from the cities. Folks from Austin, from Dallas, from other states are moving to this region in growing numbers; but so far, the little towns like Fort Davis, Alpine, and Marfa have maintained their distinctive personalities. The effort necessary just to get to these places tends to weed out the easily discouraged as well as anyone who lacks an affinity for what is already there. Unlike much of Arizona, New Mexico, and other self-consciously western locales, West Texas has almost entirely escaped the onset of glitz and trendiness. Visitors would be wrong to write it off as entirely provincial, however. Sophistication encroaches even beyond the cosmopolitan city of El Paso all the way to tiny Marfa, with its world-famous contemporary art foundation, and to the hidden-away luxury of pricey Cibolo Creek Ranch, which attracts international jet-setters to its private airstrip.

The ubiquitous Mexican influence is most pronounced, naturally, along the Rio Grande, where it combines with Indian and Texan cultures to create a vibrant and colorful atmosphere. The river itself, invariably associated with Texas, has figured in many western movies. The name Big Bend refers to the enormous bent-elbow shape of the river as it curves around mountain ranges and changes its northwest-southeast flow to head northeast, thus embracing the land's south, west, and east sides. Its Spanish name may be translated as Big, or Great, River; but it rarely lives up to that name today, its wildness now tamed by numerous dams. However, in terms of the history and tales associated with its banks, it remains magnificent.

The only large city in this region, El Paso, is in fact the largest city on the U.S.-Mexico border. Just barely in Texas to begin with and closer to three other states' capitals than to Austin, El Paso holds herself a little apart from the rest of the state; she's even in a different time zone. First discovered by Europeans in the 1580s, "El Paso del Norte," or "The Pass of the North," provided a route through the mountains for Spanish colonists in Mexico to travel into western Texas and New Mexico in their search for gold. Later the pass was used by Americans moving from east to west.

This region boasts two national parks and one state park. Big Bend National Park's 800,000-plus acres nestle in the great curve of the river just east of the Big Bend Ranch State Park. The peaks of Guadalupe Mountains National Park loom over the Texas–New Mexico border to the north. Because the Big Bend Country is so remote, these glorious wilderness areas can be savored without the hassles of the enormous crowds that descend on other magnificent parks such as Yellowstone or Grand Canyon.

Filmmakers have used this scenery to great effect at least since

1950, when *High Lonesome* was filmed in Pinto Canyon. You can experience the vast beauty of Big Bend landscapes in films as disparate as *Barbarosa* and *Fandango*. You can also observe the landscape used as a backdrop for social and psychological ills in movies like *The Border* and *Flesh and Bone*. Colorful historical characters such as Judge Roy Bean and Pancho Villa have inspired several Hollywood films with stories set in Big Bend Country, although they were filmed elsewhere. Locations just across the border have also been popular for movies such as the Robert Rodriguez low-budget hit, *El Mariachi*, and its high-budget sequel, *Desperado*, both of which were shot in Del Rio's sister city, Ciudad Acuña. But of all the movies associated with this region, *Giant* is probably the first one most people would think of. In fact, it's probably the one movie about Texas that almost everyone would cite, and for good reason. *Giant*, filmed near the little town of Marfa, presumed to define the personality of the whole state, and for at least one generation of viewers it succeeded pretty well. But many other films offer interesting perspectives also.

REEL-LIFE AND REAL-LIFE TOURS

Feature Presentations: Big Bend Country in a Starring Role

Barbarosa (1980)
Willie Nelson, Gary Busey, and Gilbert Roland
Directed by Fred Schepisi

Reel-Life Tour

With cinematography reminiscent of the spaghetti westerns of the 1970s, *Barbarosa* rewards viewers with two Texas treasures, the Big Bend and Willie Nelson. It also includes authentic details of daily life in nineteenth-century Texas while at the same time showing how mythic heroes may be created from homely sources. The opening scenes take place in central Texas—Blanco County, to be exact—whence farm boy Karl Westover, a second-generation German American played by Gary Busey, flees to the Big Bend Country to escape revenge-seeking Old World neighbors. He hooks up with Nelson's character, known as "Barbarosa," who turns out also to be on the run. He is pursued by Mexicans seeking revenge on behalf of Don Braulio, played by Gilbert Roland in his last movie role, a patriarch who has parlayed a family brawl into a mythic tragedy starring Barbarosa as the elusive archenemy.

Magnificent shots of the glorious Big Bend country abound, with its incredibly varied colors and textures showing to great advantage. Scenes of the Hill Country are not so lovingly photographed, the emphasis there being on the deprivations of the immigrant farmers' lives. The film is somewhat misleading geographically in suggesting that Blanco County and the Rio Grande aren't as far apart as they actually are. And for some reason the script has the characters who travel between those points encountering the Brazos River, although no reasonable route they might take would bring them anywhere near that great old stream. On the whole, however, *Barbarosa* ranks high on the authenticity scale.

Real-Life Tour: Big Bend Ranch State Park, Lajitas

A frequently cited Indian story says that the Great Spirit threw into the Big Bend all the rocks left over from creating the rest of the world, making it a region of great geologic diversity. The Chihuahuan Desert forms the backdrop for the entire region, but it's not all desert. Along the Rio Grande you find stands of river cane and cedar, and in the mountains you encounter oases of evergreen forests and shaded springs with cactus and ferns intermingled. Big Bend Ranch State Park encompasses almost 300,000 acres of mostly undeveloped wilderness and can be accessed at the Fort Leaton State Historic Site in Presidio or at the Barton Warnock Environmental Educational Center at Lajitas, where scenes were shot not only for *Barbarosa* but also for *Streets of Laredo* and *Spy Kids II*.

A Langtry Double Feature:
The Westerner (1940)
Gary Cooper, Walter Brennan, and Chill Wills
Directed by William Wyler

The Life and Times of Judge Roy Bean (1972)
Paul Newman, Jacqueline Bisset, Ava Gardner, and Stacy Keach
Directed by John Huston

Reel-Life Tour

Both of these movies were filmed in Arizona rather than Texas, but omitting films about one of the best-known characters associated with the Big Bend Country, the self-styled "Law West of the Pecos," Roy Bean, would be unthinkable in a collection of Texas movies. *The Westerner* also addresses the significant historical conflict between cattlemen and farmers in Texas after the Civil War. Gary Cooper plays a wandering cowboy named Cole Harden, who sides with the farmers against Bean and the cattlemen. Before the climactic showdown between Harden and Bean, played by Walter Brennan in one of his Oscar-winning roles, Harden exploits Bean's famous obsession with the English actress Lillie Langtry as a way to undermine his authority.

Bean's fascination with Langtry also figures prominently in the Paul Newman vehicle *The Life and Times of Judge Roy Bean*, a movie generally considered far inferior to *The Westerner*. In this film Roy Bean is a farcical character who engages in a series of outrageous episodes of murder and mayhem, tied loosely together by the thread of his romantic love for Lillie Langtry. Unlike *The Westerner*, this movie is not concerned directly with historical realities such as the cattleman-farmer conflict. In fact, director John Huston referred to it as an allegory in Laurence Grobel's *The Hustons*, saying, "It seemed to reflect the old American Spirit that was capable of doing so many unlikely things. There was a breadth and generosity and a carelessness about it that I fostered."

Real-Life Tour: Langtry

For whatever reason the producers decided to film two movies about Judge Roy Bean elsewhere, the fact is that the real Langtry, with a population of perhaps thirty, provides an authentic piece of rocky and barren old West Texas. Located on Highway 90 about 60 miles northwest of Del Rio and very near the Rio Grande, Langtry comprises the meticulously restored saloon and home of Judge Roy Bean, where he dispensed his own brand of justice along with the alcohol. He may not have actually named the town after Lillie Langtry as he claimed; others have said that it was named for an engineer named Langtry, who oversaw Chinese workers constructing the railroad in the 1880s. But in any case, Bean certainly did christen his saloon in honor of the actress, using her stage name, "The Jersey Lily," which is misspelled "Lilly" on the sign.

High Lonesome (1950)
John Barrymore Jr., Jack Elam, and Chill Wills
Directed by Alan LeMay

Reel-Life Tour

High Lonesome is a good companion piece for *The Sundowners*, which was filmed in the Panhandle Plains. Many of the same cast and crew worked on both of these B-westerns, and by watching the two of them you can compare scenery of the northern and the southern regions of West Texas. Alan LeMay wrote both screenplays, and he also directed *High Lonesome*, using again the actors Jack Elam, Chill Wills, and John Barrymore Jr. The plot involves a young drifter, played by Barrymore, who is accused of committing a series of murders and detained by a rancher who has been involved in a range war. Meanwhile, the real murderers are preparing to go on the rampage again and seek revenge on the rancher.

Real-Life Tour: Pinto Canyon

If you drive about forty miles southwest of Marfa on FM 2810, you will encounter some absolutely gorgeous scenery in a remote area, but be forewarned that you should have a full tank of gas and plenty of water before venturing into Pinto Canyon. The pavement ends a few miles from the canyon, but if your vehicle is tough enough to take some very rough roads, you'll find the trip worth the effort. One of the sets for *High Lonesome*, a cluster of abandoned adobe houses, can be seen along the roadway a couple of miles after you pass the remains of a perlite mine. Once you have enjoyed the journey into the canyon, just be sure to turn back toward Marfa while you have plenty of gas to get there.

The Good Old Boys (1995)
Tommy Lee Jones, Sissy Spacek, Frances McDormand,
and Matt Damon
Directed by Tommy Lee Jones

Reel-Life Tour

Texas native Tommy Lee Jones both directed and starred in this made-for-TV movie that lovingly presents an authentic picture of life in turn-of-the-century West Texas. Based on the novel of the same name by renowned Texas writer Elmer Kelton, the story focuses on Hewey Calloway, a fortyish bachelor cowboy who is tempted to renounce his love for the wide-open spaces in favor of settling down near his brother's family farm with Miss Spring Renfroe, a pretty schoolteacher. An excellent cast, including several Oscar winners, lends believability to the leisurely tale. Sissy Spacek, another Texas native, as Spring; Frances McDormand as Eve, Hewey's sharp-tongued sister-in-law; Matt Damon as Hewey's nephew Cotton; and Sam Shepard as Snort Yarnell, Hewey's main partner in good-old-boyishness, are major standouts along with Jones as Hewey.

The scenery is also a major standout. The enormous blue skies of the Big Bend Country grace the opening titles, and the movie offers great views of the flat country dotted with mesquite trees, yucca, cholla, and prickly pear, with the mountains jagged on the horizon. As you would expect from a movie produced with the input of so many real Texans, the accents are right on the money, as are the figures of speech and the characters' attitudes. Period details were important in the sets also. The homestead house was modeled after the house in which Kelton himself was born, and the song that Spring and Hewey sing in the parlor is one that Kelton had seen advertised in a 1903 newspaper.

Real-Life Tour: Fort Davis, Marfa, Alpine

Although the story is set in San Angelo and Upton County, located in the Panhandle Plains region, most of the filming of *The Good Old Boys* took place in the Big Bend Country. The first scene offers lovely views of Fort Davis, the restored historic fort itself, with its backdrop of a mountain of chocolate-colored boulders. Several of the restored buildings are seen in the background as Hewey has an unpleasant encounter with a city marshal. The church in a subsequent scene, however, was a movie set construction.

On the map, Fort Davis lies at the top of an almost equilateral triangle formed with two other towns, Marfa to the southwest and Alpine to the southeast. The *Good Old Boys* homestead set, no longer standing, was constructed in a pasture a few miles south and east of Marfa on Highway 67. Various outdoor scenes were shot in the countryside around Alpine.

Giant (1956)
Rock Hudson, Elizabeth Taylor, and James Dean
Directed by George Stevens

Reel-Life Tour

Giant may be the best Texas movie ever. It includes most of the usual twentieth-century characters and themes—cattlemen, oilmen, nouveau-riche gaudiness—the same ones that would populate the TV series *Dallas* a couple of decades later; and most Texans agree that it conveys the spirit of 1950s Texas accurately, even though Edna Ferber's novel on which it was based did not impress Texans as being accurate at all. In fact, many of them hated the book and thought it was slanderous. Even George Stevens was nervous about filming *Giant*, considering how unpopular the book was in Texas. But as he subsequently produced and directed it, the film earned the affection of Texans and has even been called "The National Movie of Texas."

Within the context of a family saga, *Giant* entertainingly traces the transformation of an aristocratic ranching economy into the wheeler-dealer atmosphere of the oil business. Socially as well as economically, the families with old money based on vast ranches and cattle herds come in conflict with the upstarts who strike it rich in oil. Another social issue addressed in *Giant*, for one of the first times in a popular movie, is the segregation between Anglos and Mexican Americans in West Texas. The rousing conclusion of the movie focuses on the formerly prejudiced Bick Benedict's passionate defense of his half-Mexican grandchild.

The spectacular cast has helped make *Giant* a classic. James Dean is seen in his last and perhaps greatest role before dying in a car crash while the film was still in production. Rock Hudson and Elizabeth Taylor are at their gorgeous best as Bick and Leslie Benedict. The landscape is so important that it is almost like another member of the cast. Mercedes McCambridge, who played Luz Benedict, recalled it in her autobiography as "the ugliest . . . on the face of the earth," but when Bick and Leslie first drive up to the mansion sitting in the middle of nowhere, the stark emptiness is offset by the glorious blue sky full of the puffy flat-bottomed white clouds so prevalent in Texas summers. Even the barrenness conveys a sense of grandeur.

Giant's release on DVD in June 2003 was the occasion of a gala premiere in Marfa, the little town that had happily allowed itself to be taken over for the filming in 1955. The exciting days when Warner Brothers Studios came to town to make the movie are brought back to life in the documentary "Return to *Giant*," included with the double-disk DVD version. You can immerse yourself in all things *Giant* with this DVD, which also includes interviews with the stars, with local citizens who worked as extras, with production crew members, and with city officials. Some of these interviews were done in 1955, some decades later, but all offer fascinating views of the interactions between the people of Marfa and the Hollywood visitors.

Real-Life Tour: Marfa

The tiny town of Marfa does not appear in *Giant*, but the cast and crew set up housekeeping there, with most of the filming done on private ranch property between Marfa and Valentine. Traveling west on Highway 90 out of Marfa, you can see the ruins of Jett Rink's "Little Reata" on your right. Just look for that familiar windmill and the arch that used to have the name on it. The ruins of the Reata mansion can be seen a few miles further along on your left. Unfortunately, all you can see now—far in the distance—is a series of poles; start looking when you are about a quarter of a mile east of the Border Patrol's Drug Interdiction station on Highway 90.

There are still plenty of folks in Marfa who remember the filming or who have been told about it all their lives. Many of the residents in 1955 worked as extras in the film. You may well run into some of them around the El Paisano Hotel, which hosted cast and crew in 1955 and which reopened in 2001 after having been closed for many years. It still features displays of *Giant* memorabilia, and you may be able to stay in one of the rooms that the stars used. The Public Library and the Marfa and Presidio County Museum also maintain archives of photos and articles related to the filming of the movie.

Fandango (1985)
Kevin Costner, Judd Nelson, and Sam Robards
Directed by Kevin Reynolds

Reel-Life Tour

The ruins of the *Giant* movie set have become such an icon that they have been featured in other movies, including this early Kevin Costner film. Set in 1971, *Fandango*'s story follows buddies from the University of Texas who set out on a road trip through West Texas to commemorate the end of their college days and their flight from Vietnam, marriage, and careers. They visit several notable Big Bend sites, filmed so as to give you a strong sense of place. The movie has become such a cult favorite that fans have documented many points of the cinematic journey on Web sites such as www.alexmusson.com/fandango.

Writer and director Kevin Reynolds based the story on some of his own adventures with Baylor University classmates, and he used a cast of relatively unknown actors. Costner, Judd Nelson, Sam Robards, Brian Cesak, and Chuck Bush play the "Groovers," the band of brothers who skip out on their graduation party to head out on the highway. Their adventures include automobile mishaps, fireworks in a cemetery, an almost disastrous parachute jump, digging up a bottle of Dom Perignon, and finally a lovely wedding that local residents are conned into underwriting. This rowdy fun is punctuated with a few rather touching moments as the Groovers express their youthful exuberance and their anxiety over facing adult responsibilities.

Real-Life Tour: Toyah, Marathon, Alpine, Marfa, Pyote, San Elizario

The opening scenes of *Fandango* are supposed to take place in a frat house on the University of Texas campus, but they were filmed in the tiny almost ghost town of Toyah, located about twenty miles west of Pecos on I-20. The set was constructed in an abandoned two-story school building on the north side of town. Just east of Toyah, near the Shaw Road exit off I-20, Chata Ortega's Bar and Grill was one of the Groovers' first stops.

The characters talk about being in Marfa; but the Sonic Drive-In, where they pick up the bubbleheaded girls, is actually located in Alpine. You can visit it and order your own chili dog at the intersection of Holland and Garrett. And the gas station where the guys get the car patched up is located in the town of Marathon, on Highway 90 at Avenue F. The cemetery where they shoot off fireworks, however, really is located in Marfa, on the western edge of town on Highway 90. And if you keep going west on 90, past the cemetery, you may be able to see what's left of the *Giant* set, where the Groovers spend the night.

The goofy scenes at the "Pecos Parachute School" were shot at the abandoned Rattlesnake Air Force Base, south of Pyote off I-20. But the later comic flying scenes, including a Cessna's landing on a Dallas freeway and taxiing into a residential neighborhood, were not shot in Texas at all, but rather in Tulsa, Oklahoma.

The climactic digging up of the bottle under a rock marked "DOM" takes place at one of the most spectacular spots along FM 170 between Presidio and Lajitas. Known as the "Big Hill," the scenic overlook about thirteen miles north of Lajitas is just a short distance from the teepee-shaped shelters of a rest stop that you will definitely notice. And if you walk toward the river, you will see the big rock marked "DOM."

The finale of the movie is supposed to take place in Presidio, but it was actually filmed in San Elizario, near El Paso. The town square was renovated in the 1990s, so it doesn't look exactly the same as it does in the movie; but the gazebo is still there, as is the magnificent mission church.

Flesh and Bone (1993)
Dennis Quaid, Meg Ryan, James Caan, and Gwyneth Paltrow
Directed by Seven Kloves

Reel-Life Tour

Flesh and Bone stars Dennis Quaid as a vending-machine supplier who drives all over West Texas, so it has much scenery in common with *Fandango;* but its story is much darker, to say the least. Those wide-open spaces that bring out exuberance in Kevin Costner and his fellow Groovers are here portrayed as oppressive in their hypnotic vastness and rural isolation. Quaid and his then wife, Meg Ryan, play lovers whose relationship is possibly doomed by a murderous secret involving Quaid's evil father, played by a really, really creepy James Caan. The loneliness and languid heat of the region are conveyed in a way that emphasizes the ominous outlines of the story, and the actors are convincingly "Texan," one and all, but especially Gwyneth Paltrow in one of her earliest film roles. Her Texas accent is impeccable.

Flesh and Bone was pretty much trounced by the critics and ignored at the box office, but that may have been partly because back in the early 1990s, Meg and Dennis were expected primarily to be cute and charming. Instead, their roles here are complex and their performances subtle. Writer-director Steven Kloves manages to weave elements of film noir into the vivid Texas locales, along with romance and even a good deal of humor—rather amazing considering the grimness of the film's basic premise.

Real-Life Tour: Marfa, Pecos

Many *Flesh and Bone* scenes were shot in Central Texas, but the overall flavor is that of West Texas—dusty, barren towns separated by lots of open space forming a backdrop for Quaid's taciturn, cowboy-like character, archetypally dealing quietly with painful memories. The Stardust Motel in Marfa was the location for several scenes. Unfortunately, it burned down a few years after the movie was filmed, but the sign still stands at the west end of town on Highway 90. Another motel featured was the Town and Country in Pecos, which is now the Budget Inn on Third Street.

Sylvester (1985)
Melissa Gilbert, Richard Farnsworth, Michael Schoeffling,
and Constance Towers
Directed by Tim Hunter

Reel-Life Tour

This tale of a teenaged girl in Big Bend Country may be seen as the counterpart of the teenaged boys' story in *Dancer, Texas Pop. 81*. Melissa Gilbert, beloved alum of *Little House on the Prairie*, plays sixteen-year-old Charlie, a tough tomboy working on the ranch of cantankerous John Foster, played by Richard Farnsworth. Her parents are dead, and Charlie tries to support herself and her two younger brothers by breaking horses for Foster. Hoping to make some real money, she decides to train the best of the horses, one named Sylvester, and enters him in the National Equestrian Trials in Kentucky. Most of the film takes place in and around Marfa, providing an enjoyable cinematic visit to this charming little town.

Real-Life Tour: Marfa, Alpine

Like Fort Davis in *Dancer, Texas Pop. 81*, Marfa gets to be a star in *Sylvester*. Many locations in the town show up on the screen, but of special interest are the historic stockyards and rodeo arena about a mile from downtown. Don't look for the supermarket in Marfa, however; that scene was shot in neighboring Alpine.

Waltz Across Texas (1982)
Anne Archer, Terry Jastrow, Richard Farnsworth,
and Mary Kay Place
Directed by Ernest Day

Reel-Life Tour

The title alludes to a wonderful song by Texas tunesmith Ernest Tubb, and the story was co-written by its two co-stars, Terry Jastrow, a Midland native, and his wife, Anne Archer. She plays a geologist from the East Coast who ends up working a wildcat oil well along with Jastrow's character, a Texan who searches for oil a bit less scientifically than she does. Inevitably his characterization of a hunch-following wildcatter suffers by comparison to Robert Duvall's more colorful performance in *The Stars Fell on Henrietta*, but the couple's screen presence is pleasant enough. The setup for the storyline produces a predictable battle of the sexes, and people who probably know have said the oil-business stuff is not very realistic. But you do get to see some good-looking Texas line dancing, true-to-life oil rig scenes, and lots of footage of Midland, Texas.

Real-Life Tour: Midland

Midland lies in the northeastern corner of the Big Bend Country, very far, both literally and figuratively, from the grandeur of the Big Bend itself. In fact, it sits in one of the flattest, dullest stretches of countryside you'll see anywhere. For that reason, this statement on the back of the VHS box describing the Jastrow/Archer story in *Waltz Across Texas* is a bit surprising: "Amidst the breathtaking beauty of Midland, Texas, they share a unique quest." Now Midland might be called handsome, considering its many high-rise buildings. And some of its arduously maintained green neighborhoods might be very pretty. But "breathtaking beauty" simply is not a quality associated with this city. It is worth visiting, however, especially if you have an interest in the oil industry. The excellent Permian

Basin Petroleum Museum, Library and Hall of Fame is handy to I-20 West, near exit 136. The reputation of this museum and library is such that the actors and producers of *The Stars Fell on Henrietta* traveled here to do research on oil wildcatting in order to make their movie historically accurate.

An El Paso Double Feature:
Lone Wolf McQuade (1983)
Chuck Norris, David Carradine, Barbara Carerra, and L. Q. Jones
Directed by Steve Carver

The Border (1982)
Jack Nicholson, Harvey Keitel, Warren Oates, and Valerie Perrine
Directed by Tony Richardson

Reel-Life Tour

Unless you have a real fondness for 1980s action movies, you'll probably watch *Lone Wolf McQuade* mainly for the shots of downtown El Paso, the racetracks, and the surrounding rugged countryside, particularly I-10 stretching out forever in the middle of

Border crossing at El Paso, area patrolled by Chuck Norris in *Lone Wolf McQuade* and by Jack Nicholson in *The Border.* Courtesy of J. Griffis Smith/TxDOT

nowhere. This movie is a precursor of Chuck Norris's popular TV series *Walker, Texas Ranger*, but it's much more violent and not as well acted. As for the way the Texas Ranger culture is portrayed, the film takes some liberties; that ultraconservative organization would hardly tolerate a renegade such as McQuade even to the grudging extent depicted in this movie. The nickname "Lone Wolf" is all that connects Norris's character with the legendary real-life Ranger Manuel Gonzaullas, who was known as *El Lobo Solo* in the 1920s.

The locations are authentic, however, and the aerial photography from a plane flying east out of El Paso is spectacular. Here's a bit of trivia that might be worth investigating: John Milius, screenwriter for *The Life and Times of Judge Roy Bean*, is listed as "Spiritual Advisor" in the credits for *Lone Wolf McQuade*.

The Border offers a more realistic portrayal of crime fighting in the El Paso area than that of the chest-thumping *McQuade*. The misdeeds involve the exploitation of illegal aliens seeking a hopeful life in America, and Jack Nicholson sympathetically plays Charley, a Border Patrol officer trying to resist the temptation to join his co-workers on the take. Under pressure from his spendthrift sexy wife, played by Valerie Perrine, Charley is lured into complicity with fellow officer Harvey Keitel, who demonstrates what seems to be a matter-of-fact corruption throughout the agency. In the end, however, Charley holds on to his sense of right and wrong. He rescues the stolen baby of a beautiful Mexican woman and makes sure all the bad guys end up dead.

This movie, even more insistently than *Lone Wolf McQuade*, focuses on the decidedly unglamorous aspects of El Paso. The vans of the Border Patrol haunt the unpaved back roads, and the Rio Grande appears only as a polluted stream full of garbage and old tires. Even the new brick house Charley buys for his wife manages to appear drab at the same time that it gleams in the unrelenting sunshine.

Real-Life Tour: El Paso

Fortunately, there's a lot more to El Paso than shows up in these two films. The downtown area you see in *Lone Wolf McQuade* is a lively, bicultural, modern city; in the film you catch glimpses of the sprawling white convention center and the adjacent historic Paso Del Norte Hotel, currently known as the Camino Real. Built around 1912, this edifice has hosted many famous folk, including Pancho Villa, and has been through several ownerships. Its Dome Bar, which was the original lobby, is definitely worth a visit to see the opulence of its original Tiffany glass dome and spectacular marble walls, columns, and floors. Venturing from downtown, you may want to head out on the Transmountain Road to visit the Border Patrol Museum and gauge for yourself the reality quotient of *The Border*.

Dancer, Texas Pop. 81 (1998)
Breckin Meyer, Peter Facinelli, Eddie Mills,
and Patricia Wettig
Directed and written by Tim McCanlies

Reel-Life Tour

Native Texan Tom McCanlies wrote and directed this indie film lauding the serene beauty of the country surrounding the Davis

Some of the "pretty country" near Fort Davis where Eddie Mills' character "wouldn't mind owning a ranch" in *Dancer, Texas Pop. 81*. Courtesy of J. Griffis Smith/TxDOT

Mountains. Serenity is, of course, not terribly exciting for observers, so *Dancer, Texas Pop. 81* strikes some viewers as dull. But for those who share the filmmaker's affection for the region and its people, it is a little gem.

The story concerns four young men who have grown up together in Dancer and who have vowed to leave town for the big city of Los Angeles as soon as they finish high school. As graduation approaches, each boy examines his own ties to the hometown, while the other inhabitants offer advice and place bets on whether or not the buddies will actually leave. In general, the townsfolk hope they don't leave, since the fellows represent four-fifths of the entire graduating class. Also, their departure would necessitate revising the city limits sign to reflect a population of only 77.

McCanlies utilized no big names in his cast, and so far none of his young actors have broken out into stardom, but the performances are appropriately low-key and likeable. The movie offers a realistic view of contemporary life in the rural Big Bend Country, with glances at the present-day oil business and a modern working ranch. The characters discuss the problems of drought and the courses of study offered at Sul Ross State University. *Dancer, Texas Pop. 81* provides a great introduction to a quiet region of the state, where most of the drama is in the landscape and people tend to live and let live.

Real-Life Tour: Fort Davis, Alpine, Valentine

Most of *Dancer, Texas* was filmed in the town of Fort Davis, not to be confused with the nearby restored fort, which you can see in *The Good Old Boys*. Several private homes; the First Presbyterian Church; and the Jeff Davis County courthouse, playing the high school, are all clearly recognizable. You also get some idea of the grandly dramatic Davis Mountains under brilliant blue skies. The remains of "The Oasis" gas station, which appeared in ads for the movie, can still be seen on FM 505 near the town of Valentine, a couple of miles east of Highway 90. The four young men were pictured sitting in lawn chairs in the middle of the road in front of this building, which had been constructed out of ticky-tacky for the movie.

Friday Night Lights (2004)
Billy Bob Thornton, Lucas Black, Garrett Hedlund,
and Derek Luke
Directed by Peter Berg

Reel-Life Tour

Billy Bob Thornton should probably be receiving his naturalization papers as a Texas citizen any day now. In the last few years, he has directed the Texas movie *All the Pretty Horses*; he portrayed Davy Crockett in *The Alamo*; and he has starred in this film about high school football. What's more, he enjoys statewide admiration not only for his talent but for his warmth and accessibility. *Friday Night Lights* is based on the best-selling nonfiction book of the same name, written by H. G. Bissinger, describing the 1988 football season at Odessa Permian High School. Thornton plays Gary Gaines, who was head coach that year.

The book angered many of Odessa's residents who felt they'd been portrayed unfairly as pathologically obsessed with the success of the high school football team, but the movie tones down that aspect of the story enough to have appeased most Odessans. The film still reflects a win-at-all-costs attitude, however, as residents place relentless pressure on the players and the coach for a state championship. The city has used school funds to build an enormous stadium and pays the coach considerably more than it pays the school's principal. After a losing game, the coach comes home to find "For Sale" signs on his lawn. A caller to the local talk-radio show complains that the players are doing "too much learning" in school at the expense of their game.

Texas high school football undeniably produces a kind of mania across the entire state, not only in Odessa. Other movies such as *Varsity Blues* have treated this same subject; and even in *The*

Last Picture Show, you see the team members for little Anarene High School suffering ridicule from the adults for their shortcomings on the field. *Friday Night Lights* offers a slice of Texas life that is authentic for a large segment of the population. On the other hand, you can contrast Odessa's stressed-out, would-be heroes with the laid-back high school students in *Dancer, Texas Pop. 81.* Each extreme is a Texas reality.

Real-Life Tour: Odessa

Friday Night Lights was filmed in Odessa, so you are seeing the real deal when you watch this movie. The lush green of the grass in the football stadium glaring in the vastness of the barren Permian Basin landscape is an effective visual kickoff to the film. But as important as football is to Odessa, the city has a variety of other attractions for the visitor. As you would expect, museums tend to focus on local history and the oil and ranching businesses. But what might be a surprise is the Globe of the Great Southwest, a theater on the campus of Odessa College modeled upon the original Globe in London. Nearby is a replica of Ann Hathaway's cottage as well. At the other cultural extreme, you will find the "World's Largest Jackrabbit," an eight-foot fiberglass statue commissioned by the Odessa Chamber of Commerce in 1962.

Short Takes: Big Bend Country in a Supporting Role

The Andromeda Strain (1971)
Arthur Hill, David Wayne, and Kate Reid
Directed by Robert Wise

Based on prolific author Michael Crichton's debut novel, this sci-fi flick was filmed in the tiny community of Shafter, which is located about forty miles south of Marfa on Highway 67. Shafter happily pretended for the sake of the movie to be a New Mexico town, and it must have done an excellent job, because *The Andromeda Strain* received an Academy Award nomination for Best Art Direction–Set Decoration. The scary story involves a U.S.

Army satellite's returning to earth with a deadly virus that scientists struggle to understand and contain. Their efforts are supported by a number of Big Bend residents appearing as extras. Little Shafter looks pretty much the same today as it did in 1971— a ghostly and largely abandoned silver-mining town.

Paris, Texas (1984)
Harry Dean Stanton, Dean Stockwell, and Nastassja Kinski
Directed by Wim Wenders

This film—and you must call it a *film* rather than a *movie*—reflects the existential anxiety of German director Wim Wenders, but not much of anything about Texas except some excellent scenery. Despite the title, the vast, empty landscapes you see here are not found anywhere near the often lush and green city of Paris in northeast Texas. Wenders chose to shoot instead in and around Terlingua, an abandoned mining town close to the Big Bend. This surreal tale, written by Sam Shepard, has been adored by critics and honored at Cannes, but it lacks any insights about Texas or Texans. Wenders performs his usual cinematic wizardry with symbolism, this time centered on myths and stereotypes of the American West, but the only authentic Texas here is provided by the great cinematography.

Blue Sky (1994)
Jessica Lange, Tommy Lee Jones, and Powers Boothe
Directed by Tony Richardson

Jessica Lange, in an Oscar-winning role, and native Texan Tommy Lee Jones star in *Blue Sky* as a couple moving from one military base to another in the early 1960s as the wife scandalizes each community with her sexually free behavior. The husband, a nuclear scientist, also makes himself unpopular with the military establishment by challenging its insistence on aboveground testing after he documents the dangers to local inhabitants. Although most of the action takes place and was shot on location in Alabama, several scenes show sites in Texas pretending to be Nevada and New Mexico. The 1880 Beach homestead and corrals located at Red Rock Ranch near Van Horn serve as the home of residents threatened by the effects of nuclear testing.

Courage Under Fire (1996)
Denzel Washington, Meg Ryan, Lou Diamond Phillips,
and Matt Damon
Directed by Edward Zwick

Here's another military tale, this time about a rescue helicopter pilot—played by Meg Ryan—who died in the first Gulf War. Denzel Washington plays an Army officer assigned to investigate her death, which appears to have been heroic enough to merit the first Medal of Honor presented to a female. The story is told mainly through flashbacks as Washington's character tries to sort out conflicting stories about the events surrounding the pilot's death. West Texas plays Iraq in this film; and you can visit one of the sets at Indian Cliffs Ranch, about thirty-five miles east of El Paso.

BIG BEND TRAVELOGUES
Scouting the Locations

When you plan your itinerary in the Big Bend Country, always remember that this region can be unforgiving to the careless traveler. Be sure you have plenty of drinking water and enough fuel in your vehicle to get you to the next town. The colors and textures in the landscape can easily mesmerize you during the day, as can the amazing brightness of the stars at night. But you must keep your wits about you, so you do not wander off onto gravel roads leading into marvelous canyons and get lost or forget that the closest town with an open gas station may be more than fifty miles away.

El Paso ➤ San Elizario ➤ Van Horn ➤ Valentine ➤ Marfa (195 miles)

If your visit to Texas starts in El Paso, you will probably want to make a stop at nearby Anthony, located on I-20, where you will find a Texas Travel Information Center operated by professional travel counselors who are happy to provide maps and information for all regions of the state. After exploring El Paso's downtown and recognizing sights from *Lone Wolf McQuade*, you might enjoy the spectacular scenic drive along the Transmountain Road, Loop 375, which is accessible either from Highway 54 northeast of the city or from I-10 on the northwest. The Border Patrol Museum is located at 4315 Transmountain Road and would likely be of interest to fans of Jack Nicholson's character in *The Border*.

If you have time, you should consider touring the old Spanish colonial missions that dot the banks of the Rio Grande in El Paso's Lower Valley, about fifteen miles southeast of downtown. The earliest settlements in Texas were established here in the 1600s, and the structures show more Indian influence than you will find in the better-known missions more recently constructed in Central Texas and California. Take the Zaragosa exit from I-10 and follow the Mission Trail signs. The first mission you come to is referred to as Ysleta and was established in 1681. The second is Socorro, also dating back to 1681; you might recognize this site from *The Bad News Bears in Breaking Training*. The third is San Elizario, the site of an eighteenth-century Spanish presidio and the location for the wedding scenes in *Fandango*. If you want to skip the others and just go to San Elizario, stay on I-10 east out of El Paso to Exit 42; then follow the signs for about five miles to the town square, with its gazebo and its historical markers detailing the sixteenth-century Spanish expeditions to the area.

Twenty miles east of El Paso on I-10 at Exit 49, to Fabens, you will find Indian Cliffs Ranch and the popular Cattleman's Steakhouse. The restaurant features big windows through which you can watch prowling coyotes; and you can view other animals in the private zoo, which includes a rattlesnake pit. Most intriguing, however, are the movie sets you can tour, which have been used for *Lone Wolf McQuade* and *Courage Under Fire*, among other films.

Back on I-10, head east for another hundred miles or so to Van Horn, a pleasant town that originated as a stagecoach stop and that still caters to travelers with its many overnight accommodations.

State Highway 54 leads north out of town all the way to the spectacular and rugged Guadalupe Mountains National Park; but also on this road, just about three miles from Van Horn, you'll find another movie lover's point of interest, Red Rock Ranch. This spot is particularly fascinating to geologists because of its unusual natural outcropping of Precambrian sandstone. But for the movie fan, a big part of its attraction is the Beach homestead and corrals, nestled into the geologic splendor as seen in *Blue Sky*. A bonus is another set, called Anton Chico, where part of *Dead Man's Walk* was filmed in 1995.

Take US 90 out of Van Horn, and you'll fly along the plains surrounded by several mountain ranges. A few miles south of Valentine, you can follow FM 505 a couple of miles to the spot in the road where the boys in *Dancer, Texas Pop. 81* set up their lawn chairs in front of the Oasis.

As you approach Marfa on US 90, look for the cemetery from *Fandango* just west of town; it's named Cemeterio de la Merced. If night is falling, you may want to head directly for the Marfa Mystery Lights Viewing Center, located about eight miles beyond the town, also on US 90. This facility offers a viewing deck, restrooms, and information about the Marfa Lights, first reported in 1883 and still unexplained. You could easily spend the next day visiting sites associated with *Giant*, *Fandango*, *Sylvester*, and *The Good Old Boys*. Another film, *Grand Champion*, mostly filmed in the Panhandle Plains, shot scenes in downtown Marfa and at the middle school. You could also make the run out to Pinto Canyon via FM 2810 to explore the location for *High Lonesome*; but allow plenty of time, and don't forget the drinking water and the full gas tank.

Marfa ➤ Shafter ➤ Presidio ➤ Lajitas ➤ Terlingua ➤ Alpine (200 miles)

US 67 south out of Marfa will take you all the way to Presidio, by way of Shafter, where you can visit the location for *The Andromeda Strain*. Presidio is a great place to begin a spectacular fifty-mile drive to Lajitas along the River Road, FM 170, which follows the course of the Rio Grande and affords breathtaking views of the river far below the highway.

Perhaps the most spectacular view is at Big Hill, which you will recognize as the spot where the Groovers dig up the bottle of wine in *Fandango*. A few miles east of Big Hill, you may see a road sign identifying the Contrabando Movie Set, which is located in the Big Bend Ranch State Park and maintained by the Texas Parks and Wildlife Department. About six miles farther on, you will reach the former ghost town of Lajitas, now partially transformed into a desert resort. Besides visiting locations for *Barbarosa* and other films, you will want to check out the "mayor" of Lajitas, a beer-drinking goat named Clay Henry.

At Lajitas FM 170 leaves the Rio Grande and heads northeast through the mountains to Terlingua, which became a true ghost town almost overnight when the quicksilver mining industry played out in the early 1940s. Its collection of abandoned adobe shacks has been reinhabited by a few hardy souls since the 1960s, and a small band of stalwarts make their living running raft trips down the river or providing services for visitors to such events as the annual International Championship Chili Cookoff. Contrasting with the crumbling ruins are some modern vacation homes and the Terlingua Ranch Resort. The overall atmosphere is one of desolation and loneliness, which was exploited in *Paris, Texas*. A livelier glimpse into the eccentricities of past and present residents may be enjoyed on a stroll through the town's cemetery, where unusual grave markers and tributes abound.

Four miles beyond Terlingua is another former mining town, Study Butte, at which point this itinerary turns north toward Alpine via FM 118 for a lonely seventy-eight miles across plains and through valleys with spectacular mountains sometimes in the distance, sometimes nearby. This is some of the countryside seen in films such as *The Good Old Boys*. When you reach Alpine, you'll see Sul Ross State University perched above the town, the alma mater contemplated by the youths in *Dancer, Texas Pop. 81*. If you're hungry, you might want to visit the Sonic Drive-In that the Groovers patronized in *Fandango*. You may also recognize landmarks from *Sylvester* and *Grand Champion*.

Alpine → Marathon → Langtry → Del Rio (205 miles)

Leaving Alpine on US 90 headed east, you drive through the Glass Mountains and arrive at Marathon, a town so named because its founder was reminded of the hills near Marathon, Greece. Here, you can visit the gas station where the Groovers' car was repaired at the intersection of the highway with Avenue F. Thereafter, US 90 leads through a raw and arid region named *malpais*, or "badlands," by the early Spanish explorers.

The mountains of Big Bend have been left behind; but upon reaching Langtry, you will happily have come back in contact with the Rio Grande. Here you can review the colorful exploits of Judge Roy Bean and take advantage of the displays and services provided by the official Texas Visitor Center, including an impressive cactus garden. About eighteen miles farther along, US 90 brings you to the highway bridge and the spectacular scenic overlook above the Pecos River Canyon, where you look down upon cave dwellings and southward into the mountains of Mexico.

When you reach the city of Del Rio, you are very near a point where three Texas regions converge—Big Bend, Hill Country, and South Texas Plains—so this city could claim identity with any one of them. As a border town, it is distinguished by many Mexican qualities as well. Several movies have shot scenes in the vicinity of Del Rio, including *Sugarland Express*, *The Good Old Boys*, and *Lonesome Dove*. Across the border in Ciudad Acuña, you may recognize locales from *El Mariachi* and *Desperado*, two highly successful films by Austin's Robert Rodriguez.

Alpine → Fort Davis → Toyah → Pecos → Pyote → Odessa → Midland (200 miles)

FM 118 leads north out of Alpine to Fort Davis, where most of *Dancer, Texas Pop. 81* was filmed; you'll recognize the courthouse, which played the high school in the movie. Fort Davis, on a plain 5,050 feet above sea level, is the highest town in Texas; consequently, it is a relatively cool oasis during the summers and historically a magnet for visitors seeking to escape the heat of other regions. Besides enjoying the town, you will want to visit the Old Fort Davis National Historic Site, which served as the backdrop for the opening scenes of *The Good Old Boys*. FM 17 winds northward along the edge of the Davis Mountains through gorgeous scenery to Balmorhea. Preferably after visiting the San Solomon Springs swimming pool, take FM 2903 out of Balmorhea north to Toyah, where you can check out *Fandango* locations; then hit I-20 east to Pecos, for *Flesh and Bone* ambience; to Pyote to view the "Pecos Parachute" hangar from *Fandango*; and on to Odessa for *Friday Night Lights* and then to Midland for *Waltz Across Texas* and *Hangar 18* locations.

BIG BEND COUNTRY CAST AND CREDITS

Some notable movie folk who were born or grew up in Big Bend Country:

Kathy Baker, actress, born in El Paso
Thomas Haden Church, actor/writer/director,
   born in El Paso
Woody Harrelson, actor, born in Midland
Judith Ivey, actress, born in El Paso
Terry Jastrow, actor/writer, born in Midland
Debbie Reynolds, actress, born in El Paso
Gene Roddenberry, writer/producer, born in El Paso
Irene Ryan, actress, born in El Paso

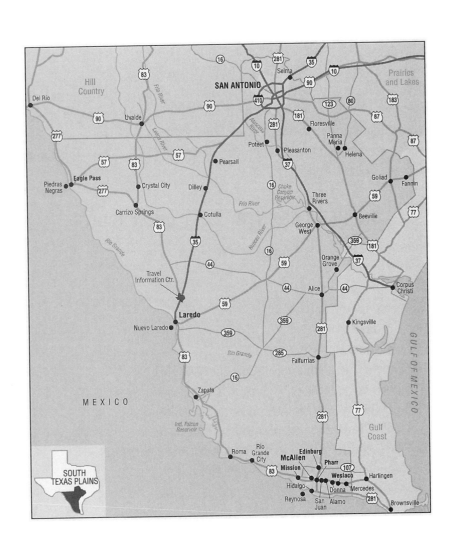

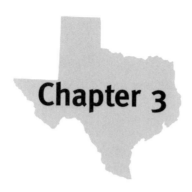

Chapter 3

South Texas Plains

This stretch of road runs between nowhere and not much else.
Indian Shop Owner in *Lone Star*

ESTABLISHING SHOTS

The Region on the Map

THE SOUTH TEXAS PLAINS region has much in common with the neighboring Big Bend Country, including strong Mexican influences, great expanses of unforgiving landscapes, and a generally sparse population. The major exception to that sparseness, metropolitan San Antonio, presides grandly from the northernmost point of the region as the irresistible city to which virtually every road you see on the map ultimately leads.

The sinuous path of the Rio Grande marks the western border of these plains, and you might surmise the inhospitable nature of its upper three-fourths when you notice on the map that only two U.S. border cities appear there, Eagle Pass and Laredo. Sometimes called "Brush Country" in reference to the predominant vegetation of mesquite, prickly pear, and dwarf oaks, the mostly wide open spaces stretch over to where the Gulf Coast begins. Though not very hospitable to humans, the minimal vegetation of the Brush Country could support large herds of cattle because of the enormous size of the ranches established there in the nineteenth century.

In contrast to the mostly empty space between Eagle Pass and Laredo and even on down to Mission, the southern quarter of the river's path is dotted with a sudden flurry of communities. McAllen, San Juan, Pharr, Weslaco, and their close neighbors owe their existence and prosperity to the richness of the soil and the length of the growing season. Here in the Lower Rio Grande Valley, known to Texans simply as The Valley, the meandering river has laid down several eons' worth of alluvial and delta deposits which, combined with the tropical climate, allow for a glorious and year-round agricultural bounty.

Along the eastern edge of the South Texas Plains, you will find scattered small towns proud of their cultural heritages and historical significance. Goliad, near the eastern extremity, is particularly important to Texas history as the site of the massacre of James Fannin and his men. "Remember Goliad!" joined "Remember the Alamo!" as the battle cry of "Texian" soldiers as they fought the Mexicans. The entire region will appeal not only to fans of movies about the fight for Texas independence but also to those who love westerns that feature cattle drives, border skirmishes, and vast ranches.

Movie lover's tours focus on a variety of settings in San Antonio and on the cities of Laredo, Eagle Pass, Mission, and Roma, each of which has starred in at least one movie. The only official Texas Travel Information Center in this region is north of Laredo at the intersection of I-35 and US 83, but San Antonio has a full-service visitor information center at 317 Alamo Plaza.

The Region Onscreen and Off

The South Texas Plains, more specifically San Antonio, welcomed some of the earliest moviemaking to the state. In 1910, Gaston

Melies established the Star Film Ranch and produced some seventy movies, including one called *The Immortal Alamo*, before moving the company to California in 1911. Other production companies briefly set up shop in San Antonio during the next decade or so, but by the mid-teens Hollywood and New York were clearly the only permanent homes of the studios. However, these studios continued to use Texas sites for location shootings. For example, San Antonio provided exteriors for *The Warrens of Virginia* in 1923; and its military installations saw the filming of many movies about flying, including the very first Oscar winner, *Wings*, in 1927. In fact, so many movies have been shot in San Antonio that there is at least one entire book devoted to the subject, *Texas Hollywood: Filmmaking in San Antonio Since 1910* (Maverick Publishing Company, 2002), by Frank Thompson.

Not until the 1950s, however, did movies filmed in Texas begin to gain the high profile that they enjoy today. And the first big-name project of that era was filmed in the South Texas Plains in and around the town of Roma. The movie was *Viva Zapata!* in 1952, a major studio production that received several Academy Award nominations and won Anthony Quinn his first Oscar. Although the story was not set in Texas, the producers chose Roma as the filming location because it resembled Zapata's Mexican hometown—a decision resulting in a movie that shows off this Texas border town and the surrounding countryside.

Ironically, perhaps the best movie about the establishment of the Texas cattle industry in South Texas was not filmed in the state at all. *Red River* was shot in Arizona and Mexico but is not to be missed if you want to appreciate the mythic qualities of huge cattle drives and the acquisition of the land north of the Rio Grande, all of major significance to Texas history. One South Texas area that evolved into enormous cattle empires is often referred to as the Nueces Strip, the land between the Nueces River and the Rio Grande, which remained in dispute between Texas and Mexico until the end of the Mexican War. Land entitlements of millions of acres had been granted first by Spain and then by Mexico to owners who depended on *vaqueros*—the original cowboys of the region—to ride the land and protect their interests. These rugged fellows are the original source of traditional cowboy attire: bandanas, boots, spurs, chaps. And they provided many familiar terms attached to cowboy life, such as *bronco, rodeo, reata,* and *sombrero.* In *Red River,* John Wayne successfully takes over the land for his ranch after killing one of the defending *vaqueros* and sending the other back with the message, "Tell Don Diego . . . that all the land north of that river's mine. . . . I'm takin' it away from him."

Even after the Mexican War had established the Rio Grande as the southern boundary of Texas, additional controversy arose because the river was continually changing its course. Since the exact border became impossible to identify, pockets of land along the river became a kind of no-man's-land for bandits who could evade each country's law enforcement there. Texas Rangers set out to end the depredations of these outlaws by methodically and ostentatiously killing them, a draconian policy that apparently helped deter the predators. Finally, in 1905, the United States and Mexico signed a treaty defining the boundary once and for all, thus eliminating the lack of jurisdiction around the shifting channels of the river.

Aside from the ranches and cattle drives featured in scores of movies, the most frequently filmed subject associated with South Texas is undeniably the Battle of the Alamo, which stands peacefully amid the downtown bustle of San Antonio. Many Alamo movies have been filmed in Texas, but almost none anywhere near the actual site. A look at just a few of them reveals dramatically different approaches to the story.

A Film Festival of Alamo Movies

The Man from the Alamo (1953), starring Glenn Ford, is mainly an "after-the-Alamo" movie, a highly fictionalized account of Moses Rose, the only man who chose not to stay and fight with the others. As Hollywood tells the story, the man, renamed "John

Stroud," does not decide on his own to leave; rather, he has had the bad luck to draw the black bean in a lottery to see who would go on a courier mission. He plans to return to fight alongside his comrades, but is unable to get back before the final battle. Consequently, he is scorned as a coward by other Texans until he redeems himself by saving a wagon train from outlaws.

Davy Crockett, King of the Wild Frontier (1955) is a nostalgic favorite of the baby boomers. This Disney epic had kids all over the world singing the theme song and wearing coonskin caps. Fess Parker's Crockett is perhaps the one most people think of first, although John Wayne's has plenty of devotees, especially among the Daughters of the Republic of Texas (DRT), the ladies who maintain the integrity of the Alamo. However, Billy Bob Thornton's portrayal in 2004's *The Alamo* may challenge these two old standards, at least for viewers who appreciate historical accuracy.

The Last Command (1956) appeared right on the heels of the televised Davy Crockett saga and presented a very different treatment of the Battle of the Alamo, one striving mightily for historical accuracy. It focused more on Jim Bowie, played by Sterling Hayden, than on Crockett, who this time was played by Arthur Hunnicutt as a man pushing fifty in contrast to Parker's more youthful Davy. Perhaps the most notable difference from earlier Alamo movies is the characterization of Santa Anna, whom J. Carrol Naish portrayed as a believably flawed human being rather than an evil caricature.

The Alamo (1960), which John Wayne directed and starred in as Davy Crockett, was a high-dollar enterprise that trumpeted its "authenticity." Experts were consulted and research was done, but more than a few errors slipped through, such as placing the Alamo near the Rio Grande rather than the San Antonio River. Also, a couple of generic fictional characters were written into the story: a beautiful Mexican woman, played by Linda Cristal, to provide love interest for Wayne; and a young survivor, played by the teen fave Frankie Avalon, to sing "The Green Leaves of Summer." Sometimes box office ambitions trump historical accuracy.

Viva Max! (1969) is a lighthearted movie that aroused anything but approval in the hearts of the Daughters of the Republic of Texas. As much as they adored John Wayne's film, they detested this adaptation of Jim Lehrer's novel about a two-bit Mexican general whose decision to march across the border and retake the Alamo is based upon the logic that Mexico had, after all, won that particular battle. Unlike most other Alamo films, this one includes scenes shot in San Antonio—along the River Walk, for example, at the Spanish Governor's Palace, and at the old police station across from the county courthouse. But since the DRT ladies were so horrified that they even closed the Alamo to all visitors for the duration of the *Viva Max!* filming, there was no thought at all of shooting this mockery inside the Alamo itself. Interiors were shot on a set constructed in Rome, Italy.

The Alamo: Thirteen Days to Glory (1987) is a made-for-TV movie that earnestly attempts to be authentic. In avoiding too-youthful actors, however, the producers leaned a little heavily toward age. Three of the main characters who were in their forties at the Alamo are played none too convincingly by actors in their sixties: James Arness, Brian Keith, and Lorne Greene, in his final role. On the other hand, Alec Baldwin and the late Raul Julia are not only age appropriate but also very effective in their roles as Travis and Santa Anna. The budget for this effort was apparently too limited to pay for extras needed in the battle sequences. The final scenes have obviously been lifted from the 1956 production *The Last Command*.

Alamo . . . The Price of Freedom (1988) has been playing since 1988 in the IMAX theater near the Alamo and is well worth its forty-minute running time. Of course, its brevity means that many details are omitted; but the film is accurate as far as it goes. It provides an excellent introduction or refresher for the visitor who wants to appreciate the history of the shrine.

The Alamo (2004) was plagued long before filming began with highly publicized changes in announced stars, directors, producers, and script. Adding to the perception of general confusion was the unfortunate delay of its much-ballyhooed premiere, and, upon the movie's release, the box office was not kind. However, this film deserves a second look on DVD, especially by viewers interested in historical accuracy. In contrast to John Wayne's version, it was made with authenticity as a primary goal, and historians have praised the results. As for movie reviewers, they have offered the most praise to the performances of Billy Bob Thornton, as Crockett, and Jason Patric, as Bowie. Dennis Quaid, as Sam Houston, has not fared so well with the critics.

The whole subject of the Alamo is obviously a perennial favorite with filmmakers, since the eight movies described here represent only a fraction of the total. In fact, Frank Thompson has written a book called *Alamo Movies* (Old Mill Books and Republic of Texas Press, 1991) that offers a full account of various television and big screen treatments of the story through 1990. And Don Graham's *Giant Country* (TCU Press, 1998) includes excellent commentary on many of those movies in the essay "Remembering the Alamo: The Story of the Texas Revolution in Popular Culture." The basic facts about the Alamo are well known, to Texans anyway, but filmmakers keep trying to answer the story's central question—why, really, did 187 men fight for thirteen days against clearly overwhelming odds?

REEL-LIFE AND REAL-LIFE TOURS
Feature Presentations: South Texas Plains in a Starring Role

Viva Zapata! (1952)
Marlon Brando, Anthony Quinn, Jean Peters,
and Joseph Wiseman
Directed by Elia Kazan

Reel-Life Tour

Though little known today, *Viva Zapata!* is a classic film that received many honors, including several Oscar nominations. John Steinbeck's screenplay was nominated, and Anthony Quinn won his

Civil War–era buildings in Roma, pretending to be in Mexico, provided a setting in 1952 for *Viva Zapata!* Courtesy of Bob Parvin/TxDOT

first Academy Award as a supporting actor, while Marlon Brando lost as best actor to Gary Cooper in *High Noon*. Although it's about Mexican history rather than Texas, the film deals with matters that had great impact on the border towns, since the Mexican Revolution inevitably imposed itself on South Texas.

Elia Kazan and screenwriter Steinbeck were both drawn to the subject by their admiration for Emiliano Zapata, the illiterate Mexican peasant who led uprisings against a dictatorship that allowed the wealthy to steal land from the poor. They wanted to make the film in Mexico, but because that country's government demanded the right to approve the script, they shot most of the movie in the Texas town of Roma and its surrounding countryside, which apparently looks much like Morelos, Zapata's home state.

Marlon Brando transformed himself with a moustache and makeup to look amazingly like the historical figure. His performance is straightforward, with none of the mumbling and eye rolling associated with many of his later roles. Quinn plays Zapata's swaggering brother Eufemio to the hilt, never letting even the great Brando overshadow his performance.

Real-Life Tour: Roma

One of the best-preserved towns in this region, Roma was, during the last half of the nineteenth century, a steamboat port where goods from the eastern United States and Europe were unloaded and transported by land into Mexico. Such foreign contacts created a taste for other cultures in the inhabitants, as reflected in the surviving Spanish and French Creole–style architecture. In 2001 the town celebrated the fiftieth anniversary of the filming of *Viva Zapata!* with a parade and film festival, attended by more than thirty-five local residents who had worked as extras in the movie. The historic buildings have recently been restored, but they are still recognizable from the film—especially the picturesque Spanish colonial church, the cobblestone plaza, and the Vale–Noah Cox House, where Anthony Quinn stood on the balcony and kissed his horse in joy at the news of the Mexican dictator's defeat. Current residents still take pride not only in the choice of Roma as a filming site, but in the colorful history of the town as an inland port, a center for ranchers from both sides of the border, and a hideout for Mexican Revolutionaries.

She Came to the Valley (1979)
Ronee Blakley, Dean Stockwell, Scott Glenn, and Freddy Fender
Directed by Albert Band

Reel-Life Tour

Based on a 1943 novel by Cleo Dawson, who grew up in the town of Mission, *She Came to the Valley* tells the story of a poor family living in the Rio Grande Valley during the Mexican Revolution. Pat Westall and his wife Willy are the pioneering couple, played by Stockwell and Blakely, who leave Oklahoma to homestead in Texas. A drifter persuades them to move to the Valley, where they discover that he is a supporter of Pancho Villa, the revolutionary leader being vilified by Mexican soldiers who raid the towns along the border and pretend to be his followers. This film is not widely known and is obviously a low-budget enterprise, but it was filmed on location in Mission and McAllen and has a certain sweetness about it. Popular Tex-Mex singer Fender gets to sing the title song, and the author of the novel shows up as a partygoer in one scene.

Real-Life Tour: Mission, McAllen

The town of Mission took its name from a nearby settlement established by Oblate Fathers in the 1820s. These priests are said to have planted one of the first orange groves in the Valley, thus originating the citrus culture about three miles from the present town. More than oranges, however, the Texas Ruby Red grapefruit is the fruit associated with Mission. The town was established about 1908, so its early years coincided with the Mexican Revolution, as the storyline of *She Came to the Valley* makes clear. Nearby McAllen is popular as a gateway to Mexico; its center is only eight miles from the Mexican town of Reynosa, a proximity that ensures the intertwining of the region's history with that of Mexico.

Eddie Macon's Run (1983)
Kirk Douglas, John Schneider, Leah Ayres, and Lee Purcell
Directed by Jeff Kanew

Reel-Life Tour

John Schneider was still hot as one of TV's "Dukes of Hazzard" when he was cast in *Eddie Macon's Run*, an action/crime thriller. He plays the title character, who is wrongly charged with murder and locked up in a Texas jail. Desperate to rejoin his family in Mexico, he breaks out of jail and is pursued by a small-town cop, played by Kirk Douglas, who is determined to bring him back. There is nothing particularly Texan about the whole enterprise, which ultimately involves a murderously deranged ranching family and a rich young woman who helps Eddie out of sheer boredom. But Laredo forms a background for much of the movie, including a wild car chase through the city streets. This movie is one to view for shots of Texas cityscapes and landscapes, not for cultural or historical insights.

Real-Life Tour: Laredo

Laredo is an interesting city, dating back to 1755 as the first nonmissionary, nonmilitary Spanish settlement in North America. Its heart was San Agustin Plaza, still in existence as part of a restored downtown. In the early nineteenth century, Laredo was caught between two wars of national independence, Mexican and Texan, ultimately being claimed by Mexico. Then when Texas joined the United States in 1845, Laredo again became a no-man's-land between two countries because the United States and Mexico could not agree on the boundary line. When the Rio Grande was finally accepted as the border, those who wanted to remain Mexican citizens moved across the river and established Nuevo Laredo in 1848.

Such a colorful history deserves its own movie someday, but for now *Eddie Macon's Run* will have to do. Martin High School, on San Bernardo Avenue, was transformed into the prison from which Schneider's character escapes; and the rodeo scene was shot at the Laredo International Fair and Exposition grounds, charmingly known as LIFE Downs. The exterior of La Posada Hotel, on Zaragoza Street, serves as a backdrop for some of the action.

Cloak and Dagger (1984)
Henry Thomas, Dabney Coleman, and Michael Murphy
Directed by Richard Franklin

Reel-Life Tour

Unfortunately, the prehistoric nature of the Atari cartridge that causes so much trouble in *Cloak and Dagger* is probably a complete turn-off to today's sophisticated high-tech kids. That may explain why the movie is currently available only in VHS. But this is a rare film truly suitable for the whole family, and it deserves a DVD release. It is suspenseful and imaginative enough to keep adults interested while the story focuses on two resourceful children who must battle the evildoers on their own. The liveliness of the writing and the acting is enough to make you forgive the improbabilities of the plot, even while realizing that those bad guys surely wouldn't shoot at kids on a city bus!

A post-*ET* Henry Thomas impeccably plays Davey Osborne, a young boy grieving for his recently deceased mother and living in a fantasy world of video spy games with an imaginary friend from one of those games, heroic Jack Flack. Davey's father, an Air Force sergeant at San Antonio's Kelly Field, is worried about his son's fantasy life; and when Davey tells of witnessing a real murder and being pursued by real bad guys, his dad is sure Davey is merely imagining all the excitement. The dad and Jack Flack are both played by Dabney Coleman, in one, or rather two, of his best roles ever; and Davey's relationship with each one is a heart-warmer.

Real-Life Tour: San Antonio

The city of San Antonio, Henry Thomas's actual hometown, is shown off to great effect in *Cloak and Dagger*, and she doesn't even seem to have aged all that much in the twenty-plus years since the filming—with the exception, perhaps, of Windsor Park Mall and the old-style boats on the River. The River Walk itself looks pretty much the same today and also sounds the same when you pass Jim Cullum's Landing, where the Jim Cullum Jazz Band still plays most nights. The Japanese Tea Gardens, referred to as the Sunken Gardens by locals, at Brackenridge Park; the Tower Life Building; the airport; and the Alamo all figure prominently in the plot, but the Alamo scenes were shot on a set in California. Apparently the guardians of the Alamo, the Daughters of the Republic of Texas, did not consider *Cloak and Dagger* worthy of permission to film on the site.

Still Breathing (1997)
Brendan Fraser, Joanna Going, Celeste Holm, and Lou Rawls
Directed and written by James F. Robinson

Reel-Life Tour

As in *Cloak and Dagger*, San Antonio gets lots of attention in *Still Breathing*, a highly unusual romance. Brendan Fraser plays Fletcher, a street performer first seen operating his marionettes near the Alamo. He becomes convinced by a series of dreams that his intended true love is a cynical, predatory young woman named Roz, whom he finally locates in Los Angeles. Roz leads a grim life of conning rich men who are attracted to her. Through a misunderstanding, she thinks Fletcher is just one of the targets set up for her. A substantial suspension of disbelief is required for this plot to work, but excellent performances, along with an almost dreamlike tone, help the viewer accept the more improbable details and simply enjoy the trip.

To describe Fletcher as eccentric is putting it mildly, but Fraser's portrayal exudes a convincing sincerity. Celeste Holm is delightful as his equally eccentric grandmother, Ida; and Joanna Going manages to make Roz sympathetic despite her unsavory lifestyle and her bitterness. But the setting is as essential to the film as the characters are. San Antonio possesses unique charms encompassing its vivid past as a Spanish outpost, then an American frontier town, and now one of the largest cosmopolitan cities in the country. At its heart is a downtown marked by a spider web of streets radiating out from its center and a river so winding that it travels fifteen miles between two points only six miles apart. Despite its skyscrapers, it manages to suggest an unhurried, old-fashioned life. Its historic missions are constant reminders of the past and the spirituality that laid the city's foundations. Fletcher and his friends spring believably from this sweet miasma that has prevailed over the violent history of battles and skirmishes that finally created a graceful, soulful old city. As Fletcher says, "It's its own world."

Real-Life Tour: San Antonio

Still Breathing's opening scene takes place on a closed street in front of the Alamo. Since filming is not allowed on Alamo property, this scene and the later one where Fletcher works his puppets show the Alamo only in the background. Fletcher takes Roz to see the San Jose Mission, where they walk along a path east of the chapel, and he shows her the Rose Window in the Mission's south wall, telling her the same story that a Park Ranger will probably tell you if you ask. The scene with Fletcher and his grandmother in boats playing their musical instruments was shot on an undeveloped stretch of the river north of town, near the Mulberry Street bridge. The other river scenes—dream sequences of Fletcher and Roz as children and the final image of them floating down a gleaming river—were shot in San Marcos, about an hour's drive north of San Antonio, in the Hill Country. Private homes were used for interiors and, understandably enough, their addresses are not public. However, you can see wonderful houses similar to Fletcher's in gracious old Alamo Heights. And finally, the coffee house where Roz and Fletcher first meet is not in Los Angeles at all, but is actually the Babylon restaurant on South Alamo Street.

Lone Star (1996)
Chris Cooper, Elizabeth Peña, Kris Kristofferson,
and Matthew McConaughey
Written and directed by John Sayles

Reel-Life Tour

Lone Star beautifully captures the Tex-Mex tapestry found in both the South Texas Plains and the Big Bend Country. The accents and speech patterns; the references to food, entertainment, and work; the personal interactions; and especially the music are all authentic to the borderlands. You have to pay attention, however, for the story is complex, reflecting both the history of the region and the intertwined lives of the characters. In fact, this movie requires and deserves at least two viewings for full appreciation. Sayles presents the blended cultures—or rather the *blending* cultures, since the process is ongoing—through the conventions of both the detective story and the western. He demonstrates how a common history can be perceived in different ways by different people.

The setting is a fictional border town called Frontera, where Sam Deeds serves as reluctant sheriff in the shadow of his late revered father, Buddy Deeds, who is credited with redeeming the sheriff's office after the monstrous tenure of his predecessor, Charley Wade. The discovery of a human skeleton in the desert causes Sam to suspect his father may have murdered Charley back in 1957. Along with Sam's investigation, occurring in the present, the movie provides frequent flashbacks to the 1950s, gradually piecing together events involving not only Buddy and Wade, but also other characters such as the teenaged Sam and his high school sweetheart.

Real-Life Tour: Eagle Pass

Lone Star was filmed in Eagle Pass, in most ways a real-life counterpart to Frontera. In fact, according to Sayles, "virtually everything we needed was there except for the drive-in, which we had to build." Other exceptions would be references to a dam and military installation within the county, but those entities certainly exist along the border; they are just attached to other cities. Del Rio, for example, is near the banks of Lake Amistad, created by the mighty Amistad Dam in the 1960s. The little town of Zapata was relocated to its present site after the original town, like the fictional Perdita mentioned in *Lone Star*, was inundated following the construction of Falcon Dam. As the seat of Maverick County, Eagle Pass boasts a proper courthouse to represent that of the fictional Rio County in *Lone Star*. The Mexican border town of Piedras Negras is within walking distance across the international bridge. Although Fort McKenzie exists only in the movie, you can visit many restored buildings of historic Fort Duncan, including a museum.

Sayles took great pains to present the racial and cultural complexity of towns like Eagle Pass, managing to include many historical references to the Spanish, the Mexicans, the Indians, the African Americans, and the Anglos. A scene at the high school in which parents and teachers argue about how local history should be taught provides a synopsis of the different ways these groups can view the events and personalities from their shared past.

Short Takes: South Texas Plains in a Supporting Role

All the Pretty Horses (2000)
Matt Damon, Henry Thomas, and Lucas Black
Directed by Billy Bob Thornton

Based on Cormac McCarthy's novel of the same name, most of this film's story is set in places other than the South Texas Plains, but much of it was filmed on the Gallagher Ranch near Helotes outside of San Antonio. The ranch house, built in the 1850s with native stone, plays the Mexican ranch *La Purisma*, surrounded with lush tropical plants brought in to make it look as though it is sitting in central Mexico. The movie stars Matt Damon and Henry Thomas, who is as impressive now that he is grown up as he was in *Cloak and Dagger*. Director Billy Bob Thornton has captured the elegiac tone of a tale about young men aspiring to a way of life that they realize is disappearing in 1940s Texas. They leave their home near San Angelo and head to Mexico in search of a cowboy's life. One of the establishments they visit on the way is played by San Antonio's Cadillac Bar, located at 212 S. Flores Street. The Scottish Rite Cathedral on Avenue E in San Antonio plays a fancy restaurant in Mexico where Damon and Penelope Cruz enjoy a rendezvous.

Pee Wee's Big Adventure (1985)
Paul Reubens, Elizabeth Daily, and Jan Hooks
Directed by Tim Burton

Most people don't associate Texas with Pee Wee Herman, aka Paul Reubens, but this film includes memorable scenes filmed in San Antonio. Reubens and the late Phil Hartman wrote the very funny script that recounts Pee Wee's search for his stolen bicycle. After a psychic tells him that the bike is hidden in the basement of an important landmark in Texas, Pee Wee sets out to retrieve his beloved possession. He gets to San Antonio by hitchhiking and by hopping a train. When he gets there he finds out, of course, that the Alamo has no basement. The humorous "Alamo tour" led by

Jan Hooks was, needless to say, not approved by the DRT for filming inside the shrine. It was shot instead at a California mission.

Father Hood (1992)
Patrick Swayze, Halle Berry, Sabrina Lloyd, and Brian Bonsall
Directed by Darrell Roodt

Patrick Swayze seems to have great fun in *Father Hood*, a humorous dad-and-kids road picture. Even though his being a native Texan is not part of the story, he does not disguise his real Texas accent. He plays a small-time hood who is a completely uninvolved father until he is convinced he must rescue his daughter and son from an abusive juvenile home in California. The teenaged girl and small boy join him on a cross-country trek to New Orleans, with several colorful stops in Texas—notably at Floore's Country Store in Helotes and at Cascade Caverns in Boerne—all eventually resulting in chase scenes as the police pursue the father who has technically kidnapped his children.

Miss Congeniality (2000)
Sandra Bullock, Michael Caine, Benjamin Bratt,
and Candice Bergen
Directed by Donald Petrie

The ever-charming Sandra Bullock produced and stars in *Miss Congeniality*, a bit of entertaining fluff. She plays an FBI agent completely out of touch with her inner beauty queen until she goes undercover to prevent a terrorist attack by pretending to be a contestant in a beauty pageant. Coached by a very funny Michael Caine, she, of course, blossoms into the gorgeous woman that was never really disguised and also manages to identify and disarm the bad guys. Partially shot in San Antonio, the film offers lots of colorful scenes filmed along the River Walk, in front of the Alamo, at the Convention Center, and at the Institute of Texas Cultures.

Border Bandits (2004)
Narrated by Roland Warnock et al.
Directed and produced by Kirby Warnock

Border Bandits is a documentary based on a story told to the director/producer by his grandfather Roland Warnock, recounting violent events that took place near Edinburg in 1915. Roland told his grandson about witnessing the murders of two unarmed men by Texas Rangers and then burying the bodies himself two days later. Kirby spent years investigating the story, interviewing historians and the victims' descendants, studying Texas Ranger reports, trying to nail down the facts for his film. He then produced *Border Bandits*, which includes the actual recorded narration by his grandfather, accompanying a reenactment of the events for the screen. The documentary is also enhanced by the voices of a female mariachi band, The Ramirez Family from Odessa.

SOUTH TEXAS PLAINS TRAVELOGUES
Scouting the Locations

You could spend several days visiting San Antonio's movie locations, and the city's many charms will probably make you want to stay even longer. It makes a great headquarters for exploring the South Texas Plains; in fact, all of the movie lover's itineraries start from there. Before you even venture outside the city limits, however, take time to appreciate its unique personality.

The City of San Antonio

The mission that ultimately became San Antonio was established by Spain in 1718, half a century earlier than the creation of the United States, and a certain Old World quality was permanently imprinted on what is now a bustling modern city. Its residents tend to display a decidedly relaxed attitude, but not in the

Romantic, festive River Walk in San Antonio, site of suspenseful chase scenes in *Cloak and Dagger* and *The Getaway.* Courtesy of J. Griffis Smith/TxDOT

sense of a lack of industriousness. As *Still Breathing* illustrates, the folks in San Antonio, or "San'tone" as many Texans call it, live and work with an infectious exuberance that blossoms into the numerous fiestas and celebrations held throughout the year. Virtually everyone who visits San Antonio falls in love with the city.

The Alamo is usually at the top of a visitor's to-see list, and even though most of the films about it have been shot elsewhere, any movie lover will want to pay homage to the actual shrine. *Cloak and Dagger's* set of the interior may have looked realistic, and films such as *Miss Congeniality*, *Still Breathing*, and *Pee Wee's Big Adventure* offer good looks at the chapel's exterior; but getting behind that façade and exploring what remains of the original mission can be rather thrilling.

Not far from the Alamo is *El Paseo del Rio*, "the River Walk," a level below the downtown streets and a delightful place for strolling, dining, and people watching. Among the hotels, boutiques, and sidewalk cafes, you will find Jim Cullum's Landing, where you can listen to the jazz band that plays in *Still Breathing*. A naturally romantic and dreamy setting among giant cypress trees, tropical greenery, and arched bridges for films such as *Selena* and *Still Breathing*, the River Walk can also provide a scary ambience for exciting chase scenes like those in *Cloak and Dagger* and *The Getaway*.

Numerous downtown landmarks besides Alamo Plaza and the River Walk will look familiar to the moviegoer, such as the Tower Life Building, with the Tower of the Americas in the background, from *Cloak and Dagger*; the Scottish Rite Cathedral from *All the Pretty Horses* and *The Newton Boys*; the Alamodome from *Selena*; the downtown U.S. Post Office from *Father Hood*, *The Big Brawl*, *Toy Soldiers*, and *Johnny Be Good*; the St. Anthony Hotel from *The Newton Boys*; the San Antonio International Airport from *Cloak and Dagger* and *Still Breathing*; and La Villita Plaza from *American Outlaws*.

Brackenridge Park, two miles north of downtown, offers a lovely retreat of winding paths, rustic bridges, and tranquil pools. It made its movie debut in 1923 playing Appomattox in *The Warrens of Virginia*. More recently, its Japanese Tea Gardens, created from an old limestone quarry, were seen in *Cloak and Dagger*, where a nostalgic viewer may catch sight of the now demolished sky ride, a system of Swiss-made cable cars that once provided a panoramic view of the gardens and the adjacent San Antonio Zoo. The distinctive Sunken Gardens' appearance in *The Big Brawl* tends to undercut the pretense that the story is taking place in Chicago.

Also north of downtown is the Monte Vista Historic District, with its grand homes built mostly during San Antonio's "Gilded Age" (1890–1930), and Alamo Heights, the neighborhood in which *Still Breathing*'s Fletcher lives. South of downtown another residential area, the King William Historic District, has been tapped for scenes in films such as *The Newton Boys* and *Nadine*.

The Missions and the Military in San Antonio

In addition to the Alamo, four other early eighteenth-century missions comprise the San Antonio Missions National Historical

Park. The Mission Trail is marked with signs on the city streets directing visitors to each of the majestic structures presiding over the banks of the San Antonio River. Mission San Jose, known as the "Queen of Missions," is the one with the Rose Window featured in *Still Breathing*. But not mentioned in the movie is the delightful fact that mariachi masses take place there each Sunday. The other three missions are worth visiting as well. Mission Concepción, with its massive twin towers and cupola, boasts acoustics said to equal those of Utah's Mormon Tabernacle, and you can admire its beauty in the last scenes of *Outlaw Blues*, where it pretends to be a church in Mexico. Mission San Francisco and Mission San Juan are still active churches today, ready to serve descendants of the first Indians who were converted and who worshipped within their restored walls.

These missions, along with the Alamo, were established near the river during the town's struggles for existence, first against Apaches and Comanches. Ever since being founded as a presidio, San Antonio's identity has had a strong military component. From the 1920s through the 1940s, the area provided locations for numerous movies about military men, pilots especially. Randolph Air Force Base is famous for its "Taj Mahal," a training facility built in 1931 with a rotating beacon on a tower 147 feet tall. Its blue-and-yellow glazed tile roof could be seen by pilots from miles away. Hollywood presented this structure as a rallying point for heroic aviators in such films as *West Point of the Air* (1934), *I Wanted Wings* (1941), and *Air Cadet* (1951). Even earlier, the first full-length feature to win an Oscar, *Wings*, was filmed at Camp Stanley in 1926. Camp Stanley was part of the Leon Springs Military Reservation, where other movies were also filmed, including King Vidor's acclaimed 1925 drama, *The Big Parade*. Leon Springs Military Reservation, located twenty miles northwest of San Antonio, also includes Camp Bullis, named for a commander of the Black Seminole Scouts, whose history is discussed by a character in John Sayles's *Lone Star*.

San Antonio ➤ Boerne ➤ Helotes ➤ San Antonio (70 miles round trip)

This itinerary would make a nice little day trip out of San Antonio for anyone, but especially for fans of *Father Hood*. Take I-10W toward Boerne to exit 543; then follow the signs to Cascade Caverns, a living cave named for its hundred-foot waterfall. *Father Hood*'s viewers will see plenty to recognize in the cave itself and on its grounds, which served as the setting for one of the movie's big chase scenes. After you've enjoyed these caverns, you might want to continue with your spelunking by visiting Boerne's Cave Without a Name and then head toward San Antonio via a back road or two.

Take State Highway 46 out of Boerne over to Highway 16, and turn back toward San Antonio. You will encounter the little town of Helotes, where Floore's Country Store has reigned for more than sixty years as one of the state's greatest dance halls and was another location for *Father Hood*. If your timing is right, you may hear some great Texas music. Many of the biggest names have performed there and continue to do so. The founder, John T. Floore, was for a time the business partner in the original Willie Nelson Music Company and was immortalized in Nelson's song "Shotgun Willie."

Not far from Helotes is the Gallagher Ranch Headquarters, the first dude ranch in Texas, dating back to 1927. Scenes for *All the Pretty Horses* and the 1995 remake of *Lolita* were shot here. You can go to www.gallagherheadquarters.com for information and photographs.

San Antonio ➤ Eagle Pass ➤ San Antonio (280 miles round trip)

Another day trip out of San Antonio is especially for fans of *Lone Star*. You might even want to make it more than a day trip and stay overnight to experience the local culture on both sides of the

border. The very fact that it is not a tourist mecca can make Eagle
Pass, along with its Mexican sister city, Piedras Negras, an appeal-
ing destination to many folks. The mix of races and cultures, dom-
inated by the Mexican, is easily observed even by the casual visitor.
One interesting historical fact that is not mentioned in *Lone Star* is
that Eagle Pass is considered the "burial plot of the Confederacy."
On July 4, 1865, General Joe Shelby was riding to Mexico with his
troops to offer assistance to the French Emperor Maximilian when
he decided to bury the last Confederate flag carried by his men.
The spot he chose was in the middle of the Rio Grande as he
crossed the border from Eagle Pass. Most of the major history of
the area, however, is referenced in Sayles's film, including the grad-
ual ascendancy of Hispanic leadership, the ongoing plight of the
Kickapoo tribe, and the unresolved conflicts over the Texas Revolution, especially regarding the legends of the Alamo.

San Antonio ➤ Laredo ➤ Roma ➤ Mission ➤ Edinburg (305 miles)

The stretch of I-35 between San Antonio and Laredo makes up
more than half of this itinerary; and frankly, there is not much variety in the Brush Country landscape, nor are there any major
movie-related sites to recommend. However, you may want to
visit one or more of the perfectly nice little towns you will encounter along the interstate. Cotulla, for instance, houses its
Brush Country Museum in a former school where President Lyndon Johnson taught, and it also claims some movie lore connections by virtue of its proximity to La Mota Ranch, where most of
The Texans was filmed in 1938. North of Cotulla, the little towns
of Pearsall and Dilley offer expressions of agricultural pride char-
acteristic of the South Texas Plains. A giant peanut monument
graces Pearsall's downtown, and a huge watermelon presides over
Dilley's City Park. This South Texas propensity to erect monuments to agricultural products is slyly referred to by Sam Deeds in
Lone Star, when he mentions the possibility of a giant catfish to

boost tourism for his town. Other real-life examples are Poteet's World's Largest Strawberry, Floresville's giant peanut, and Crystal City's somewhat more imaginative tribute to the spinach crop: a statue of Popeye.

Besides providing the landscape and buildings you might recognize from *Eddie Macon's Run*, Laredo is a fascinating place for its culture and its history. Actually, there are two Laredos. The first Laredo is on the U.S. side of the Rio Grande, and Nuevo Laredo is on the Mexican side. Most residents are bilingual, and holidays as diverse as Washington's Birthday and Mexican Independence Day are celebrated with equal enthusiasm in both Laredos. The hybrid culture depicted in *Lone Star* is found here also, but in a big-city setting rather than the small-town milieu of Eagle Pass.

Highway 83 out of Laredo tends to hug the path of the Rio Grande as it curves south and east, being one of the major "Roads of the River," *Los Caminos del Rio*. Before you've gone fifty miles, you come to Zapata, named for a famous Indian fighter, Antonio Zapata, and not the character Marlon Brando played in *Viva Zapata!* The original town of Zapata was completely submerged when the Rio Grande was dammed to create Falcon International Reservoir in 1953; the current town was built to replace it. A somewhat fictionalized version of the construction of Falcon Dam and Reservoir and the resultant destruction of the old town is significant to the plot of *Lone Star*. Photos of the old Zapata are displayed in San Ygnacio's La Paz Museum, housed in a two-hundred-year-old Mexican home located between Laredo and present-day Zapata.

About forty miles south of Zapata the flat terrain becomes hilly, and you come upon Roma, with its enchanting Old World atmosphere. The European-style nineteenth-century buildings with iron-barred windows and overhanging balconies blend Spanish and French Creole influences, and according to the makers of *Viva Zapata!* they mirror perfectly a nineteenth-century Mexican town. Roma's National Historic Landmark District includes thirty-eight structures that were built between 1848 and 1928. Just about fourteen miles on down the highway, Rio Grande City sits among hills similar to those of Roma; but during the thirty-mile drive to Mission, you will notice a change in the scenery.

Instead of the monotonous expanses of rolling Brush Country mesquite and cactus interrupted only occasionally by a small town, the landscape flattens out again to fields of onions, aloe vera, and cabbage. Dusty greens and browns give way to vivid color. Purplish pink bougainvillea in the spring and crimson poinsettias in winter accent the many vibrant shades of green among the citrus orchards edged with towering palms and dotted with yellow-and-orange globes of fruit. You have entered the Rio Grande Valley.

Mission sits on the edge of an urbanized stretch of the highway, but it has maintained its small-town atmosphere. Its primary significance for the movie lover resides in its being both the setting and the filming location for *She Came to the Valley*. But, in addition, its main street boasts the still thriving Border Theater, a stunning Pueblo-style movie palace built in 1942 and decorated with colorful ceramic tiles and murals, a wonderful place to enjoy a picture show.

McAllen, just a few miles east, is the major city of this area and caters to thousands of visitors, especially those called "Winter Texans," or "Snowbirds." These folks are mainly Midwesterners or Canadians who spend the whole winter here, enjoying this subtropical paradise year after year. Leaving McAllen on Highway 83, the movie lover's tour continues north on Highway 281 just a few miles to Edinburg, which serves as the western gateway to the Lower Valley. Near these two towns, the events of *Border Bandits* took place in 1915. Edinburg's Museum of South Texas History is a good place to get an overview of the history and prehistory of this entire region. And the Sheriff's Posse Rodeo, every Saturday night at an arena two miles south of Edinburg, provides a firsthand view of cowboys doing their thing—just like in the movies!

SOUTH TEXAS PLAINS CAST AND CREDITS

Some notable movie folk who were born or grew up in the South Texas Plains:

Carol Burnett, actress, born in San Antonio
Joan Crawford, actress, born in San Antonio
Al Freeman Jr., actor, born in San Antonio
Ann Harding, actress, born in Fort Sam Houston
    (San Antonio)
Richard Jones, actor, born in San Antonio
Paula Prentiss, actress, born in San Antonio
Robert Rodriguez, director/writer/producer/actor, born in
    San Antonio
Henry Thomas, actor, born in San Antonio
Peter Weller, actor, graduated from Alamo Heights High
    School, San Antonio

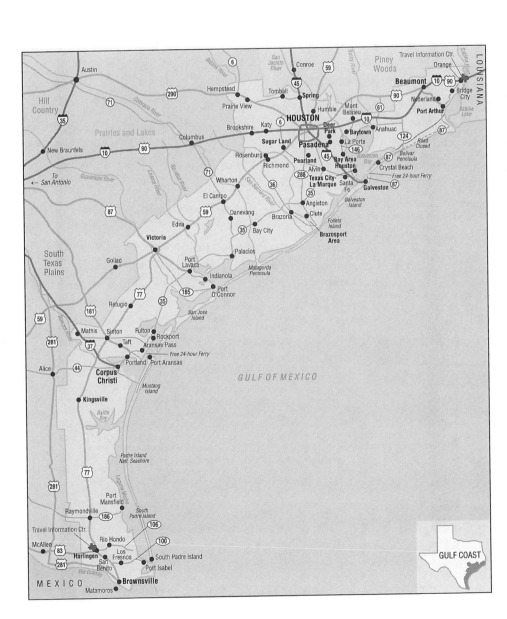

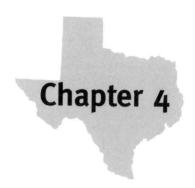

Chapter 4

Gulf Coast

Some Texas where real cowboys seem
Lost in a movie-cowboy's dream.
W. H. Auden, "New Year's Letter"

ESTABLISHING SHOTS

The Region on the Map

STATE TOURISM BOOSTERS have been known to refer to the Gulf Coast as the Texas Riviera. Slightly more modestly, perhaps, they have also called it the Texas Gold Coast, but in reality the region has its own unique personality and need not make false claims of either a Cannes or a Miami Beach. Between Brownsville, at the southwestern tip, and Orange, at the northeastern point of this crescent-shaped region, you will encounter islands and peninsulas, beaches and parks, laid-back fishing communities and wildlife refuges, and big-city as well as seashore attractions of all kinds.

The distance between Brownsville and Orange is about 365 miles as the crow flies, but if you drive the major highways that connect them, you will travel about a hundred miles more than that. The driving is relatively easy along excellent major highways I-10, US 59, and US 77; but you will not see much of the Gulf of Mexico unless you head toward the shoreline on one of the eastbound or southbound roads off the main thoroughfares. Along the whole length of the coastline, you will find a series of narrow barrier islands and peninsulas separated from the inner shorelines by wide, shallow lagoons, such as the Laguna Madre between Padre Island and the mainland.

The region designated as the Gulf Coast encompasses the entire Texas coastline and arcs inland as much as a hundred miles to the town of Hempstead at its widest point. Most of the region's towns are no more than fifty miles from the shore, however, including southernmost Harlingen and Brownsville, both within the eastern reaches of the Lower Rio Grande Valley; Victoria, just beyond the South Texas Plains near the center of the arc's path; and Beaumont, a major port near the edge of the Piney Woods, where it anchors two sides of the "Golden Triangle" along with the cities of Port Arthur and Orange. Boasting two of the excellent Texas Travel Information Centers, one at Harlingen and the other at Orange, the Gulf Coast beckons visitors to delight in its shimmering seaside attractions, its fascinating history, and its urban cultural amenities.

The Region Onscreen and Off

The Gulf Coast holds special interest for movie lovers as the location for the earliest moving pictures ever shot in Texas—at least the earliest still in existence. These silent film clips, which document the devastation of Galveston by the hurricane of 1900, can be viewed on the Internet at www.1900storm.com for an eerie look at the storm's destruction and for a glimpse of the Texas island and some of the people who lived there more than a century ago.

The cities of Brownsville and Harlingen are considered by most Texans to be in the Valley rather than on the Coast, but they are as much like the coastal towns to their east as they are like the border towns to the west along the Rio Grande. In common with the latter, they saw their share of border skirmishes during the early 1900s, and they enjoy the agricultural productivity of the Valley; but Brownsville is also an international seaport, connected to the Gulf of Mexico by a seventeen-mile-long ship channel. And both Brownsville and Harlingen are only a very short distance from the premiere beach resort of South Padre Island.

North of Brownsville sprawl the eastern reaches of the South Texas Plains; and, just over into the Gulf Coast, you'll find the city of Kingsville, known as the "birthplace of the American ranching industry" as it continues to service the huge King Ranch, established in 1853 and encompassing 825,000 acres. Open to guided tours, the ranch is still a working operation with thousands of head of cattle and hundreds of horses. It is often cited as the inspiration for Bick Benedict's ranch in *Giant*.

Corpus Christi, the next city up the shoreline, marks the beginning of what is sometimes called the central coast, which stretches roughly to Bay City and forms a transition zone between the arid lower coast and the moisture-laden upper coast. Corpus—Texans generally drop the *Christi*—sits where the humid coastal plains meet the dry Rio Grande plains. The city's Hispanic-majority culture, as depicted in *Selena*, allies it with the lower coast; the city's humid climate allies it with the upper coast.

East of Corpus, protecting its glittering downtown high-rise buildings and sailboat masts from the full power of the mighty Gulf of Mexico, Mustang Island and Padre Island have merged into one barrier island since the channel that once split them in two has silted up. North of Mustang Island, folks living along several bays and on the Rockport-Fulton Peninsula enjoy an economy based largely on sport fishing and the shrimping industry. Following the shoreline to the upper coast, you encounter Galveston Island, and at its northern tip the magical city of Galveston, where acclaimed producer/director King Vidor was born in 1894; and where, at age 18, he produced and directed a movie about the 1900 hurricane.

Galveston's direct access to the ocean would seem to have made it the most important port in the region; but instead, Houston, fifty miles inland, became the Gulf Coast's primary seaport and trading center. Connected to Galveston Bay by Buffalo Bayou, Houston attracted leaders who quickly saw the value of developing a ship channel. Later, the discovery of oil inspired petroleum companies to build refineries, and Houston subsequently became a leading petrochemical and natural gas center. This industry has provided the movies with many stereotypical Texas oilmen, but another group of movie characters are also attached to Houston—the astronauts and their mission control managers at the Space Center. In addition, the bustling city has served as the urban backdrop for several movies about generational conflict, such as *Terms of Endearment* and *Jason's Lyric*; and the soaring façades of Houston's gleaming skyscrapers have visually energized futuristic films like *Robocop 2* and *Futureworld*.

Despite the variety of films associated with the Gulf Coast, and with all of Texas for that matter, the phrase "Texas movie" still initially calls to mind for most people a western, starring cowboys. The Gulf Coast, with its decidedly un-western terrain of islands, seashores, and modern urban landscapes, would seem an unlikely location for such a movie. But in fact, one of the quintessential western movie motifs, the cattle drive, was born in this region.

In the early 1920s a silent film called *North of 36*, based on a novel of the same name, was shot on location at a ranch near Houston and included footage of one of the last actual cattle drives. The story deals with the Reconstruction era in Texas, when the devastated local economy necessitated transporting cattle to distant markets, and it was told again in two remakes of the film: *The Conquering Horde* (1931) and *The Texans* (1938), both of which incorporated some of the original cattle drive footage. The realism of the scenes shot for *North of 36* greatly pleased historian J. Frank Dobie, who had criticized other movies for showing the cattle being driven northward always at a run. However, some additional footage of cattle appearing in *The*

Texans, which was shot on location near Cotulla, in the South Texas Plains, was not at all authentic, according to Dobie, who complained that an uninformed viewer of the movie might think that the cattle "never quit running over the entire two-thousand-mile trail."

The Gulf Coast has not been the location for a traditional western movie in a long time, but filmmakers continue to tell stories about the culturally diverse people who live in this region of colorful history and sparkling seascapes and who often exhibit a contemporary worldliness attained over decades of economic booms and busts. Several films offer entertaining and authentic views of this enticing slice of the Lone Star State.

REEL-LIFE AND REAL-LIFE TOURS

Feature Presentations: Gulf Coast in a Starring Role

Red River (1948)
John Wayne, Montgomery Clift, Walter Brennan,
and Joanne Dru
Directed by Howard Hawks

Reel-Life Tour

Even though it was filmed in Arizona and Mexico rather than Texas, *Red River* so quintessentially depicts certain historical and cultural realities, as well as Texan archetypes, that it deserves to be called a classic Texas movie. Its setting can be generally represented by a swath reaching from the Red River itself, where it meanders north of the Wichita Falls area, all the way to the Rio Grande, perhaps to Brownsville. The mythic tale embodies some of the most compelling events of the nineteenth century in West and South Texas, namely the successful defiance of Indian attacks and harsh landscapes in order to create great cattle herds, which were then transported to Kansas in an epic cattle drive. The old-fashioned scrolling prologue that follows the opening credits immediately sets the stage for some heavy-duty iconic footage to follow: "Among the annals of the great state of Texas may be found the story of the first drive on the famous Chisholm Trail, a story of one of the great cattle herds of the world."

The story begins in 1851. Dunson (John Wayne) and his friend Groot (Walter Brennan) depart from a California-bound wagon train to head south for Texas, where Dunson intends to start his own cattle herd. Shortly thereafter they are joined by an orphaned boy leading a cow. The recurring visual of a cowhide-bound journal is opened to a page reading, "And that was the meeting of a boy with a cow and a man with a bull and the beginning of a great herd. In search of land they traveled South through Texas . . . through the Panhandle . . . nearing the Rio Grande."

The intervening years melt into a montage with Dunson's voice-over predicting the huge ranching empire he'll create. By 1865 the now white-haired Dunson has fulfilled his dream of producing "thousands of head of good beef," and the boy has grown up to be his surrogate son, Matt, played by Montgomery Clift. But the Civil War's aftermath has destroyed the Texas economy, and there is no local market for the cattle. Like the characters in *North of 36*, Dunson faces financial ruin unless he can move them north, so he orders all of his and his neighbors' cattle to be rounded up and branded in preparation for driving them to Missouri.

In one of the film's most memorable scenes, the men are all ready to start the drive near dawn. The camera pans around the mounted cowboys and the cattle, coming to rest on Dunson as he says, "Take 'em to Missouri, Matt." The picture explodes with quick close-ups of individual cowboys waving their hats and whirling their horses around as they shout to get the cattle moving. This is the scene that Peter Bogdanovich chose to show on the movie theater's screen in *The Last Picture Show*, perhaps to emphasize the contrast between the malaise of his 1950s characters and the idealized, exuberant energy of their pioneering forebears.

After this optimistic kickoff, however, *Red River* focuses on realistic details of the grueling trail drive—the tedium, the physical exhaustion and injuries, the tight rations of food and water. After many hardships and adventures, the herd arrives successfully—in Abilene, Kansas, rather than Missouri—and the cowboys are welcomed as the first to drive their cattle along the route that will be named the Chisholm Trail.

Real-Life Tour: Brownsville, Raymondville, Sarita, Kingsville, Victoria

Although *Red River* was filmed elsewhere, most of the story takes place in Texas, and an appropriate tribute to this movie would be to follow an itinerary organized around the meanderings of the old Chisholm Trail itself. Originally, the name applied only to that part of the trail north of the Red River, where wagon tracks made by a trader called Jesse Chisholm were followed by a herd of 2400 steers being driven from San Antonio. Eventually, however, the entire network of trails from the Rio Grande to central Kansas would be called the Chisholm Trail and would extend eight hundred miles from various points in south Texas. The trail has become a major symbol of the romantic Old West, even though its life span as an important transportation route was only about twenty years.

The main trail stretched from San Antonio to Fort Worth and then west to cross the Red River near what is now called Spanish Fort. But feeder trails converged on the main trail, so one can argue that these branches can correctly be called part of the Chisholm Trail. In the Gulf Coast, Brownsville is often cited as the southernmost point where cattle drives began, so the Chisholm Trail/*Red River* tourist might start there and move on up through Raymondville, still a ranching town; Sarita, home of the huge Kenedy ranch; Kingsville, home of the even huger King Ranch; and Victoria, home and burial place of one of the few female drovers, Margaret Heffernan-Borland.

Baby, the Rain Must Fall (1965)
Steve McQueen, Lee Remick, and Don Murray
Directed by Robert Mulligan

Reel-Life Tour

Adapted by highly acclaimed Texas author and screenwriter Horton Foote from his play *The Traveling Lady*, this movie's script showcases the southern more than the western characteristics of Texas. The movie's setting is in Columbus, a town in the Prairies and Lakes region, and much of the film was shot in the Gulf Coast region; but the Piney Woods area of far East Texas is nearby, and the Piney Woods is where the southern roots of the Texas personality run deep. Lee Remick's character, whose accent sounds very southern, mentions more than once that she has traveled from East Texas to Columbus.

The story is very dark, almost Southern gothic in tone, emphasizing mood and character over plot. McQueen plays Henry Thomas, a paroled convict who returns to his sleepy hometown of Columbus, where the judgmental residents have no sympathy for his dream of a career singing with a string band. His wife, Georgette, played by Remick, has been notified of his release from prison and travels to Columbus with their young daughter. She hopes to set up a real household with Henry, and even he expresses some desire to fulfill his domestic responsibilities. But his violent temper, his hatred of his abusive adoptive mother, and his drinking all conspire to defeat Georgette's dream of a happy family.

Reviews were mixed on the artistic quality of this film, but it contains many authentic details of life in small Texas towns during the early 1960s. Particularly good are the scenes involving Georgette's struggles to find work, the scenes filmed in the honky-tonks where Henry plays with his band, and those revealing the stern attitudes of the locals toward the man they watched grow up and go bad. Particularly unauthentic, however, are the scenes depicting Henry's singing, in which McQueen's lame attempt at lip-synching is simply excruciating. At least the uncredited appearance of Glen Campbell as one of the musicians offers a bit of welcome distraction.

Real-Life Tour: Wharton, Bay City

Wharton is the hometown of Horton Foote, who wrote *Baby, the Rain Must Fall*, and maybe that is one reason the residential scenes were filmed there instead of in Columbus, where the story is set and where scenes in the courthouse were shot. Columbus is less than forty miles north of Wharton via FM 102. Steve McQueen is said to have stayed in a motel in Bay City, twenty-five miles south of Wharton on Highway 60, during the filming. Among other pastimes, he apparently spent a good deal of time at the Bay City Ford dealership working on his car.

My Sweet Charlie (1970)
Patty Duke and Al Freeman Jr.
Directed by Lamont Johnson

Reel-Life Tour

This TV movie not only earned eight Emmy nominations and great critical acclaim but also received very high viewer ratings, thus helping to pave the way for other serious and high-quality TV productions during the 1970s. In her Emmy-winning performance, Patty Duke plays an uneducated, frightened southern girl whose pregnancy has caused her lover and her family to abandon her. She ends up in a deserted house by the sea to await the birth of her child, only to have her solitude broken by the arrival of an African American lawyer played by Al Freeman Jr., who is being hunted for the killing of a white policeman.

The movie was shot at Port Bolivar, where one of the caretaker's dwellings at the historic lighthouse becomes the refuge sought by these two desperate souls. In addition to views of a magnificent Gulf Coast landmark, this movie offers a touching account of how the

racial tensions and misunderstandings of the 1960s—not so different from those of today, perhaps—can be overcome by two people
whose hearts are finally receptive to each other. The realistic conflict between the ignorant southern white teenager and the militant
northern black attorney gradually evolves into a love story as a result of the circumstances that brought them together, circumstances
created by different but equally oppressive kinds of social prejudice.

Real-Life Tour: Port Bolivar

The lighthouse featured so prominently in *My Sweet Charlie* is
located on the southern tip of Bolivar Peninsula, a sparsely populated strip of land fifty miles long northeast of Galveston Island. If
you tire of the tourists in Galveston, you can hop the free ferry that
travels between Galveston and Bolivar Point and enjoy the relative
solitude in the area of the lighthouse. However you manage to get
there, you will be visiting an important historic site. In addition to
being the home of many fascinating stories about the lighthouse,
dating back to 1845, Port Bolivar also claims to have been the birthplace in 1821 of the first Anglo baby in what was to become Texas.
Jane Wilkinson Long became known as the "Mother of Texas" after
giving birth in a mud fort near the current Port Bolivar. You should
know, however, that the Piney Woods has perhaps a stronger claim
for that first Anglo birth; for in 1804, Helena Kimble Dill's daughter
was born in what is now Nacogdoches County.

Terms of Endearment (1983)
Shirley MacLaine, Debra Winger, Jack Nicholson,
and Jeff Daniels
Directed by James L. Brooks

Reel-Life Tour

Based on Larry McMurtry's novel of the same name, *Terms of
Endearment* is not nearly so drenched in pure Texas ambience as

the other films made from his novels, such as *The Last Picture Show*; but it was filmed largely, and recognizably, in Houston. The story focuses on the turbulent, ultimately loving relationship between two strong-willed women, Aurora Greenway (MacLaine) and her rebellious daughter, Emma (Winger), and does not emphasize Texas or any other particular region of the country. The scenes involving Aurora's love interest suggest something of a tie with Houston since he, Garrett Breedlove (Nicholson), happens to be an ex-astronaut. Their scenes together of sharp-tongued repartee and genuine affection are delightful respites from what turns out to be a world-class tearjerker.

This uniformly excellent production was rewarded with a bit of a sweep at the Academy Awards, winning the Best Picture award along with Best Director, Best Actress (MacLaine), and Best Supporting Actor (Nicholson) and a slew of nominations. A sequel to *Terms of Endearment* in 1996, *The Evening Star*, had trouble living up to its predecessor; but it is actually quite watchable and offers many of the same actors and location shots, only a decade or so older.

Real-Life Tour: Houston, Galveston Island

Aurora and Garrett live in posh homes representative of the stylish Houston enclaves, such as Avalon and River Oaks, the latter having recently attracted such notable residents as former President and Mrs. George H. W. Bush. The movie characters' homes are actually located on Locke Lane in the Avalon section of the city. For their contentious first date, Aurora and Garrett have lunch at Brennan's, a popular downtown restaurant, and then go for a wild drive along East Beach on Galveston Island. Emma and her husband, Flap, set up housekeeping in a garage apartment located in Houston Heights, which features lovely Victorian houses, many on the National Register of Historic Places.

Urban Cowboy (1980)
John Travolta, Debra Winger, Scott Glenn, Madolyn Smith,
and Barry Corbin
Directed by James Bridges

Reel-Life Tour

A few years before *Terms of Endearment*, Houston starred in another movie, and this one was more thoroughly Texan. It also focused on a different social level; the main characters reside in a
trailer park rather than in swanky River Oaks. The time frame as
well as the location is intrinsic to *Urban Cowboy*, since the movie
depicts a specific period and subculture in Houston—the late
1970s, when young oil-industry workers crowded into singer
Mickey Gilley's enormous honky-tonk to drink, dance the two-
step, and test their machismo by riding the mechanical bull. This
movie coincided with and undoubtedly contributed to the nationwide fad of western styles of dress and entertainment, sometimes
called redneck chic. Consequently, it inevitably seems dated, but
the movie still features believable portrayals of the young Texans
who flocked to Gilley's a quarter-century ago, and not everything
has changed since then.

The plot is nothing to brag about. Young, not-too-bright, work-
ing-class couple Bud and Sissy hang out and try to work out their
problems at Gilley's, whose synthetic Old West atmosphere is reflected in the film's storyline. The bad guy (Scott Glenn) actually
attempts a holdup at the dance hall, and Bud swiftly foils him,
thereby winning back his lovely wife. But, as Don Graham points
out in his book *Cowboys and Cadillacs: How Hollywood Looks at
Texas*, the movie is not all about pseudo-cowboys. In addition to its
fake western glamour, *Urban Cowboy* also includes gritty, true-to-
life details about contemporary Houston. Sissy's job, for instance, is
driving a tow truck for her father's business; she drags crashed vehicles from the freeways to the wrecking yard. Her Uncle Bob's house
is typical of the cookie-cutter developments that have eaten up the

previously open marsh prairies. And the dreary disorder of Sissy and Bud's mobile home reflects the reality of their having married too young and without a clue as to who they really are.

Real-Life Tour: Houston, Pasadena, Deer Park, Pearland

Unfortunately, for those who would like to tackle the mechanical bull themselves, Gilley's watering hole burned down in 1990 after enjoying immense popularity throughout the 1980s in suburban Pasadena. In the film's opening montage, the skyline is recognizable as Houston's; and during Bud's trip down Memorial Drive, nostalgic Houstonians can lament long-gone landmarks such as the Jeff Davis Hospital and Allen Parkway Village. Locations still standing are Uncle Bob's house on West Side Drive in suburban Deer Park, the oil refinery where Bud works in Pasadena, and the cemetery in Pearland. You needn't look for the mobile home park where Sissy and Bud live, however; those scenes were shot in California.

Alamo Bay (1980)
Ed Harris, Amy Madigan, Ho Nguyen, Donald Moffat, and
Truyen V. Tran
Directed by Louis Malle

Reel-Life Tour

Alamo Bay is based on actual events related to a painful topic for Texas, or any other state for that matter: racism. The victims of racial prejudice in this film are Vietnamese immigrants who settled in a Gulf Coast town after the fall of Saigon in 1975 to make their living as fishermen. The local shrimpers are understandably concerned when the hardworking newcomers seem to threaten their livelihoods, and the situation escalates into violent hostility. The Ku Klux Klan shows up and tries to gain control of the town by fanning the flames. Alice Arlen wrote the script, which was based on Ross E. Milloy's articles published in the *New York Times*.

Ed Harris, in one of his early roles, does his usual effective job in portraying Shang Pierce, a down-on-his-luck Vietnam veteran facing repossession of his fishing boat. His former lover, Glory, is played by Harris's real-life wife, Amy Madigan. The fictional town of Port Alamo, not far from Corpus Christi, is the setting; the movie was filmed in the Rockport-Fulton area. The conclusion is tragic for the main characters, but despite its incendiary subject, the film conveys compassion for the despondent Vietnam veteran as well as for the targets of his hatred. A rather uplifting follow-up to the subject of this movie is found in a *Newsweek International* article written by Adam Piore in January 2001. Entitled "Breaking Down Barriers," it relates the story of Dallas Cowboy football star Dat Nguyen, whose family experienced hostilities similar to those depicted in *Alamo Bay* but whose subsequent success as an American sports figure is indicative of positive developments in relations between the Vietnamese immigrants and their neighbors.

Real-Life Tour: Rockport-Fulton

Obviously, *Alamo Bay* deals with events that residents probably do not enjoy discussing with visitors, but there is plenty to enjoy in Rockport and Fulton without inquiring directly into the dark period of cultural hostilities along the coast. The two municipalities are separate; but they have so much in common, especially recreational areas, that they have joined forces as a single desirable destination for tourists and tourist-related businesses. Saltwater recreation is especially abundant since the towns are located on a peninsula between Copana Bay and Aransas Bay. Viewers of *Alamo Bay* will be especially interested in the fishing, and they will find many public fishing piers as well as private ones for the guests of motels and hotels. Professional fishing guides and charter boats are available as well, and you can visit Rockport Harbor to admire the local fishermen's daily catch and perhaps elicit some firsthand tales that may be of exotic interest to the landlubber.

The Legend of Billie Jean (1985)
Helen Slater, Keith Gordon, Christian Slater, Yeardley Smith,
Peter Coyote, and Dean Stockwell
Directed by Matthew Robbins

Reel-Life Tour

"Guilty pleasure" is the phrase some fans use to describe *The Legend of Billie Jean*. Most people find its feverishly self-righteous teen heroine a bit over the top, but the movie offers lots of adolescent energy and great shots of Corpus Christi. Billie Jean Davy (Helen Slater), who is seventeen, and her younger brother Binx (Christian Slater) are used to suffering indignities as a result of being poor orphans; but when some rich bullies trash Binx's beloved motor bike, Billie Jean wants justice. Since the authorities are no help, she tries to get the father of one of the bullies to pay for a new bike. He instead offers her cash for sexual favors, and an enraged Binx accidentally shoots him.

In going on the run from the police, the siblings are accompanied by two friends, one of whom is played by Yeardley Smith—

USS *Lexington*, seen in *Pearl Harbor*, and city of Corpus Christi, setting for *The Legend of Billie Jean* and *Selena*. Courtesy of J. Griffis Smith/TxDOT

now famous as the voice of Lisa Simpson. Intensely feeling the injustice of it all, Billie Jean manages to make a video that becomes a media sensation, and she gains fame as "an outlaw, a hero, and the voice of a generation." Girls all over the country start cutting their hair and dressing the way she does while chanting her battle cry, "Fair is fair!" When the younger members of her gang decide to go home, Billie Jean stays the course, continuing to fight for fairness while struggling with the demands of her notoriety.

Real-Life Tour: Corpus Christi

The setting and the location coincide in this movie, and most of the shots of 1980s Corpus Christi are easy to recognize. The site of frantic chase scenes, Sunrise Mall, is located on South Padre Drive. The parking garage is not connected to the mall, however, but rather to the downtown Bank of America. Bob Hall Pier on Padre Island, not far from Corpus, was used for the beach scene; and the final shots, where Billie Jean's effigy burns, were filmed in the parking lot of the Dockside Surf Shop. But you won't find the miniature golf course, where the gang hides out; it was built just for the movie near the Harbor Bridge in downtown Corpus.

Jason's Lyric (1994)
Forest Whitaker, Allen Payne, Jada Pinkett,
and Bokeem Woodbine
Directed by Doug McHenry

Reel-Life Tour

Some of the more well-to-do areas and some of the struggling blue-collar areas of Houston are presented in *Terms of Endearment* and *Urban Cowboy*. A third part of Houston is depicted in *Jason's Lyric*—the inner city. Filmed mostly in the Fourth and Fifth Wards, neighborhoods named for the voting precincts established in the nineteenth century, this movie captures the desperation of some of the city's poorest African American citizens, who live there among the shabby houses and brick-paved streets.

Native Texan Forest Whitaker is featured as Maddog, a happily loving father until he is sent to Vietnam and loses a leg. After he returns home, he becomes a drunk and a wife-beater. His two sons, Joshua (Woodbine) and Jason (Payne), are understandably traumatized, and all the familial anguish ends up with Joshua's accidentally shooting Maddog. The two brothers grow up, Joshua to a life of drugs, petty crime, and jail time; Jason to a plodding existence of working in a TV repair shop and taking care of his religious mother.

The movie's title refers to a young waitress named Lyric, played by Jada Pinkett, who is given to quoting poetry. As the title suggests, she becomes Jason's passion, triggering his desire to change his life, but their plans to escape on a Greyhound bus meet with obstacles personified by Joshua and by Lyric's brother. The publicity for this movie said it combined the story of Cain and Abel with that of Romeo and Juliet.

Real-Life Tour: Houston

In 1839, Houston's city charter divided the city into several sections called wards, and even though these political divisions were abolished in the early 1900s, residents still identify certain neighborhoods with the old names. For example, the Fourth Ward, located southwest of downtown, and the Fifth Ward, east of downtown, along the banks of Buffalo Bayou, denote areas where much of *Jason's Lyric* was shot, and they encompass some of the oldest and most significant African American communities in Houston. After the Civil War until the early twentieth century, the Fourth Ward enjoyed prominence as the cultural and economic center for Houston's black population. During the 1920s, however, the Third Ward began to grow rapidly, attracting black institutions and affluent professionals into new developments. By the 1980s, only one residential area was left in the Fourth Ward, and it had become the poorest black area in Houston, as is painfully represented in *Jason's Lyric*. You may enjoy checking out one of the film's major settings, however. This Is It restaurant, where Lyric works, is located at 207 West Gray Street and is famous for its excellent soul food. It has the distinction of having been mentioned, along with *Jason's Lyric*, in Texas Senate Resolution No. 472, which honored the memory of Frank Jones, the eatery's owner.

Short Takes: Gulf Coast in a Supporting Role

Hellfighters (1968)
John Wayne, Jim Hutton, and Katharine Ross
Directed by Andrew V. McLaglen

A semi-biopic, *Hellfighters* tells the story of men who put out oil-well fires. John Wayne plays Chance Buckman, a character loosely based on Red Adair, the famous Texas oil-rig firefighter, who served as technical advisor for the film. A precursor to later major disaster movies such as *The Towering Inferno* and *Armageddon*, *Hellfighters* focuses on the stressful personal relationships that seem inevitable for movie characters who enjoy life-threatening professions, but you also see great shots of the Goose Creek oilfield in Galveston Bay just outside Houston at Baytown.

A NASA Double Feature:
Apollo 13 (1995)
Tom Hanks, Bill Paxton, Kevin Bacon, and Gary Sinise
Directed by Ron Howard

Space Cowboys (2000)
Clint Eastwood, Tommy Lee Jones, James Garner,
and Donald Sutherland
Directed by Clint Eastwood

These two movies are representative of others dealing with America's space program in that they utilize footage from the NASA center. Houston is not known as Space City for nothing, and some residents will be quick to tell you that the name of their city was the first word spoken on the moon, as in "Houston, Tranquility Base here, the Eagle has landed." The Lyndon B. Johnson Space Center, which was established as the "Manned Spacecraft Center" back in 1961 after a nationwide search for an appropriate site, sits between Houston and Galveston. It houses the real Mission Control, which looks just as it does in the movies. *Apollo 13*, like *The Right Stuff*, is an entertaining movie that relates actual events of the U.S. space program in a straightforward and matter-of-fact way. *Space Cowboys*, on the other hand, is a romantic tale of over-the-hill former astronauts who are called back to duty and heroic deeds. Their training sequences, filmed at the Space Center where real astronauts are prepared for their journeys, emphasize the humor in the old guys' struggles to regain their youthful skills and tolerances.

Rushmore (1998)
Jason Schwartzman, Bill Murray, Olivia Williams,
Seymour Cassel, and Brian Cox
Directed by Wes Anderson

This strange little comedy is not to everyone's taste, but it garnered a good bit of critical praise when it was released. Its creator, native Houstonian Wes Anderson, has referred to it as something of a fable, without a recognizable time or setting; but he ended up filming much of it at his own alma mater, St. John's School in Houston. The movie's Rushmore Academy is a tony private school where Max Fischer (Schwartzman) devotes his time to extracurricular activities instead of to his class assignments. His poor grades get him booted out of his beloved school and sent to the huge Grover Cleveland High School just across the street from Rushmore. Houston's Lamar High School played that role and, in an instance of life imitating art, just happens to be right across Westheimer Street from St. John's. Other locations in the movie are a barber shop at 219 East Eleventh Street, Max's family's home on Emerald Street, the Hollywood Cemetery at N. Main at I-45, and the Warwick Hotel at 5701 Main Street.

Pearl Harbor (2001)
Ben Affleck, Josh Hartnett, Kate Beckinsale, Jon Voight,
and Cuba Gooding Jr.
Directed by Michael Bay

The box-office disappointment of this huge-budget movie is rumored to have been part of the reason that the budget was slashed for *The Alamo* (2004), which in turn was a box-office disaster, perhaps partly due to those very budget cuts. But the critics were not kind to *Pearl Harbor* either. Although the title suggests a serious historical drama, the emphasis in the film is on the love triangle among fictional characters played by Affleck, Hartnett, and Beckinsale. Obviously, a story set in the Pacific during World War II would not seem to be Texan, and it's not. However, two venerable ocean vessels that are docked in the Gulf Coast region appear in *Pearl Harbor*.

Battleship *Texas*, which served in World War I as well as in the 1944 D-Day invasion, is moored at the San Jacinto Battleground State Historic Site at Deer Park. Exterior shots of this unique monument were used to represent various ships under attack at Pearl Harbor. Interior compartments were also used as sets for the scenes aboard the aircraft carrier USS *Hornet*. Also used for scenes representing the *Hornet* was the USS *Lexington*, now a floating museum anchored in Corpus Christi Bay.

Local Hero (1983)
Peter Riegert, Burt Lancaster, Fulton Mackay, Denis Lawson,
Jenny Seagrove, and Jennifer Black
Directed and written by Bill Forsyth

This wryly humorous film is mostly set in a small village in Scotland, but the opening and closing shots offer glimpses of Houston.

Burt Lancaster is funny and rather touching as a rich Texas oilman with palatial offices and a penchant for meteor showers and comets, but his Mr. Happer is too uniquely eccentric to be exemplary of anything particularly Texan. Although this gentle movie does not depict Houston as a bad place, it does represent the city as sterile and impersonal, in contrast to the Scottish countryside, which is more than tolerant of small-town human foibles. The movie opens with Peter Riegert's character, Mac, tooling along Houston's congested freeways in his Porsche, with the glittering skyline in the background. His rather coldly elegant apartment was located in one of the first high-rise apartment buildings in Greenway Plaza; and the fictional Knox Oil Company enjoyed the splendor of the dramatic bronze towers that comprise the Pennzoil Building on Milam Street. You see the crowded downtown streets as Burt Lancaster strides to his limousine at the curb while the police brush by him on their way to arrest his profane counselor, who is perched on a window washer's scaffold outside Happer's plush office. Happer is on his way to join his employee Mac in the Scottish village which Mac was sent to purchase for the oil company. Houston is a pleasant and efficient place in this movie, but Scotland is where the heart is for both Happer and Mac.

Robocop 2 (1990)
Peter Weller, Nancy Allen, Dan O'Herlihy, Tom Noonan,
and John Glover
Directed by Irvin Kershner

The *Robocop* series producers wanted locations that could look like a futuristic version of Detroit, so they chose two Texas cities: for the first one, Dallas, and for the second one, Houston. Needless to say, there's nothing Texan about the storyline, but if you've seen *Robocop 2*, you might be interested in some of the locations. For instance, the exterior of "Civic Centrum" is actually the Wortham Center, on Smith Street in Houston's Theatre District. During the big finale at that site, you can catch a glimpse in the background of the lovely Alley Theatre and of Jones Plaza. The auditorium of Civic Centrum, where the *Robocop 2* incarnation is first seen, however, was shot inside the George R. Brown Convention Center. The Cullen Center, at 1600 Smith Street, portrayed the OCP office. Mayor Kuzak's shouting press conference was filmed in front of Houston City Hall, the east entrance. The abandoned hospital was the former Jefferson Davis Hospital, the exterior of which is seen in *Urban Cowboy's* opening montage and which has since been torn down.

Reality Bites (1994)
Winona Ryder, Ethan Hawke, Janeane Garofalo, Steve Zahn, Ben Stiller, Swoosie Kurtz, and John Mahoney
Directed by Ben Stiller

Though set in Houston, where many of the exteriors were also filmed, this movie is a generic youthful angst picture that could have been set most anywhere in 1990s urban America. In *Reality Bites*, recent college graduates try to decide what to do with their lives while constantly referring to the brand names they've grown up with, such as Big Gulps, Coco Puffs, and the Brady Bunch. Obviously a viewer who also came of age in the nineties will find this group more sympathetic than will some older movie lovers. Ryder's character must choose between the lackadaisical but oh-so-intelligent Ethan Hawke and the ultra-responsible but rather dull Ben Stiller. After Ryder loses her job with a TV show, Hawke comforts her with a visit to Tranquility Park, a downtown oasis of water fountains and cylindrical structures built to honor the moon landing in the Sea of Tranquility. This couple is also joined by Garofalo and Zahn on a rooftop near Hawke's home in the Montrose area. Trendy Montrose is definitely the site where these characters would have landed in Houston.

Selena (1997)
Jennifer Lopez, Edward James Olmos, John Seda,
Constance Marie, Jacob Vargas, and Jackie Guerra
Directed by Gregory Nava

This biopic traces the tragically short life of Tejano singer Selena, a phenomenally popular personality among a large segment of the Texas population. Played convincingly by Lopez, Selena managed to combine sweetness and sexiness in her persona, and she was on the verge of crossing over into mainstream popular music when she was murdered. In depicting her childhood as well as her successful career, the film offers a glimpse of Mexican American culture in contemporary Texas. Her strict yet supportive father is played by the excellent Edward James Olmos; the closeness of family ties is evidenced by the presence of her brother and sister in her band and their mutual dependence in dealing with the pitfalls of fame. Much of this film was shot in other regions of Texas; but one of the Gulf Coast's most glorious jewels, Corpus Christi, shines beautifully in the scenes about Selena's childhood.

GULF COAST TRAVELOGUES

Scouting the Locations

Brownsville ➤ Raymondville ➤ Sarita ➤ Kingsville ➤ Corpus Christi (160 miles)

A logical place to start the grand tour of the Gulf Coast is Brownsville, at the southern tip of the crescent-shaped region. Fans of the 1980 movie *Back Roads* can revisit some of the escapades of Sally Field and Tommy Lee Jones, and history buffs will find much to savor in the Brownsville Heritage Complex and Stillman House Museum as well as in the downtown area's historic structures dating back to the mid-1800s. Anyone with a special affection for war movies will enjoy the museum of the Commemorative Air Force Rio Grande Valley Wing, located at the Brownsville/South Padre Island International Airport. Many World War II films have featured vintage aircraft such as those displayed here. North of Brownsville you can visit the Palo Alto Battlefield, where the first shots of the Mexican war were fired in 1846. Declared a national historic site in 1993, it is required by Congress to offer exhibits that depict the war and its consequences from the perspectives of both the United States and Mexico. In addition to visiting this site marking the very first battle of one war, you can also visit nearby the location of the last battle of another, the Civil War. About twelve miles east of Brownsville stands the historical marker identifying the Palmito Ranch Battlefield, where Confederate forces defeated a band of Federals only to learn that the war had ended a month earlier. And, of course, Brownsville is the southernmost starting point for the legendary Chisholm Trail, celebrated in *Red River*.

Traveling north out of Brownsville, you will encounter at Harlingen one of the excellent Texas Travel Information Centers. There you'll find all kinds of printed information and friendly folks to dispense it, along with special recommendations for what to see and do. Among the city's colorful public murals, be sure to see the one called The Golden Age of Hollywood and Mexican Cinema, painted by Angel Hernandez. It graces the historic Rialto Theatre building and is seventy-six feet long.

Just a few miles farther north on US 77, Raymondville signals the beginning of the plains area of the coast and another marker of the Chisholm Trail. Between here and Kingsville stretches a swath of brush country for almost seventy-five miles, the eastern extreme of the vast South Texas ranches established in the mid-1800s in much the same way that *Red River's* fictional ranch grew up. About fifty miles into these mesquite-studded plains, you will pass through Sarita. Although it is a county seat, Sarita is little more than a ranch headquarters for the 235,000 acres comprising Kenedy Ranch. Sarita, named after the daughter of the ranch's founder, is home to the Kenedy Ranch Museum, which honors the rich family heritage.

Twenty miles north of Sarita and the Kenedy Ranch on Highway 77 is the much larger town of Kingsville, which is, in turn, home of the much larger King Ranch, a National Historic Landmark. For an idea of the ranch's size, consider this frequently made comparison: It is bigger than the state of Rhode Island. Guided tours of the ranch are available, and much of its history is depicted at the King Ranch Museum, located in a downtown restored ice plant. The lively little city boasts other museums along with a variety of boutiques and antique shops in historic buildings. You may also recognize the Kleberg County Courthouse, at 700 E. Kleberg, from its scenes in *The Legend of Billie Jean.*

From Kingsville, Corpus Christi and an entirely different world are only thirty miles away. In less than an hour's drive from the Wild Horse Desert and the birthplace of the ranching industry, you find yourself in a sparkling seaside resort town. To orient yourself before beginning any serious sightseeing, you may want simply to walk along the downtown waterfront. The sculptor who created Mount Rushmore, Gutzon Borglum, designed the impressive seawall that runs along Shoreline Blvd. The seawall features a walkway and seating along the top and steps leading down to the water—a great place to unwind and breathe in the spirit of this lovely city. You can also visit here the Mirador del Flor, a memorial to Selena featuring a statue of the beloved singer.

Corpus Christi ➤ Rockport-Fulton ➤ Refugio ➤ Victoria ➤ Wharton ➤ Houston (230 miles)

Corpus Christi locations for *The Legend of Billie Jean* and for *Selena* are easily recognizable. In addition, Selena fans will want to visit the Selena Museum, established by the singer's father to house various memorabilia including a *Selena* movie script. At one of the Corpus Christi Visitors Centers, you can pick up a map that will direct you to various Selena-related points of interest, such as her home and her gravesite.

When leaving Corpus for points east, you will take the immense Harbor Bridge, US 181, that spans the ship channel and offers a magnificent panoramic view of the coastline. The majestic USS *Lexington*, the aircraft carrier seen in *Pearl Harbor*, is anchored next to the bridge. A tour of its historic premises, now a floating museum, is highly recommended. Once you've crossed the Harbor Bridge, start looking for Highway 361, which will take you toward Aransas Pass and through Ingleside, an early ranching town where one of the first cattle drives commenced. Aransas Pass is a good place to observe the shrimping industry. This city of palm-tree-lined streets hosts the annual Official Shrimporee of Texas, but it generally concentrates on commercial fishing and leaves the resort functions to its island counterpart, Port Aransas.

Leaving Aransas Pass on Highway B35, you will drive mostly through coastal marshlands and occasionally catch sight of the deep blue Gulf waters. After only about eleven miles, you will encounter Rockport's pretty harbor, a seaside recreational paradise. As seen in *Alamo Bay*, the fleets of shrimp trawlers are in constant evidence beyond the windswept trees lining the shoreline. The nearby town of Fulton, established along with Rockport as a separate city in the 1860s, began its life as a ranching town, and both cities were important cattle processing and shipping points till the railroads took over the transporting of cattle and their products. Today they are thriving tourist communities noted for their concentration of artists as well as for fishing, for all sorts of water recreation, and for birding.

Once you can tear yourself away from the sparkling coastline, head northeast out of Fulton on Highway 35 for a trek back inland through cattle and oil-producing country. At the intersection with FM 774, turn left, and go west about twenty miles to Refugio, a busy cattle-market town during the Chisholm Trail days. Its ranching history is vividly depicted at the Refugio County Museum, and this proud heritage mixes with the contemporary bustle of oil production. US Highway 77 leads out of Refugio to

Victoria, some forty-three miles away. Victoria is a gracious city that sits serenely at a distance from the modern bisecting highways that reflect its origins as a major historical crossroads. Many cattle drivers called it home, and one of the few women who ventured onto the trail, Margaret Heffernan-Borland, was returned here for burial after she died in Kansas at the end of a drive in 1873. The McNamara House Museum offers an extensive exhibit detailing everyday life and culture of late nineteenth-century South Texas—a chance to compare the versions seen in movies with the real thing.

US Highway 59 east out of Victoria will carry you toward Houston, and a little over halfway there, you will come to Wharton, acclaimed writer Horton Foote's hometown. Residential scenes for *Baby, the Rain Must Fall* were shot here way back in the early 1960s, but the comfortable old homes look much the same as they did then with their broad porches and neat flower beds.

Just outside the town, on US 59, you will almost certainly notice the Tee-Pee Motel. This eye-catching tourist court from the 1940s was seen in the 1995 remake of *Lolita*, as were the postwar buildings in the nearby tiny towns of Egypt and Glen Flora, which lie on FM 102.

Powder featured Wharton's courthouse in the role of a high school, and that 1995 film also includes scenery that you may recognize as you travel farther on US 59 toward Houston, including Sugar Land's state prison, the exterior of which was used to represent a boys' school. Sugar Land itself, however, despite what you might expect, does not appear in the 1973 film *The Sugarland Express*. Perhaps if it had been included with the other Texas cities that provided locations for that film, the producers would not have misspelled the city's name as one word instead of two.

If this itinerary has been completed in one day, the arrival in Houston will probably coincide not only with the end of daylight but very likely with the end of a traveler's energy. There is so much for the movie lover to see in Houston and the immediate vicinity that a fresh start the next day is recommended.

Houston, Inside Loop 610

Most Texans have a strong opinion about Houston; they either love it or hate it, and each viewpoint can be defended. The city has much to love, for sure, including great museums and art galleries; excellent ballet, opera, and symphony companies; top-flight restaurants with exotic menus. On the other hand, its detractors can cite its lack of zoning regulations, horrific traffic, polluted air, and oppressively humid climate. In the end, though, the pluses outweigh the minuses for a visitor, since the drawbacks would mainly be a problem for residents and the positive features are perfect for a vacationer.

The downtown area of Houston is a good place to begin a movie lover's tour; it is full of landmarks featured in several popular films. Since the city is one of the largest in the entire nation, you will need to orient yourself and plan your rambles to make the most of your visit. A first stop, then, should be the Visitor Information Center at 901 Bagby Street in the City Hall. Coincidentally, the east entrance of this building served as the backdrop for the mayor's press conference scene in *Robocop 2*.

Other *Robocop 2* sites are within the Theatre District, which covers seventeen downtown blocks and is second only to New York City in the total number of seats for all its venues. The imposing Wortham Center provides a permanent home for both the Houston Grand Opera and the Houston Ballet, rather incongruous residents for the site of the violent finale of *Robocop 2*. That explosive footage also includes background shots of the nearby Alley Theatre and Jones Plaza, equally genteel entities in real life. The damage you see in the movie was, thankfully, computer generated. Other major scenes for *Robocop 2* were shot at the Cullen Center and at the George R. Brown Convention Center.

Tranquility Park, featured in *Reality Bites*, commemorates the first moon landing on the Sea of Tranquility and is a lovely downtown oasis of towering cylindrical shapes and flowing water. Built on top of a three-level underground parking garage, the stainless steel cylinders are the transformed underground garage exhaust vents discharging air high above the walkways. Seating areas among trees and grass counter the space-travel suggestions of the towers and provide good vantage points from which to view the architecture of downtown and relax to the cooling sounds of flowing water.

Also downtown you can visit Brennan's restaurant, where Aurora and Garrett have lunch in *Terms of Endearment*; you can gawk up at skyscrapers like the Pennzoil Building, where Burt Lancaster reigned over Knox Oil Company in *Local Hero*, and One Shell Plaza, which portrayed Washington DC's FBI building in *Arlington Road*; you can admire the Warwick Hotel, where Bill Murray's character moved when his marriage crumbled in *Rushmore*. Not far away, the Fourth and Fifth Wards stretch along Buffalo Bayou, where the poignant characters in *Jason's Lyric* seek escape from their individual demons and where you can stoke up on soul food at Lyric's workplace, the funky This Is It cafe. Another colorful eatery, a bit northwest of downtown, is the Pig Stand No. 7 on Washington Avenue, where Aurora dines with a younger suitor in *The Evening Star*, the not-too-successful sequel to *Terms of Endearment*.

To the east of I-45, you'll find Houston Heights and Avalon Place, where characters in *Terms of Endearment* and *The Evening Star* resided. The young, hip seekers of *Reality Bites* lived south of the Heights in Montrose. Also in the heart of Montrose, at 3921 Yoakum Street, is the former home of Howard Hughes. Nearby is the ritziest neighborhood of all, River Oaks, also seen in *Terms of Endearment*. And you will also find in this area St. John's School and Lamar High School, both of which were locations for *Rushmore*. Down in the southwest quadrant of the area enclosed by

Houston's Tranquility Park, visited by Winona Ryder and Ethan Hawke in *Reality Bites,* and part of the skyline as seen in *Local Hero, Urban Cowboy, Jason's Lyric,* and other films. Courtesy of J. Griffis Smith/TxDOT

Loop 610, you can visit the Houston Museum of Natural Sciences to experience its intriguing exhibits—or just because you saw it pretending to be a Washington, DC, museum in *Arlington Road*. If you particularly liked that 1994 movie, you may want to drive outside the Loop and farther south on Highway 288 to Pearland's Dixie Woods subdivision, where the residential scenes were shot. Finally, the aging behemoth that is the Astrodome sits just inside the Loop. You can view it as a young "Eighth Wonder of the World" in the 1970 cult film *Brewster McCloud*.

Pasadena and Deer Park

Pasadena is southeast of downtown Houston, and its sister suburb Deer Park is directly to its east. You can see the site where Gilley's Country and Western Club teemed with young would-be cowboys and cowgirls before it burned down at 4500 Spencer Highway. In the northern part of the city, along the Houston Ship Channel, you'll see refineries where many of those youngsters, including *Urban Cowboy's* Bud, worked to pay for their boisterous nights at Gilley's. Over in Deer Park the filmmakers found the perfect house for Sissy's Uncle Bob, on West Side Drive.

And for something completely different, head up Battleground Road, Highway 134, on the eastern edge of Deer Park to the San Jacinto Battleground State Historic Site. This is where Texas won its independence from Mexico on April 21, 1836, as depicted most recently by Hollywood in 2004's *The Alamo*. The great battleship *Texas* is here also, which you can tour while recalling its performance in *Pearl Harbor*.

Houston ➤ Baytown ➤ Clear Lake Area (NASA) ➤ Galveston (75 miles)

People are sometimes surprised to learn that Galveston's seaside fun is only about an hour's drive from the urban amenities of Houston. In fact, it's so close, you'll probably have time for a side trip east just a few miles to Baytown and a visit to Evergreen Road, where the opening oil-rig scene was shot for *Hellfighters*. Take Highway 146 across the spectacular Fred Hartman Bridge and follow 146 to Highway 1, which will take you west to the Lyndon B. Johnson Space Center. You will probably want to spend some time touring this exciting location, which you likely have seen in many movies besides *Space Cowboys* and *Apollo 13*. Continuing south on I-45, you will cross the bridge to Galveston Island, whereupon the Interstate becomes Broadway Avenue. If you follow Broadway to Seawall Blvd. and turn left, you will be on your way to East Beach, along which Shirley MacLaine and Jack Nicholson take drives in both *Terms of Endearment* and *The Evening Star*. In the latter film they also enjoy a meal at Clary's, a popular seafood restaurant located not far off I-45 on Teichman Road.

Galveston ➤ Port Bolivar ➤ Beaumont ➤ Nederland ➤ Port Arthur ➤ Orange (125 miles)

A rather pleasant excursion for its own sake is the free ferry ride from Galveston Island to Port Bolivar. You drive your automobile onto the ferry from the pier at the end of Ferry Road. The trip lasts only about fifteen minutes, but the wait to board can be an hour or so on busy summer weekends and holidays. The historic lighthouse where *My Sweet Charlie* was filmed is about a mile from the ferry landing at Port Bolivar on the north side of Highway 87. At its foot is the site of the mud fort where Jane Long became "The Mother of Texas" when she gave birth in 1821.

Highway 87 used to trace a leisurely route from Port Bolivar to Port Arthur, hugging the coast and providing quite a change from either of the two usual concepts of Texas highways, urban freeways full of bumper-to-bumper speeding automobiles or lonely interstates where isolated vehicles hurtle through vast western spaces. Instead, this route has been traveled by folks willing to slow or even stop periodically to enjoy the sights and sounds of ocean breezes and whirring flocks of feeding birds. The marshes and rice fields spread inland; the Gulf waters stretch to the other horizon; and an amazing variety of waterfowl can be spotted along this coastline, where the flyways from all directions cross paths. Unfortunately, a twenty-mile stretch of Highway 86, east of High Island, succumbed to the destructive forces of nature and has been closed for many years; but you can still travel along the peninsula from Port Bolivar to High Island, where you will be diverted north toward I-10, which you can follow east into Beaumont.

Beaumont is another port city and home to an array of museums. Its population grew by tens of thousands within a month in 1901 after the world's first oil gusher came in at Spindletop, and a replica of the resulting boomtown has been constructed as a tourist attraction. Movie lovers will want to visit Beaumont's opulent and beautifully restored Jefferson Theatre, on Fannin Street.

Traveling south on US 96 from Beaumont, you will encounter the small city of Nederland, which commemorates its Dutch heritage with a Windmill Museum featuring artifacts from the city's beginnings. Of more interest to the movie lover, however, is the museum's exhibit of Tex Ritter memorabilia, honoring the actor/singer who grew up here and considered Nederland his hometown.

Nederland is located at the northern city limits of Port Arthur, which any visitor will notice is an industrial center with no shortage of unaesthetic landmarks related to the oil business. In fact, the refineries at its southern outskirts may appear to be a movie setting for technological hell. Nevertheless, German filmmaker Wim Wenders, in discussing locations for *Paris, Texas*, was certainly too harsh in calling it "The most desperate town I have ever seen. Its only claim to fame being [sic] that Janis Joplin went to high school there." That view may have coincided with the gloominess he sought for his strange little movie, but it hardly reflects the city, at least the parts of it beyond the intersection of Highways 87 and 82. "Port Ar'Tour," as it is pronounced by its sizable Cajun population, is a year-round fisherman's delight with a variety of attractions for the history buff and the nature lover as well as for those curious about the business of a major port where, from an observation deck, you can watch Big Arthur, the seventy-five-ton gantry crane, at work with the big ships. And if you manage to arrive during Mardi Gras, you can celebrate with a family-oriented version of the New Orleans madhouse.

Orange is about twenty miles north of Port Arthur, and travel between the cities features two lovely bridges spanning the Neches River. The gracefully arched Rainbow Bridge, completed in 1938, is one of the tallest bridges in the nation. The Veterans Memorial Bridge, the first cable-stayed bridge on a Texas highway, was opened in 1991. Orange, Port Arthur, and Beaumont represent three corners of a triangle, the area of which comprises two counties that border southwestern Louisiana. It is sometimes called the Cajun Triangle because of the influential Cajun culture, but more often it has been called the Golden Triangle because of the riches brought by the discovery of oil. Like its sister cities, Orange has a deepwater port, oil refineries, and a varied economy that has attracted a multicultural population. It also boasts one of the most interesting of all the Texas Travel Information Centers. Besides offering the usual helpful, friendly staff and informative travel information, the Orange center includes a 650-foot boardwalk extending into Blue Elbow Swamp, a great place to see otters, alligators, and numerous varieties of birds.

GULF COAST CAST AND CREDITS

Some notable movie folk who were born or grew up in the Texas Gulf Coast region:

> Wes Anderson, writer/director/actor, born in Houston
> G. W. Bailey, actor, born in Port Arthur
> Barbara Barrie, actress, graduated Miller High School in
>   Corpus Christi
> Gary Busey, actor, born in Goose Creek (now part of Baytown)
> Dabney Coleman, actor, graduated Corpus Christi High School
> Hilary Duff, actress, born in Houston

Shelley Duvall, actress/producer, born in Houston
Farrah Fawcett, actress, born in Corpus Christi
Freddy Fender, composer/actor, born in San Benito
Sean Patrick Flanery, actor, grew up in Houston
Irma P. Hall, actress, born in Beaumont
Katherine Helmond, actress, born in Galveston
Howard Hughes, producer/director, born in Humble
Evelyn Keyes, actress, born in Port Arthur
Beyoncé Knowles, actress/composer, born in Houston
Kris Kristofferson, actor/composer, born in Brownsville
Richard Linklater, director/writer, born in Houston
Tara Lipinski, actress, born in Houston
Lyle Lovett, actor/composer, born in Klein
Annette O'Toole, actress, born in Houston
Valerie Perrine, actress, born in Galveston
Dennis Quaid, actor, born in Houston
Randy Quaid, actor, born in Houston
Tex Ritter, actor, grew up in Nederland
Patrick Swayze, actor, born in Houston
King Vidor, director/producer, born in Galveston
JoBeth Williams, actress, born in Houston
Renée Zellweger, actress, born in Katy

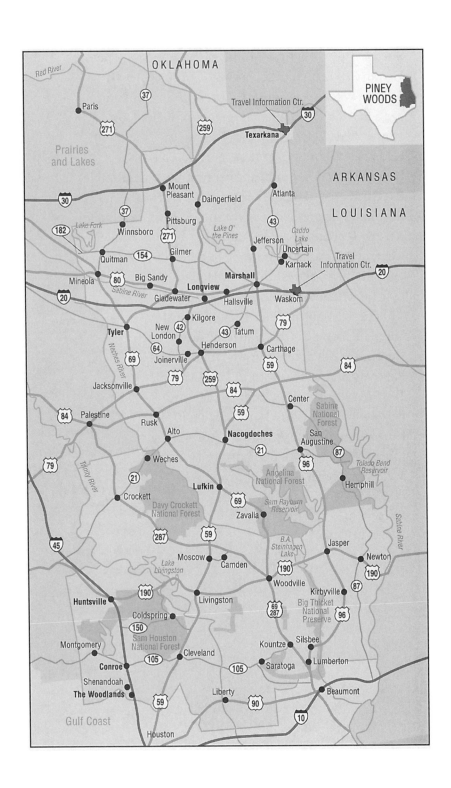

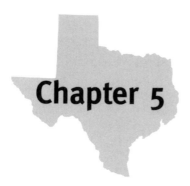

Chapter 5

Piney Woods

*Do you know how we small-town Texans get
our name for violence? Grown men still playing
with guns and cars.*
Ray Teal to Robert Mitchum in *Home from the Hill*

ESTABLISHING SHOTS
The Region on the Map

THE PINEY WOODS does not fit the usual stereotypes of Texas, except for the oil wells and a proud history of residents willing to fight for their independence. You'll find no large metropolitan areas with skyscrapers and ritzy malls, nor will you encounter wide-open dusty spaces dotted with longhorns herded by cowboys. Instead, you will find rich farmlands, dense forests, historic villages, Indian mounds, and ghostly swamps. The Piney Woods encompasses the eastern portion of the state, with Texarkana marking its northeastern corner. On the official Texas tourism maps, it stretches south along the border with Arkansas and Louisiana almost to Interstate 10, very near Beaumont, and then reaches west to include Houston's elegant suburb The Wood-lands. Northward from there, the region takes in Huntsville and Tyler. For the movie lover's tour of Texas, the cities of Palestine and Paris mark the western boundary of the Piney Woods.

Travelers entering the state from Arkansas or Louisiana are greeted with full-service state Travel Information Centers at Texarkana and Waskom. Several of the larger towns—Longview, Marshall, Lufkin, Nacogdoches—cluster in the middle of the region. Noticing the pattern of forests and lakes, you might surmise that the Piney Woods offers many delightful drives through a scenic and historic countryside. You would be right.

The Region Onscreen and Off

The Piney Woods comprises the heart of East Texas, where people have found shelter and sustenance for many centuries. The dens-est part of these forest communities is known as the Big Thicket, which was so nearly impenetrable that it successfully resisted the onslaught of settlers until the westward migration of Americans began in earnest. The lumber industry started its defoliation in the 1800s, and, helped by the petroleum industry, within a century had reduced the Big Thicket to less than a tenth of its original 3.5 million acres.

That's the bad news. The good news is that the Big Thicket Na-tional Preserve, established in 1974, now protects 97,000 acres, recognized by UNESCO as an International Biosphere Reserve. Sometimes called the "biological crossroads of North America," the Big Thicket includes several distinctive ecological systems—swamps, forests, plains, and deserts—resulting in an amazing vari-ety of plant life. The federal government has also given other parts of the Piney Woods some protection through the creation of four National Forests: the Angelina, the Davy Crockett, the Sabine, and the Sam Houston.

These humid and lush landscapes are believed to have welcomed the first paleo-Indian inhabitants some 37,000 years ago. By the 1500s, when the Spanish and French began exploring the woods, they found a thriving Caddo Indian culture. The Spanish apparently admired the Caddo word *tejas*, which they interpreted as "friend" and which ultimately was used to designate the area as "Texas."

By the early nineteenth century two major overland routes into Texas cut through the Piney Woods, one crossing the Red River near present-day Texarkana and the other crossing the Sabine River and following the Old San Antonio Road through San Augustine, Nacogdoches, and Crockett. Indians from the southeastern states also began to move into East Texas during the 1800s. The only tribes allowed to remain were the Alabamas and the Coushattas, who have resisted offers of the timber and oil industries to buy them out; they continue to maintain their reservation of nearly five thousand acres in its natural state. The reservation is supported mainly by tourism; tribe members offer guided tours through the Big Thicket, present Indian dance performances, and operate gift shops, a campground, and a museum.

The Indians and most of the Anglo settlers came to East Texas from the Deep South, and the Piney Woods forest itself is the western part of the ancient forest that stretched across the lower southern states. Consequently, many people agree with historian T. R. Fehrenbach's assessment of East Texas as "an extension—cultural as well as topographical—of the Deep South across the Texas line." The original American settlers farmed the land, either as a self-sustaining family enterprise or, in some cases, as a plantation, with slaves brought in to work the cotton and sugar fields in support of the owners' genteel lifestyle.

By the last decade of the nineteenth century, the railroads had helped overcome the post–Civil War economic disaster, and lumber emerged as the first major new industry, marking the rise of towns such as Tyler and Texarkana. At the dawn of the twentieth century oil was discovered, and within three decades the enormous and rambunctious East Texas Oil Field was in full boom in cities such as Kilgore, where a downtown block for a time contained the greatest concentration of oil wells in the world.

Today the Piney Woods is drenched in its rich and colorful history as well as in the green atmosphere of its much-diminished but still impressive deep forests. The remains of old plantations, the Indian mounds, the historical cemeteries and villages all beckon the visitor who relishes a glimpse into the past, but Hollywood has so far not devoted much attention to this part of Texas. After all, it just doesn't fit many of the stereotypes; and if moviemakers want an Old South setting, they're not likely to think first of Texas.

The southern influence in Texas is not limited to the Piney Woods, although the typical accents of folks from East Texas have remained noticeably more "southern" than have those of their neighbors who moved farther to the west. The farming culture the settlers brought to Texas from the Deep South quickly spread into Central Texas, with its inviting expanses of rich bottomlands; and Hollywood has occasionally connected Texas, if not the Piney Woods specifically, with the southern agricultural lifestyle. In fact, one classic 1945 movie about Texas is called *The Southerner*. Based on the acclaimed novel *Hold Autumn in Your Hand*, by George Perry Sessions, this film portrays a man's struggle to make a living for his family on a small farm—a familiar story in the Piney Woods. Even though it was made by a Frenchman, Jean Renoir, and was filmed in California, *The Southerner* accurately represents the life of a 1930s tenant cotton farmer in Texas. It also stars a native Texan, Zachary Scott, although critics have complained that his persona is too urbane for the role of a humble agrarian hero.

Fred Gipson's novels provide the sources for two other films depicting families living on small Texas farms. The first one, *The Return of the Texan* (1952), stars Dale Robertson and even scored an Oscar nomination for Walter Brennan, but it was not a box-office success. Perhaps a modern western about a grieving widower who returns to a small Texas farm to raise his young sons was just too far from the usual shoot-'em-up to satisfy most moviegoers. *Old Yeller* (1957), on the other hand, was not only a success when first released, but has become known over the years as a children's classic. It is set in 1859, still the frontier days, which brings it a bit closer to the usual Texas movie even though it takes place on a family farm.

None of these movies were filmed in Texas, but they acknowledge the farming lives of many early settlers in the Piney Woods and elsewhere in the state, offering a realistic contrast to the usual Texas stereotypes. Sharecroppers were at least as important to the history of the state as cowboys were; they just didn't strike so many cinematic sparks. As a result, popular films made in and about East Texas are relatively rare.

REEL-LIFE AND REAL-LIFE TOURS
Feature Presentations: Piney Woods in a Starring Role

Home from the Hill (1960)
Robert Mitchum, Eleanor Parker, George Hamilton,
and George Peppard
Directed by Vincente Minnelli

Reel-Life Tour

Home from the Hill can be considered in some ways to be an East Texas counterpart to the West Texas family saga of *Giant*. However, the difference in terrain—lushly wooded countryside versus a dusty mesquite- and cactus-dotted landscape—is not the only contrast between the two films. The family in *Giant* ultimately resolves its conflicts, and Bick and Leslie's marriage is strong and loving. In *Home from the Hill* the marriage of wealthy landowner Wade Hunni-cutt (Mitchum) and Hannah (Parker) is a disaster. Wade is a noto-rious philanderer, and Hannah has been his wife in name only since the birth of their son.

In many respects a typical late 1950s melodrama, complete with overwrought musical score, *Home from the Hill* nevertheless tells a compelling story. Since it reflects the culture and mores of a Texas small town in the postwar years, it requires the viewer to accept some attitudes and behaviors that seem rather quaint today, not to mention some rather stilted dialogue. For instance, Dr. Carson warns Wade about the dangers of "poaching on preserves of love," after yet another jealous husband has taken a shot at him.

The writing, direction, and casting are generally excellent, however, and viewers who have come to know George Hamilton as the genial self-parodying celebrity of recent years may be surprised at how good he is in the role of the incredibly naïve seventeen-year-old Theron Hunnicutt. He and another George—Peppard, playing Wade's unacknowledged illegitimate son—kicked off their movie-star careers with this successful project. The accents are not perfect, but most of the actors exhibit a passable East Texas drawl, with its soft echoes of the Deep South.

Although not all the movie was shot in East Texas, the terrain on the screen is accurate for its setting. The Sulphur River bottom, the Victorian houses, the downtown streets are similar to what you will see in the area of Paris and Clarksville today. And many scenes reflect the lifestyles and culture of the area: a lavish barbecue at the Hunnicutts' home; the annual cleaning up, sometimes called "decoration day," at the cemetery; gossiping men whittling on the town square; hunters with their dogs in the fields. The scenes in the cotton compress, where Theron takes a job, reflect an industry that has now been taken over by cotton gins; but when the first cotton compress was built in Paris in 1880, it was part of a thriving industry that made the shipping of cotton more economical. In keeping with the characterization of Wade Hunnicutt as the "lord of the realm," Wade tells Theron that he holds the mortgage on the compress. Throughout the film, the social status of the Hunnicutts is made clear. Most of the town is beholden to Wade for at least a part of their livelihood, a fact that explains how he has been able to get away with his arrogant behavior.

Real-Life Tour: Clarksville, Paris

As if to emphasize the deep southern qualities of East Texas, many exteriors for *Home from the Hill* were shot in Oxford, Mississippi. However, the woods and fields around the Texas towns of Clarksville and Paris also show up in the film, and Paris was the site of the movie's premiere. William Humphrey's novel, on which the movie was based, drew much from his childhood in Clarksville, so the location shooting in that area lends authenticity to the movie. If you want to visit a cemetery like the one in which Rafe and Hannah have their heart-tugging encounters, a perfect one is Paris's Evergreen Cemetery, which dates from 1866 and provides a resting place for over 40,000 souls. It is also the site of many unusual headstones and monuments, the most famous of which is probably the statue of Jesus wearing cowboy boots. Hunting in the Sulphur River bottom and elsewhere is still a major activity in the Piney Woods; in fact, Clarksville is known as the eastern "Wild Turkey Capital of Texas."

The Long Hot Summer (1985)
Don Johnson, Judith Ivey, Jason Robards,
and Cybill Shepherd
Directed by Stuart Cooper

Reel-Life Tour

The very idea of this made-for-TV film may offend those with fond memories of the youthful charms of Paul Newman, Joanne Woodward, and Lee Remick in the 1958 original. And for William Faulkner's admirers even the original was a bit of a travesty in the way its script played fast and loose with his characters and plots. However, this remake has its share of fans, many of them Don Johnson admirers, and it even garnered an Emmy nomination for Best Miniseries in 1986. Set in Mississippi, the story reflects the culture of the Deep South, and some of the more antebellum-looking scenes were shot in Louisiana. But a good deal of the movie used areas around Marshall and Caddo Lake to portray Mississippi, thus settling the score with *Home from the Hill*, perhaps, for using Mississippi as a stand-in for East Texas.

Judith Ivey, a Texan from El Paso, plays Noel Varner—the role originated by Joanne Woodward—the ultimately rebelling daughter of overbearing Will Varner, played by Jason Robards. The attraction between Noel and Don Johnson's Ben Quick drives the story between various melodramatic scenes that mainly involve the weaselly son, Jody Varner, and his sassy wife Eula, played by Cybill Shepherd. The rather cavalier handling of Faulkner's original settings results in a movie not very authentically southern for any particular time and place, but the location shots offer actual views of the Piney Woods as well as of neighboring Louisiana.

Real-Life Tour: Marshall, Waskom, Uncertain

The connections and similarities between the Deep South and the Piney Woods are historically supported by the fact that Marshall was one of the largest and most prosperous cities in the state when Texas seceded from the Union in 1861. In fact, after the fall of Vicksburg, Marshall became the headquarters of Confederate civil authority west of the Mississippi. In common with many southern towns, its courthouse lawn boasts a Confederate Monument; and late-eighteenth-century architecture similar to that found throughout the South makes up its Ginocchio National Historic District. About three miles west of the town of Waskom on FM 134, you'll find T. C. Lindsey & Co., the old-fashioned general store featured in *The Long Hot Summer*. And if you continue northward on 134, you'll come to the tiny town of Uncertain, located on the shores of ghostly Caddo Lake, which also makes an appearance in the film.

Southern Comfort (1981)
Keith Carradine, Powers Boothe, Fred Ward,
and T. K. Carter
Directed by Walter Hill

Reel-Life Tour

Southern Comfort's story is set in Louisiana, but much of the movie was filmed on the Texas side of the swampy borderland in the Caddo Lake area. Moreover, one of the main characters is from El Paso and is played by Texan Powers Boothe, so Lone Star

Caddo Lake, alluring and mysterious, can provide ominous settings for movies such as *Southern Comfort.* Courtesy of John Suhrstedt/TxDOT

connections abound in this atmospheric tale of murderous encounters. Sometimes compared to John Boorman's *Deliverance*, the film follows a group of mostly undisciplined National Guardsmen on a training exercise in a Louisiana swamp. Ill prepared for even basic survival in the dense vegetation, they quickly become lost and arrogantly commandeer some boats to cross a river. When the boats' owners take exception, one of the soldiers foolishly shoots at them with his blanks-loaded rifle. The owners shoot back with real bullets and kill Sgt. Poole, played by Peter Coyote.

This bloodshed sets off a violent struggle between the interlopers and the Cajun inhabitants of the swamps, with the military components and the junglelike terrain inviting comparisons with the Vietnam War. Although the Cajun hunters and fishermen are depicted as fiendish in defending their homes and the means of their livelihood, the Guardsmen themselves are hardly heroic. The final scenes in a Cajun village show the inhabitants as peaceable, friendly folks enjoying their distinctive music and dancing while the remaining soldiers seek to escape their would-be killers.

Real-Life Tour: Caddo Lake

Caddo Lake provides the perfect location for shooting a film requiring an ominous atmosphere. One of the largest natural lakes in the southern United States, Caddo stretches across the eastern border of Texas into Louisiana with about a third of its 26,800 acres of eerie wilderness. This labyrinth of dark waterways is thick with moss-draped tupelo and cypress trees rising up out of the stillness, creating a perfect backdrop for the terror the soldiers encounter in *Southern Comfort*. The history of the lake has mystical overtones as well. Caddo Indian legend claims that angry earthshaking spirits created it; and, indeed, it may have been created by the New Madrid earthquake of 1811, which was centered in Missouri. Some experts, however, believe the lake appeared a decade or so earlier when a natural raft of fallen trees dammed up the Red River. On the south side of the lake a State Park offers camping and fishing facilities, but newcomers to the boat trails that cut through this realm of hidden coves and adjoining creeks and bayous are advised to engage a local guide. Remember how quickly those soldiers in *Southern Comfort* became lost!

A Charles B. Pierce Double Feature:
The Legend of Boggy Creek (1973)
Local residents play themselves.
Directed by Charles B. Pierce

The Town That Dreaded Sundown (1976)
Ben Johnson, Andrew Prine, Dawn Wells, and Jimmy Clem
Directed by Charles B. Pierce

Reel-Life Tour

Texarkana native Charles B. Pierce mined some scary history of his hometown for these two 1970s horror films. *The Legend of Boggy Creek* is an ancestor of the more famous *Blair Witch Project* of the 1990s, for Pierce adopted the manner of a documentary filmmaker in approaching the sensational story of a bigfoot creature terrorizing the countryside around Texarkana. He recruited local inhabitants, many from the Arkansas hamlet called Fouke, located about ten miles from the Texas border, to tell their stories and play themselves in reenacting some of the events for the big screen.

Some viewers react very favorably to this "realism," which seeks to lend credibility to the story and thus make it all the more frightening; others are put off by the amateurishness of the performances and the low production quality of the film. In any case, *Boggy Creek* has attained a minor cult status, and the unconvincing appearance of the "monster" only adds to the movie's campy pleasures as the terrified residents earnestly proclaim their belief in the Sasquatch-like denizen of their woods.

Another sort of monster preyed upon Texarkana's folks in 1946, and this all-too-real serial killer's depredations are dramatized in

Pierce's later film, *The Town That Dreaded Sundown*. The brutal murders of five people, as well as the vicious attacks on three others who survived, have never been solved. And even though the rampage was brief—from February to May—the city of 44,000 people did not quickly recover from its trauma. Pierce's treatment of the story invites comparison with many later slasher films, although most of his violence occurs off screen. His hooded predator is thought by some critics to have inspired the white-masked Jason of more recent horror films.

Although obviously a small-budget film, *The Town That Dreaded Sundown* manages to convey a sense of 1940s Texarkana in telling a suspenseful story based on actual events. Pierce stays with the essential facts of the murders, but he changes the names of the persons involved along with some details of the crimes. Ben Johnson, for example, plays Capt. J. D. Morales, a character clearly based on Texas Ranger Capt. Manuel "Lone Wolf" Gonzaullas, who was called in to investigate the killings. Gonzaullas, who also figured prominently in quelling the lawlessness of the East Texas oil boom years, wrote a book about his long career in law enforcement, including the case of Texarkana's "Phantom Killer." After retiring from the Rangers, he enjoyed a second career for a few years as a technical adviser in Hollywood. He should not, however, be confused with the Chuck Norris character in *Lone Wolf McQuade*. The nickname is all they have in common.

Real-Life Tour: Texarkana

Texarkana has the distinction of being a bi-state city; the line between Texas and Arkansas runs right down the middle of its main street, and the line is literally straddled by the post office and the Bi-State Justice Center. Although the city was not founded until late in the nineteenth century, the area around it is rich with earlier historical significance. Caddo Indians were some of the first inhabitants, and seventy of their ceremonial mounds remain nearby. Spanish explorers in the 1600s and American colonists in the 1800s arrived by way of the Red River, but the growth of the city had to wait for the coming of the railroads in 1873. Its colorful past has not yet attracted a major commercial moviemaker, but native Charles B. Pierce's two horror flicks offer a view of the landscape only slightly distorted by the scariness of his tales.

Hands on a Hardbody: The Documentary (1997)
Sid Allen, Greg Cox II, J. C. Crum et al.
(all playing themselves)
Directed by S. R. Bindler

Reel-Life Tour

The winner of numerous festival awards for documentary filmmaking, *Hands on a Hardbody* offers a straightforward account of an annual event staged by a car dealer in Longview. Director S. R. Bindler built this film around the Nissan dealership's 1995 contest in which a new hard-body pickup is awarded to the person who can keep his or her hands on it the longest. The contestants, chosen by means of a drawing, stand in hundred-degree heat for up to four days with only short breaks, eventually lapsing into predictably erratic behavior after a couple of days.

However unappealing this setup sounds, the fact is that Bindler treats his subjects with such genuine affection and empathy that their stories take on an unpretentious poignancy and become something of a meditation on human aspiration. The spontaneous action of the contest itself is interspersed with previously staged interviews so that the participants ultimately are allowed to tell their own stories, providing direct insight into a subculture of a small East Texas city. The appeal of the contest has not abated since the film was made. In 2004, twenty-four contestants vied for the prize, and for the first time, the competition was broadcast in Tokyo, Japan.

Real-Life Tour: Longview

Like Texarkana, its neighbor to the northeast, Longview grew up with the railroad and first established itself as a terminal for the area's cotton and timber industries. But in the 1930s it joined its sister boomtown, Kilgore, in welcoming hordes of newcomers intent on making their fortunes in the newly discovered oil fields. The folks you meet in *Hands on a Hardbody* are representative of many you'll encounter all over the Piney Woods, and you can visit the site of the Hands on a Hard Body contest at Patterson Nissan on McCann Road in Longview. The contest takes place every September.

Short Takes: Piney Woods in a Supporting Role

Big Bad John (1990)
Ned Beatty, Jimmy Dean, Jack Elam, Doug English,
and Bo Hopkins
Directed by Burt Kennedy

Most of *Big Bad John*, a good-ol'-boy movie, was filmed in New Mexico as Jimmy Dean, playing a retired sheriff, drives around in search of the title character. However, the story begins in the sheriff's swampy retirement home, filmed in the neighborhood of Caddo Lake, where Beatty and Elam come calling to convince him he should take out after Big Bad John, who has not only killed a man but also run off with Dean's daughter. In addition to offering views of the swampy lake areas, the film includes scenes shot at the historic T. C. Lindsey & Co. store located near Waskom. Viewers old enough to remember the title song, which was a hit for Dean way back in 1961, may wonder why it took so long to make a movie based on the song, and why someone other than Dean sings it in the movie. Although the answers to those questions are not readily available, most folks probably will agree that Jimmy

Dean's persona has attained almost iconic status as a genuine Texan, born in Plainview, and as a singer and sausage spokesperson. Back when this movie was first released, according to Joe Bob Briggs, "If you rent *Big Bad John* at a video store, you get a coupon good at the supermarket for seventy-five cents off 'any Jimmy Dean meat product.'" Presumably, the expiration date on such a coupon will have passed by now, so potential renters should probably not expect anything more rewarding than the movie itself.

A Jesse James Double Feature:
American Outlaws (2001)
Colin Farrell, Scott Caan, Ali Larter, and Timothy Dalton
Directed by Les Mayfield

The Long Riders (1980)
David Carradine, Keith Carradine, James Keach, Stacy Keach,
Dennis Quaid, and Randy Quaid
Directed by Walter Hill

If the movies revisit another subject as frequently as that of the Alamo, that subject is probably the Jesse James gang. *American Outlaws* and *The Long Riders*, made twenty years apart, take on the legends in their own distinctive ways, but each utilized the Texas State Railroad Historical Park in the Piney Woods, showcasing its vintage trains, tracks, and depots. Not only does the Park's century-old locomotive pull tourists in passenger cars on a four-hour round trip between the towns of Rusk and Palestine, but it also serves moviemakers who need shots evoking the Golden Age of Steam. In a scene filmed on the tracks near Palestine for *American Outlaws*, the James Gang dramatically goes to the rescue of their leader, who is being held on a speeding prison train. Colin Farrell, who played Jesse, has expressed his delight in performing some of his own stunts, running along the tops of the cars and jumping off onto an airbag. The train stations at Palestine and at Rusk are both seen in *American Outlaws*; the latter de-

Locomotive and cars, Texas State Railroad at Palestine, featured in movies such as *American Outlaws* and *The Long Riders*. Courtesy of Stan Williams/TxDOT

pot, disguised with a few planks and some sawdust, also plays a bank robbed by the gang.

The Long Riders is another retelling of the Jesse James saga, with the added gimmick of real-life brothers playing the sibling members of the gang. The Carradines play the Younger brothers; the Keaches play Jesse and Frank James; and the Quaids play Ed and Clell Miller. Train scenes in this movie also feature some of the Texas State Railroad's twenty-five miles of track, which winds through the dense Piney Woods and hardwood creek bottoms and over numerous bridges.

A Texas Prison Scenes Film Festival:
The Getaway (1972)
Steve McQueen, Ali McGraw, and Ben Johnson
Directed by Sam Peckinpah

Outlaw Blues (1977)
Peter Fonda, Susan St. James, and Steve Fromholz
Directed by Richard T. Heffron

A Perfect World (1994)
Kevin Costner, Clint Eastwood, and Laura Dern
Directed by Clint Eastwood

The Life of David Gale (2003)
Kevin Spacey, Kate Winslett, Laura Linney, and Gabriel Mann
Directed by Alan Parker

These four movies were shot mostly on location around Austin in the Hill Country, but they nevertheless have significant scenes connecting them with prison units located in the Piney Woods. The city of Huntsville, which has attractive features other than those associated with the penal system, is the one most frequently associated with movie characters' incarcerations. It is the home of the Texas Department of Criminal Justice Institutional Division, aka headquarters of the Texas prison system, and the site of the historic Walls Unit, which housed its first convict in 1849. Tours may be arranged through the Chamber of Commerce if you want to see for yourself some of the backdrops for cinematic prison breaks and inmate activities.

Changing practices in prison management have been documented in the Texas Prison Museum, on Huntsville's downtown square. Here visitors can view a replica of a cell, old ball-and-chain shackles, and even "Old Sparky" itself, the electric chair used from 1924 until 1964—all reminiscent of many a film about crime and its consequences. Additionally, the museum features rotating exhibits, actual rifles used by Bonnie and Clyde, and crafts produced by inmates.

The Getaway, the original and not the Alec Baldwin/Kim Basinger remake, establishes its tone with opening scenes of Steve McQueen serving time inside Huntsville's walls and then being released, thanks to the maneuvering of his girlfriend, played by Ali McGraw. *Outlaw Blues* also begins inside the prison. In this film, Peter Fonda plays a songwriting inmate who aspires to country music stardom. When a famous performer comes to play for the prisoners, Fonda sings one of his own songs during the sound check, and the big star subsequently records the song as his own. This perfidy inspires Fonda's character, upon his release, to track the fellow down in Austin. *A Perfect World*, like *The Getaway* and *Outlaw Blues*, builds its plot from opening scenes in Huntsville, where Kevin Costner breaks out and goes on the run to, first of all, Austin.

Unlike these three films, *The Life of David Gale* reverses the trip: Kevin Spacey's character begins in Austin and ends up in Huntsville. This movie also carries a more serious purpose than the others do. Besides being a suspenseful action movie, it reflects the filmmaker's obvious concern with the controversial issue of capital punishment.

Before filming *The Life of David Gale*, director Alan Parker says he scouted the Ellis Unit at Huntsville because the story's writer had set it there. Parker discovered, however, that death row had been moved from Ellis to the Polunsky Unit, near another Piney Woods town, Livingston. Wanting to stay with the writer's original setting, Parker recreated the Ellis Unit in an abandoned airport hanger in Austin and shot the scenes there. However, the exterior scenes were shot in Huntsville, and those dealing with an execution—complete with helicopters, fifty-some-odd vehicles, and a couple of hundred crew members— were staged so realistically that some Huntsville residents assumed an actual execution was taking place. But because of its high profile as the site of Death Row, this small Piney Woods town is inhabited by folks used to onslaughts from the media, so they took in stride the buzzing helicopters and shouting in-mates. The DVD version of *The Life of David Gale* includes an informative extra called "Death in Texas," featuring a tour of the physical layout of Huntsville and interviews with some state prison employees, who Parker says were very cooperative with the production.

PINEY WOODS TRAVELOGUES

Scouting the Locations

Texarkana ➤ Clarksville ➤ Paris ➤ Mount Pleasant (140 miles)

If you happen to be driving from the east along I-30, Texarkana provides a great entry into Texas, with its excellent Texas Travel Information Center, where you can stock up on printed tourist materials and glean all sorts of helpful suggestions from the friendly people who work there. An interesting feature of this city is its unique status as a single city with two separate municipalities, one in Texas and one in Arkansas. You can visit the nation's only Federal Building and U.S. Post Office built to straddle the line separating two states. Besides providing location shots for *The Town That Dreaded Sundown* and *The Legend of Boggy Creek*, Texarkana has a more indirect movie connection as the hometown of Scott Joplin, the composer known as America's "King of Ragtime." One of his compositions became very popular as the score of the 1973 Redford/Newman vehicle *The Sting*. Other movies utilizing Joplin's work as background music include such disparate productions as *Pretty Baby* (1978), *Crumb* (1994), and *The Golden Bowl* (2000). A downtown mural celebrates this native son, and the Texarkana Historical Museum houses a piano he is said to have used for practice as a child.

Heading west out of Texarkana on I-30, take the US 82 exit and you'll be on the way to *Home from the Hill* country. Clarksville, the birthplace of the story's author, lies about forty miles west; and Paris, where much of the filming was done, is another thirty miles or so. The ambience of these two towns reflects the southern roots of their founders. Touring their gracious old homes is highly recommended. For glimpses of the countryside—especially the Sulphur River Bottom—where the Hunnicutt men honed their hunting skills, take US 271 south out of Paris. You'll also see the blackland farm country leading into the northern reaches of the East Texas forests. Many of the people living in these rural areas still enjoy old customs such as singing conventions and religious revivals. Mount Pleasant lives up to its name as the final destination of this itinerary, with its beautifully wooded hills and stately old homes. Its Historical Museum displays antique farm implements, Caddo Indian artifacts, and memorabilia of the town's original settlers. The Old Martin Theater, built in 1913, is now the Pleasant Jamboree, site of live stage shows; but for years, it was the only movie theater between Texarkana and Dallas.

Waskom ➤ Karnack ➤ Uncertain ➤ Caddo Lake ➤ Jefferson (35 miles)

Surrounded by lovely deep forests, the little town of Waskom serves as the gateway to Texas from northern Louisiana via I-20, with another of the excellent Texas Travel Information Centers situated on the state line nearby. A short jaunt up FM 134 will take you to the T. C. Lindsey & Co. establishment, which has provided the old-fashioned general store settings for several movies, including *The Long Hot Summer* and *Big Bad John*. A slightly longer jaunt, about fifteen miles, will bring you to Karnack, famous as the birthplace of former first lady Mrs. Lyndon B. Johnson.

Just north of Karnack, off State Highway 43, FM 2198 leads to the magical realm of Caddo Lake and the tiny town with the whimsical name of Uncertain, which has grown up along the lakeshore. Here you can relive the chills of some of the scarier scenes in *Southern Comfort* as well as enjoy the misty beauty of mossy cypress trees and meandering fingers of still water. Although Indian legend attributes the lake's origin to an earthquake, many scientists now believe it was formed by a natural logjam that backed the Red River into Cypress Bayou, creating a navigable body of water. In fact, by the time of the Civil War, steamboat travel from Caddo Lake to the Mississippi River had made the city of Jefferson a commercial center. In the 1870s, however, the U.S. Army Corps of Engineers cleared the logjam, known as the Great Raft; they thereby lowered the water levels to no more than four feet in Cypress Bayou and landlocked the formerly booming river port city.

One of the most historic cities in Texas, Jefferson lies not more than fifteen miles beyond Karnack on FM 134, and it is an ideal destination for visitors who wish to savor a quiet reflection of a bygone era when steamboats lined the docks and the city was elegant and prosperous. Today, besides all the historic homes, inns, and museums dedicated to local Texas history, Jefferson's Deep South connection is further emphasized with its popular Scarlett O'Hardy's *Gone with the Wind* Museum. This large private collection of memorabilia is bound to interest most movie lovers with its concentration of foreign and domestic movie posters and various items associated with the original release of the quintessential film about the Old South.

Waskom ➤ Marshall ➤ Longview ➤ Kilgore ➤ Henderson ➤ Carthage (100 miles)

If you travel less than twenty miles east on I-20 out of Waskom, you'll reach another Old South city, Marshall. Nestled serenely in the forested red hills and laid out with brick streets named for Confederate heroes, Marshall provided a perfectly realistic location for *The Long, Hot Summer*, a film based on several of William Faulkner's Mississippian short stories. The hardy souls who survived Reconstruction to create a prosperous town following the Civil War must have spawned descendants with the same determination to do more than just survive the most negative circumstances: One of Marshall's gala annual events is a Fire Ant Festival.

Another twenty miles or so east on I-20 will bring you to Longview, which was, like Marshall, set in a rich plantation area before the Civil War. Languishing a bit after the war, it flourished again as a center of the East Texas oil boom in the 1930s; and it gained fame during World War II as the loading end of the Big Inch pipeline that was built to send oil to the northeast when German U-boats were sinking oil tankers in the Gulf of Mexico. The Gregg County Historical Museum features exhibits focusing on the local industries of cotton, timber, oil, and railroads. But the movie lover will eventually want to head for the site of the annual Hands on a Hard Body contest; that is the Patterson Nissan dealership at 1201 McCann Road.

The East Texas oil boom spawned countless exciting tales, but so far no major movie has been made about that exact location and time. However, there have been plenty of films about oil booms in general. If you have enjoyed those movies, you'll want to travel on to Kilgore, probably taking US 259 out of Longview. Kilgore's highly praised East Texas Oil Museum recreates every aspect of the boom days through dioramas, films, and artifacts of the oil fields and the daily lives of the residents. You can also stand on the "World's Richest Acre," now a park, where twenty-four wells pumped 2.5 million barrels of oil over thirty years. Restored derricks stand proudly as a reminder of the early days when unregulated production approached a million barrels a day, prompting a shutdown order from the Texas governor and the beginnings of energy conservation.

From Kilgore, it's less than twenty miles down US 259 to Henderson. This is the town that grew up from the very first East Texas gusher, the Daisy Bradford No. 3, which struck oil on October 3, 1930, near the present-day community of Joinerville. Columbus M. "Dad" Joiner, who persisted in seeking his fortune in oil despite lack of resources and encouragement from anyone else, drilled this first well, which foretold the whole East Texas oil boom. Robert Duvall's character in *The Stars Fell on Henrietta* has much in common with Joiner, even though the movie is set in a different region of Texas and makes no overt reference to this historical figure.

Carthage, some thirty miles to the east of Henderson, shared in the oil wealth to some degree; but its rural nature and modest rate of progress changed only with the discovery in 1944 of a huge gas field nearby. Today it is a center for gas, oil, and petro-chemical processing. The movie lover visiting Carthage will be interested in its Tex Ritter Museum, where memorabilia of this Texas-born actor/singer may be viewed along with a handsome bronze statue of Tex and his horse, White Flash.

Huntsville ➤ Crockett ➤ Weches ➤ Alto ➤ Rusk ➤ Palestine (125 miles)

This itinerary begins down near the southwest edge of the Piney Woods. Huntsville is almost synonymous with "Texas prison," but it also was home to one of the most famous Texans of all, Sam Houston. His continuing influence is reflected in the name of Sam Houston State University, located there, and most strikingly by his sixty-seven-foot-tall statue that towers over I-45 and is visible from as far away as six miles. Touring the headquarters of the Texas prison system and the Texas Prison Museum may be the biggest draw for fans of movies such as *The Life of David Gale* and *A Perfect World*, but fans of Texas history movies won't want to miss the Sam Houston Memorial Complex. It not only features some of Houston's personal items but also displays items taken from Santa Anna when he was captured at San Jacinto.

To continue the theme of the Texas battle for independence, take Highway 19 out of Huntsville for about fifty miles to Crock-ett, named for the frontiersman hero who is said to have camped there on his way to the Alamo. That campsite is referred to as Davy Crockett Spring, marked only by a plaque where the spring still flows on W. Goliad Street. There is also a wooded municipal Davy Crockett Memorial Park of some thirty-five acres; and you can en-ter the Davy Crockett National Forest about ten miles east of town on Highway 7.

Heading northeast out of town on Highway 21 will also take

you through part of that forest. Just before you reach the tiny community of Weches, about twenty-one miles from Crockett, you can visit the Mission Tejas State Park. This park commemorates the first Spanish mission built in East Texas; the mission closed in 1663 after only three years. The lovely scenic drive continues along Highway 21 to Alto, where the grave of Helena Kimble Dill is honored as that of the woman who bore the first Anglo child in Texas in 1804. You may want to question the locals about the status of that claim versus the one that Jane Long was the mother of the first Texas-born Anglo in 1821 on the Gulf Coast.

From Alto, Rusk is only about twelve miles up Highway 69, another scenic drive to the eastern point of the nation's longest, thinnest state park. The Texas State Railroad operates antique steam engines pulling coaches along twenty-five miles of track to the western end of the park at Palestine. If you arrive during operating hours, you may want to take the round-trip train ride between Rusk and Palestine. It is a nostalgic journey back to the early days of train travel, and it will spark your memories of movies like *American Outlaws* and *The Long Riders*. If the train ride does not work for you, the drive from Rusk to Palestine is worth the time to experience the densely forested countryside and the historical structures and sites to be found in each of the towns.

PINEY WOODS CAST AND CREDITS

Some notable movie folk who were born or grew up in the Piney Woods region:

Sandy Duncan, actress, born in Henderson
Steve Forrest, actor, born in Huntsville
John Lee Hancock, director/writer, born in Longview
Joshua Logan, director, born in Texarkana
Matthew McConaughey, actor, grew up in Longview

Ann Miller, dancer/actress, born in Cherino
Tex Ritter, actor, born in Carthage
Sissy Spacek, actress, born in Quitman
Forest Whitaker, actor/director, born in Longview
Noble Willingham, actor, born in Mineola

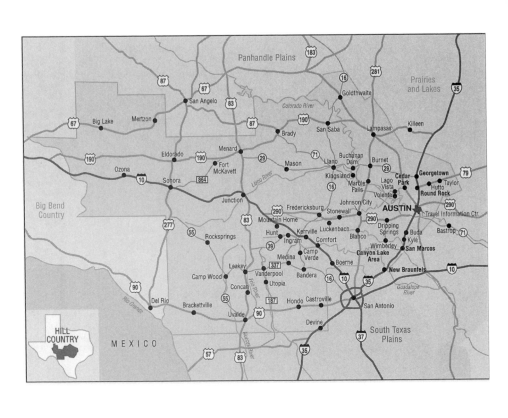

Chapter 6

Hill Country

*In Russia they got it mapped out so everyone pulls
for everyone else. . . . But what I know about is Texas,
and down here you're on your own.*
M. Emmet Walsh in *Blood Simple*

ESTABLISHING SHOTS

The Region on the Map

YOU WILL FIND some strong disagreements among
Texans about the exact boundaries of the Hill Country.
The Texas Department of Transportation, which is responsible for the official state travel guides and maps recommended to
readers of this book, defines the region as taking in Austin and Taylor at the eastern extreme, Uvalde and Brackettville to the south,
Ozona and Big Lake to the west, and Goldthwaite to the north. But
there are folks who want to expand the region to include San Antonio and Del Rio. Still others want to designate as the Hill Country
only that area of hills marking the southeastern edge of the Edwards
Plateau, where it meets the Balcones Escarpment. The hills around

Austin, they insist, represent a geologically separate formation called the Llano Uplift; and they would consider Big Lake to be part of West Texas.

The reason these boundaries matter so much is that the concept of the Hill Country is exceptionally dear to most Texans. In fact, it has been called the true heart of Texas, the state's equivalent to England's Lake District, a place where one longs to retire, perhaps, or at least to visit regularly on holiday. It is indeed literally the heart, since the geographic center of the state, at Brady, is located here; but that aspect is only incidental. The real attractions are primarily associated with its relatively mild climate, its charming historic towns founded mostly by Europeans in the mid-1800s, and its narrow but scenic rivers. The movie lover's tours go along with the TxDOT mapping and make the vibrant capital city of Austin the jumping-off point for traveling some of the winding roads of the Hill Country.

The Region Onscreen and Off

Even if you accept Austin as geographically part of the Hill Country, its urban nature as the seat of both the state government and the state's higher education system sets it apart culturally from the rest of the region. The charm of the Hill Country resides primarily in quaint small towns, populated by proudly self-sufficient Texans. The soil is thin and rocky, but stubborn farmers and ranchers have held onto their modest spreads through generations. Artists and writers, inspired by the natural beauties as well as the lingering characteristics of the original Old Country settlers, find the quiet lifestyle conducive to their work. Tourists flock to the riotous colors of the wildflowers and the magnificent sunrises and sunsets; they marvel at the caverns, the bubbling clear spring waters, and the dramatic tales of Indian-settler conflicts. But when the tourists leave, local residents happily go on with their lives. They welcome visitors graciously but display little interest in promoting additions to the permanent population. They like their communities as they are.

Movies came to the Hill Country shortly after their invention. As early as 1894, individual Austin residents had the opportunity to watch the moving images inside a box Thomas Edison called a kinetoscope. A few years later, people in Austin could all watch the images together as the film was projected onto a screen. As for movies made in and about Texas, however, those nearly all focused on the arid western regions of the state—until the 1960s, when *Bonnie and Clyde*, *Hellfighters*, and *Home from the Hill* showcased locations among Texas Prairies and Lakes, along the Gulf Coast, and amid the lushness of the Piney Woods. Not until the 1970s did Hollywood begin to notice the Hill Country, when some of its charms showed up in the successful action film *The Getaway* as well as in the somewhat less successful *The Great Waldo Pepper*. Meanwhile, several locations in the Austin area attained cult status with horror-movie fans after they found their thrills in *The Texas Chainsaw Massacre*.

In fact, toward the end of the 1970s, Texas began to call itself the Third Coast of filmmaking, a boast supported by a flurry of Academy Award–winning films made in Texas in the 1980s, including *Terms of Endearment*, *Tender Mercies*, *The Trip to Bountiful*, *Places in the Heart*, and *Born on the Fourth of July*. Increased filmmaking activity in the state was due at least partly to the establishment, in Austin, of the Texas Film Commission in 1971. Created by Governor Preston Smith to provide a liaison between filmmakers and local authorities, the Commission and its regional affiliates have succeeded over the decades in attracting numerous major filming projects to the state. In 2004 the New York magazine *MovieMaker* named Austin as the best city in the entire country for making movies, outranking both New York City and Los Angeles.

Austin has become a filmmaker's paradise for several reasons, many of them, of course, economic. But the real lures have been its unusually rich resources of artistic talent, most famously exhibited in the works of such independent filmmakers as Richard Linklater and Robert Rodriguez, along with a broad geographic and aesthetic diversity. In Austin's immediate vicinity the camera can shoot backgrounds of grassy prairies, tropical-looking rivers, cactus-dotted desert, or rolling hills that surround sparking lakes. Additionally, a number of nearby small towns are made to order for street scenes in period films or for portraying a typical Any Town, USA. Finally, the recent transformation of the old Robert Mueller airport into Austin Studios has provided twenty acres dedicated to film and video production facilities.

The Hill Country's ongoing relationship with Hollywood dates back at least to the 1950s, when Brackettville's Mayor James T. "Happy" Shahan sought a solution to his small town's economic woes after a severe drought and the closing of nearby Fort Clark. He went to California armed with photos of Brackettville's western terrain and managed to convince the makers of *Arrowhead* to film on location there in 1951. Then he teamed up with John Wayne, who wanted to make a big-budget version of the Alamo story, and built the multimillion-dollar Alamo Village just outside Brackettville as a set for Wayne's movie. Alamo Village is more than just a set, however. The re-created Alamo itself is a meticulously constructed reproduction, and all the other buildings in the village are completely functional, including the cantina, the trading post, the church, and the blacksmith shop. Scenes for many films have been shot there since Wayne's *The Alamo* in 1959, including *The Good Old Boys*, *Barbarosa*, and *Lonesome Dove*. Alamo Village continues to serve as a popular location for all kinds of film projects, but it is also a major tourist attraction for those wishing to visit an authentically re-created Texas town of the 1880s. It is open to the public year-round, with live entertainment in the summer.

Almost half a century after Happy Shahan built his hugely successful village, another replica of the Alamo was built in the Hill Country, near the little town of Dripping Springs, as part of the largest standing set in North America. But this set, built for 2004's *The Alamo*, was constructed as little more than a façade, albeit a lovingly detailed façade, and was not designed to be permanent.

Located on a private ranch about thirty miles west of Austin, the set is not open to visitors.

REEL-LIFE AND REAL-LIFE TOURS

Feature Presentations: Hill Country in a Starring Role

The Newton Boys (1998)
Matthew McConaughey, Skeet Ulrich, Ethan Hawke,
Vincent D'Onofrio, and Julianna Margulies
Directed by Richard Linklater

Reel-Life Tour

The Newton Boys is Texan through and through: based on a true Texas story, written and directed by Texans, featuring a couple of Texas-born movie stars, and filmed on location in Texas, even though most of the locations had to pretend to be in other states or even in Canada. The movie is a lively account of the four Newton brothers, who became known as America's most successful train robbers during the 1920s. McConaughey plays Willis Newton, the leader of the clan, which included his brothers Joe, Jess, and Dock. He encourages his gang in their criminal adventures by maintaining the view that they are just "little crooks stealin' from the big crooks."

In addition to Willis's rather quirky insistence that when he and his guys hold up a bank or a train they are simply engaging in an entrepreneurial enterprise, the film is unusual in that the outlaws face no final, fatal shootout. These fellows survived to tell their stories after growing old back in Texas. In fact, one of the delights of *The Newton Boys* comes at the very end. Over the final credits, we see footage of interviews with the real Willis and Joe Newton, then in their seventies, who remained unrepentant till the end of their lives.

Although much of the film involves the Newton gang's exploits outside Texas, several references are made to their background in rural Uvalde, which coincidentally is where star Matthew McConaughey was born. The understandable desire to escape their harsh lives working on hardscrabble farms led the brothers to seek other ways of making a living, and the film suggests how grim their daily lives were, and how limited their prospects, in the places they grew up.

Real-Life Tour: Austin, San Marcos, Liberty Hill, Martindale, Uvalde

Various sites in and around Austin form the backdrops for this film. One bank the Newton gang actually robbed is the old State Bank of San Marcos, which still stands on the corner of Hopkins and Guadalupe streets. Although the bank was not used to play itself in *The Newton Boys*, you can see it at some length portraying the "First Bank of Beacon City" for *The Getaway* in 1972. The old-fashioned storefronts in downtown Martindale show up in *The Newton Boys*; and so does Sullivan's Steak House, on Austin's Colorado Street, playing a twenties-era supper club patronized by Willis Newton. The Hill Country Flyer, a passenger train pulled by an antique steam locomotive that runs between Cedar Park and Burnet, was used to portray the train robbed by the Newton gang in Illinois. The reenactment of the 1924 robbery was staged at Liberty Hill, located on Highway 29. The oil derrick where Willis's hopes for a gusher are dashed was constructed just east of I-35 near the Niederwald exit on land that has since been developed. Although Uvalde is only mentioned and not shown in the film, you still might want to visit that little town to see where the Newtons lived and where Willis and Joe are buried in Hillcrest Memorial Cemetery. You can find photographs and other information on the boys in the History Room at the Uvalde Grand Opera House and at the El Progresso Memorial Library.

A Perfect World (1993)
Kevin Costner, Clint Eastwood, Laura Dern,
and T. J. Lowther
Directed by Clint Eastwood

Reel-Life Tour

Set in 1963 just before John F. Kennedy's trip to Dallas, *A Perfect World* strikes some nostalgic tones as it focuses on the relationship that develops between a likeable, smart escaped convict, Butch Haynes—played by Costner—and the endearing little boy that he takes hostage. These two are the quarry of a crusty Texas Ranger named Red Garnett, played by Eastwood, who pursues them after appropriating the governor's campaign trailer. The scenes involving Eastwood's exaggerated Texas character and Laura Dern's "criminologist" from Huntsville veer off into farce, but Costner and the kid are sweetly believable and touching.

Texas State Capitol, a grand presence in such movies as *A Perfect World, The Life of David Gale, D.O.A.,* and *The Best Little Whorehouse in Texas.* Courtesy of J. Griffis Smith/TxDOT

The chase begins in Austin, at the capitol itself, and supposedly ends in the Panhandle; but in fact, as the credits attest, the movie was "filmed entirely on location in Austin and Central Texas." Therefore, the final shots show a gently rolling, live-oak-studded green meadow rather than the dusty flatness that you would expect in Swisher County. The rural landscapes are beautifully photographed, and the interactions with storekeepers and waitresses are believable. Although the down-home friendliness in a couple of scenes is carried to the point of satire, most of the movie sounds and looks right for a Texas story. Even Eastwood's portrayal of the Texas Ranger, which reaches a bit too far in search of laughs, demonstrates the uniqueness of this mythic Texan entity as Garnett must deal with problems created by other law enforcement agencies. His difficulties demonstrate how a Ranger's authority must be exercised somewhere between that of the local law enforcement officials and that of the FBI.

Real-Life Tour: Austin, Martindale, Canyon Lake

The grounds of the Texas State Capitol are easily recognizable in the scenes of Red Garnett's gearing up to go after Butch Haynes. The house where the little boy is kidnapped is located on Austin's Columbus Street. About forty miles southeast of Austin, you'll find Martindale, which plays Noodle, a real town lying between Austin and the Panhandle. Not satisfied with Martindale's existing structures, the filmmakers created a false front for the Friendly's dry goods store that Haynes robs. Not far from Martindale, Mack's Squat and Gobble Barbeque restaurant, where Haynes and the boy stop to eat, has gone out of business; but you can still see the building in Canyon Lake on FM 2673.

Slacker (1991)
A host of Austin nonprofessional actors and artists
perform the brief speaking roles.
Written and directed by Richard Linklater

Reel-Life Tour

The popular success of *Slacker* marks the beginning of Austin's preeminence as a hotbed of unconventional filmmaking. But *Slacker* was much more than a local phenomenon; critics cite it as a major inspiration for the still booming independent film era that began with the 1990s. Linklater, an unknown at the time, managed to make the movie with almost no money, convincing his actors to work for free in roles he had written based on his observations of Austin's eccentrics and their Bohemian lifestyles.

The result is a plotless ramble in the company of one character after another, each expressing a highly individualistic social commentary while sharing with all the others a determined aimlessness. Avoiding any sort of traditional narrative, Linklater depicts a subculture of his hometown through short monologues and conversations among enough intriguing characters to populate several movies. Linklater calls his subjects "slackers," a term that has since become part of the popular vernacular; but the viewer familiar with any university campus will probably remember similar individuals, perhaps called "hippies" or just plain "weirdos."

The pattern of the movie is simple and brisk, opening with Linklater himself playing a taxi passenger holding forth on the nature of reality and possibility. When the uninterested driver drops him off, another car races away after apparently striking a woman, and a passerby calls for help. The camera then moves to the hit-and-run car as its driver goes home to his apartment, where he is soon arrested by the police. As he is led outside, the camera switches its focus to a conversation between bystanders there; and so the movie continues, ultimately presenting a collection of amusing work-avoiders who are eager to expound upon their theories about all kinds of topics including space travel; politics; literature; and general, everyday angst. The technique of moving so quickly from character to character, seeming to drop in on one spontaneous exchange after another, creates a sense of eavesdropping on other people's lives.

Real-Life Tour: Austin

A gala tenth-anniversary screening in 2001, sponsored by the Austin Film Society, attests to the continuing popularity of *Slacker* and to its importance in the launching of the modern Austin film-making scene. By this time, however, Austin was showing the effects of the high-tech boom that during the nineties speeded up its transformation from sleepy college town to "Silicon Hills." Companies like Dell Computer, Motorola, and Trilogy grew up and created cadres of highly paid techies whose tastes ran to fancier restaurants than the now defunct Les Amis Café, with its cheap food and lackadaisical service. These changes may have priced some of the original slackers out of Austin or into gainful employment, although the so-called correction in the technology industry, dating back to 2000, slowed things down a bit with widespread layoffs and failed start-up companies. And a university campus is still a university campus. You can usually find an assortment of folk singers, paranoids, do-gooders, and philosophizers if you check out the coffee houses and shops along the "Drag"—Guadalupe Street at the University of Texas, around 24th Street. And the Continental Club is still thriving and a great place to hear live music, although the performance in *Slacker* is not particularly riveting. The final scenes of cavorting young folks include some exhilarating shots of and from the heights of Mount Bonnell, which overlooks Lake Austin and miles of the Hill Country.

Dazed and Confused (1993)
Jason London, Joey Lauren Adams, Milla Jovovich,
Parker Posey, and Matthew McConaughey
Written and directed by Richard Linklater

Reel-Life Tour

As he does in *Slacker*, Linklater treats us to a tasty slice of life in *Dazed and Confused*. This time he takes us back to 1976 on the last day of school in Austin, Texas, and shows us a collection of teenage character types seeking adventures. The jocks, the nerds, the potheads, the cheerleaders, and so on are presented in the context of a wealth of period detail but without overt nostalgia. Comparison with the earlier *American Graffiti* is inevitable, but whereas George Lucas tied his 1960s story to Vietnam and commitment issues, Linklater avoids imputing any weighty significance to his characters' activities or the decisions they might make. He has said that he wanted to show how "some things never change in teenagerland . . . driving around and looking for something to do." Judging by the film's cult status with viewers not even born in 1976, Linklater succeeded in striking some unchanging chords.

The plot is generally limited to playing out the social dynamics among the characters; but a simple narrative focuses on "Pink" Floyd, the football team's quarterback, whose coach has given him an ultimatum: He must sign a contract to be drug free if he wants to continue to play. As he mulls over his decision, he hangs out with his friends and invites an incoming freshman to join them as they frequent such usual teen haunts as a pool hall, a hamburger joint, and finally a beer bust.

Another obvious *American Graffiti* comparison is the casting of relative unknowns who later hit it big. Several *Dazed and Confused* actors have approached the upper echelons of Hollywood or of the indie film scene. Matthew McConaughey, playing David Wooderson, the twenty-year-old who still wants to hang with the high school kids, started his ascendancy with this marvelous role, while the likes of Ben Affleck and Parker Posey played relatively unheralded parts. You can even catch sight of Renée Zellweger in a parking lot scene if you don't blink. And if you're interested in filming details and trivia as remembered by the cast and crew, check out an entertaining article called "The Spirit of '76" in the October 2003 issue of *Texas Monthly* magazine, with McConaughey on the cover.

Real-Life Tour: Austin, Georgetown

The movie's Robert E. Lee High School is played by Bedichek Middle School, located on Bill Hughes Road; the junior high school is played by Williams Elementary in Georgetown. The drive-in burger joint, the Top Notch, is on Burnet Road in Austin. The Moonlight Tower party was shot at Lake Walter E. Long Metropolitan Park, on Blue Bluff Road, but don't look for the tower. It was a temporary structure built for the movie. And yes, *Dazed and Confused* had its own tenth-anniversary screening and reunion party, sponsored by the Austin Film Society in May of 2003. It was held at the Moonlight-Tower-less park.

The Life of David Gale (2003)
Kevin Spacey, Kate Winslet, Laura Linney,
and Gabriel Mann
Directed by Alan Parker

Reel-Life Tour

The citizens of Austin in *The Life of David Gale*, like those in *Slacker*, are highly educated and interested in ideas, but the similarity ends there. The *David Gale* characters have a profound sense of direction in their lives. This movie is a mystery/thriller on one level, but it is also a serious film about the death penalty. And since Texas has earned a reputation for its high rate of executions, the setting is most appropriate for the subject. Adding realism to the film are details such as a scene with the governor explaining his support for capital punishment in biblical terms, but the script avoids cheap shots and does not stereotype all Texans as gun-toting zealots.

The scriptwriter, Charles Randolph, has strong ties to Texas; and as a professor of philosophy, he has good credentials for creating a believable story in terms of both its setting and its subject. Kevin Spacey stars as the title character, a popular University of Texas faculty member and an activist against the death penalty, who has ended up on Death Row. The events leading up to his conviction are related in flashbacks as he is interviewed by a reporter (Kate Winslet) days before his scheduled execution.

Director Alan Parker, who does not shy away from political issues, creates a thriller built on an intellectual argument. This anchoring of a mystery story in ideas is made possible by David Gale's identity as both a university professor and a political activist, and the city of Austin is an appropriate setting for this combination as well as for the subject of capital punishment. Filming was done on the University of Texas campus and on the grounds of the capitol, lending authentic backgrounds. In his Director's Notes, Parker writes at length about the experience of filming both in the Austin area and in Huntsville, where he obviously sought to make a movie true to its locale. One of his anecdotes, however, does belie his unfamiliarity with Texas weather. He says that while filming a diner scene near Austin, he and his cast and crew were "hit by a tornado." His description of their huddling in the kitchen to get away from plate-glass windows sounds exactly right, but his final comment that two hours later "the eye of the storm had passed" sounds as though he has tornadoes confused with hurricanes. Both of those horrors menace Texas, all right; but the hurricanes are limited to the coast and, unlike the tornado, they give you a day or two of warning before they strike.

Real-Life Tour: Austin, Taylor

Most of the action in *The Life of David Gale* is set in Austin or in the Piney Woods town of Huntsville, and Parker conscientiously shot as much on actual locations as he could. The DVD includes informative "filming of" extras that will be of interest to those wishing to visit actual sites. In Austin, locations included the University of Texas campus, various bars on Sixth Street, and the now abandoned municipal airport, redecorated to look like it's up and running again. The DeathWatch offices were created in the nearby town of

Taylor. One detail that may jar a viewer familiar with Texas is the characters' running back and forth between Austin and Huntsville. You get the impression that the two cities are only minutes apart, but we're talking Texas distances here—in this case, at least a two-hour drive.

A Texas Music Film Festival:
Outlaw Blues (1977)
Peter Fonda, Susan St. James, and Steve Fromholz
Directed by Richard T. Heffron

Honeysuckle Rose (1980)
Willie Nelson, Dyan Cannon, Amy Irving, and Slim Pickens
Directed by Jerry Schatzberg

Songwriter (1984)
Willie Nelson, Kris Kristofferson, Melinda Dillon,
and Rip Torn
Directed by Alan Rudolph

Reel-Life Tour

Singer/songwriters are so much a part of the Austin scene that any movie lover's tour must include some films about them. *Outlaw Blues* is the least authentic of this triple feature, primarily because Peter Fonda is not very convincing as either a Texan or a singer. However, the film offers some great shots of mid-seventies Austin, which will be enlightening to people familiar with only the stereotypical far-western terrain of Texas. Far from being a southwestern desert city, Austin sits in the midst of numerous waterways and lakes, several of which appear in *Outlaw Blues*. The movie also features a genuine jewel of an Austin singer/songwriter, Steve Fromholz, whose talents could have offset Fonda's awful pretense at musicianship if he had not, inexplicably, been assigned a non-singing role.

Honeysuckle Rose, aka *On the Road Again*, is a rollicking account of Willie Nelson's life as a touring Texas music star. He plays a character called Buck Bonham, but of course, he's really pretty much Willie all the time. He gets to sing his own songs with his own band at several recognizable venues, mostly in the Austin area, although there is nice footage of Padre Island as well. The family reunion scene at Fischer Hall captures beautifully the atmosphere of these traditional Texas gatherings where people of all ages enjoy the music, the food, the beer, and the inevitable domestic dramas.

Kris Kristofferson co-stars with old friend Willie in *Songwriter*, and this time the apparently requisite name "Buck" is assigned to him; only it's a surname this time, following "Blackie." Willie plays Doc Jenkins, a performer who makes the mistake of trying to become a music businessman. When he needs to be extricated from a bad deal, his cronies help him out. His domestic difficulties involve an ex-wife, played by Melinda Dillon, and some of the plot's incidents reportedly came straight from Willie's life. Like *Honeysuckle Rose*, this film offers backstage glimpses of singers' lives along with good songs by Willie and Kris. In addition, *Songwriter* addresses some of the darker side of the music business, which tends to treat artists as nothing more than commodities.

Real-Life Tour: Austin, Fischer, Gruene

Austin bills itself as the "Live Music Capital of the World," and its offerings of all kinds of music—including blues, country, Tejano, swing, and rock—lend credence to the claim. The TV show *Austin City Limits* has helped spread the word about Austin's music for decades; and if you are not lucky enough to score tickets to a taping of that show, you can catch other live performances almost any time at various clubs, parks, and bars all over town. Plenty of the venues have long, colorful histories of their own: the Continental Club, La Zona Rosa, Threadgill's, Antone's, Saxon Pub, Broken Spoke, and Cactus Café, to name only a few.

Outside of Austin, you'll find other great venues for live music.

The beautifully weathered Fischer Hall, off FM 484 from Highway 32 and showcased in *Honeysuckle Rose*, was established in 1875 by ancestors of the current operators. These days, it is mainly used for private parties; but if you want a lively music scene that is hopping almost all the time, head for Gruene Hall, located on the Guadalupe River south of Austin. Built by Heinrich Gruene in the 1880s, this old place continues to function as a rousing dance hall with live music every day during the summer and several times a week in the winter. Inspired by Gruene Hall's success since the 1970s, the rest of the town of Gruene has blossomed into a quaint collection of antique shops and art galleries built to harmonize with the old-fashioned hall, which has become a center for various folksy festivals year-round. Big-name performers have graced its stage and the dance floor over the years, including John Travolta, who performed his angelic dance routine there in *Michael*.

The Rookie (2002)
Dennis Quaid, Rachel Griffiths, Jay Hernandez,
and Brian Cox
Directed by John Lee Hancock

Reel-Life Tour

Although most of this film was shot in the Prairies and Lakes region, the mostly true story it tells is rooted in Big Lake, near the northwestern corner of the Hill Country. *The Rookie* is also somewhat of a rarity these days—a movie that is suitable for the whole family. The fact that you may have to look for it in the children's section of your video store suggests, unfortunately, that "G" rated films, by definition, have been deemed unacceptable to adults— only one tiny societal trend that speaks volumes about standards of taste in popular culture.

As its producers have acknowledged, *The Rookie* would probably never have been made if it were not based on a true story; it would have sounded too far-fetched. Jim Morris, a thirty-five-year-old high school baseball coach who briefly pitched in the minor leagues until injuries sidelined him, promises his team that if they win their district championship, he will try out for the major leagues. They do, and he does, becoming one of the oldest rookies in major league history.

The movie shows how Morris, played by Dennis Quaid, grew up in Big Lake, where, as in most small Texas towns, high school football is the dominant sport. However, from earliest childhood, Morris had loved baseball exclusively. Except for the strangely mystical framing device that opens the movie—something about nuns praying for oil—*The Rookie* offers an unusually honest glimpse into contemporary small-town Texas life, middle-class routines, and the push-pull of family members continually adjusting priorities. The school, the houses, the faces of the townspeople all project an authentic homeliness.

Real-Life Tour: Big Lake

The Rookie does not totally avoid factual shortcuts and clichés. For instance, not only did the producers choose not to film in Big Lake, but they also changed the name of Morris's school to Big Lake High School. However, if you visit Reagan County High School at 1111 12th Street in Big Lake, you'll see an oil pump in front, just like in the movie. Oil is very important to the town's economy, and even the opening fantasy scene of the movie has some basis in fact since the Santa Rita No. 1 was a gusher in 1923 and made Big Lake an oil boom town. The oil derrick used in this scene to represent the Santa Rita was the same one used in *The Newton Boys*, standing in the green fields south of Austin; but through the magic of cinema, in *The Rookie*, a desert landscape appears to stretch all around it.

Minor discrepancies occur, perhaps in deference to convenience or budget limitations, or maybe no one thought it was important to be meticulously accurate. For instance, in the movie Morris drives to San Angelo to try out for the Devil Rays, whereas he actually went to Brownwood. And for his big-league debut in

Arlington, the whole town shows up in the movie, but Morris says most people actually stayed home and watched him on TV. The film's version is more exciting, all right, with all his high school team rooting there in the stands; but realistically, they would have had a hard time getting there in time for the game after school as the movie suggests. The distances between towns in Texas are easy to underestimate; from Big Lake to Arlington is over three hundred miles. The DVD version of the movie provides details about the making of the film and how it differs from some of the facts, but after seeing the interview with the real Jim Morris and shots of Big Lake, one is convinced that the movie stayed true to the spirit of its source.

Short Takes: Hill Country in a Supporting Role

The Texas Chainsaw Massacre (1974)
Sally Hardesty, Allen Danziger, Edwin Neal, and Gunnar Hansen
Directed by Tobe Hooper

So many bright people admire this film that those who find its charms elusive are nevertheless compelled to accept its importance as a Texas movie. Horror-movie fans consider it a classic, and its continuing influence on the genre has established it as some sort of standard. Its production by unknowns on a shoe-string budget also makes for an exciting story of unexpected success, as recounted in the November 2004 *Texas Monthly* article "They Came. They Sawed," by John Bloom.

The plot is loosely based on a series of murders by a man named Ed Gein in 1957 in Wisconsin, the same crimes that inspired the movie *Psycho*. There is nothing specifically Texan about all that, but the locations for *The Texas Chainsaw Massacre* continue to attract the movie's fans to the Hill Country decades after the film's release. The word *obsession* may be too strong here, but a recent Google search for "Texas Chainsaw Massacre" yielded no fewer than 9,240 listings. Four of the most popular spots to visit are the Bagdad Cemetery in Leander; the Hills Prairie Grocery in Bastrop; the site where the "Leatherface House" used to stand, on Quick Hill Road in Round Rock; and the Four Bears Restaurant, the current incarnation of the infamous house in its new location in Kingsland. Details for ardent fans may be found on Tim Harden's website: www.texaschainsawmassacre.net.

A Robert Rodriguez Double Feature:
The Faculty (1998)
Josh Hartnett, Elijah Wood, Jordana Brewster, Clea DuVall,
Laura Harris, and Shawn Hatosy
Directed by Robert Rodriguez

Spy Kids (2001)
Antonio Banderas, Carla Gugino, Alexa Vega, Daryl Sabara, and
Alan Cumming
Written and directed by Robert Rodriguez

Robert Rodriguez, like Richard Linklater, has been a major force in establishing Austin as a hotbed of independent film making. He first made headlines in 1993 as the young Austin guy who financed his $7,000 wonder, *El Mariachi*, by renting out his body to medical science for drug testing. Since then he's made big-budget follow-ups to that initial surprise hit, and he has returned to Austin for other projects such as *The Faculty* and *Spy Kids*, neither of which is particularly Texan except for the locations. In fact, *The Faculty*, a delightful tongue-in-cheek teen horror flick, is set in Ohio, but its Herrington High School is played by the Texas School for the Deaf at 1102 S. Congress in Austin. And a house on Hopkins Street in San Marcos portrays the home of one of the students, who has an entire drug factory in the garage.

Spy Kids is an even bigger departure for Rodriguez, whose reputation was made with violent action films, including a collaboration with Quentin Tarantino on *From Dusk Till Dawn*. *Spy Kids* is a children's film, although plenty of adults enjoy it and its sequels as well; and Rodriguez is totally responsible for the writing, directing, producing, and editing. The simple plot involves a couple who have retired from the espionage business to raise a family. When they agree to go on one last mission, they get into trouble, and their two young children have to rescue them. Recognizable locations include interiors and the rooftop of the Millennium Center at Fourth and Lavaca in Austin, and the Spanish-mission-like Trois Estate on the picturesque shores of Lake Travis, where the water chase scenes were shot. The opening sequence of the movie's second sequel, *Spy Kids 3-D: Game Over* (2003), provides great shots of the Schlitterbahn Waterpark Resort in New Braunfels, although the summertime wonderland looks rather strange in the winter with dead leaves swirling about.

The Getaway (1972)
Steve McQueen, Ali MacGraw, and Ben Johnson
Directed by Sam Peckinpah

Publicity about behind-the-scenes shenanigans overshadowed the initial release of this film, but the years have been kind to its reputation as an excellent action/suspense movie that used its Texas locations to good advantage. The off-screen affair between McQueen and MacGraw, who was married to Bob Evans at the time, no doubt lent additional tension to their fictional characters' troubled relationship as husband and wife. McQueen plays Doc McCoy, paroled early from Huntsville on the condition that he pull off another bank robbery for the benefit of the crooked parole board chairman. The bank robbery takes place in fictitious Beacon City, which is played by the pretty town of San Marcos, south of Austin on I-35. The historic State Bank of San Marcos, which has since been restored, was decked out as the First Bank of Beacon City, and moveable vault bars were installed for the robbery scenes. The scenes at the veterinarian's office were shot in New Braunfels, a little farther south of Austin; and in addition to these Hill Country sites, this cross-Texas chase movie features a fistful of locations in three other Lone Star regions: the South Texas Plains (San Antonio), the Piney Woods (Huntsville), and the Big Bend Country (El Paso, Fabens).

D.O.A. (1988)
Dennis Quaid, Meg Ryan, Charlotte Rampling, Daniel Sterne,
and Jane Kaczmarek
Directed by Rocky Morton and Annabel Jankel

This remake of the 1950 film noir starring Edmond O'Brien follows the main storyline of the original and is not Texan in anything but the scenery. However, there is a lot of that scenery, much of it associated with a university campus. The main character, Dexter Cornell (Quaid), is a professor who reports his own murder to the police and spends the rest of the life left to him trying to find out who fed him the radioactive substance that is killing him. Along the way, he falls in love with a student (Ryan) and tries to unravel various academic intrigues as well as family secrets that may have led to his poisoning.

The opening scenes of Dexter's classroom will strike Texans as a bit strange since they were obviously shot in the capitol building, pretty fancy digs for the literature professor. Real campus scenes were shot at Southwest Texas State University, which has since been renamed Texas State University-San Marcos. The peculiarly windowed J. C. Kellum Building portrayed the freshman girls' dorm, where Meg Ryan lived; but if you visit it now, you'll see the windows have been redone in a less bizarre style, rendering inappropriate the building's early nickname, "the giant cheese grater." Another unusual building on the San Marcos campus is unchanged from its appearance in *D.O.A.*, however, and that's the Theater Center: a red, round building that looks like nothing so much as a hatbox floating in a lake.

Besides the capitol building interiors, a number of other recognizable locations in Austin appear in *D.O.A.*, including the Travis County Courthouse, in the opening scene; the Continental Club, where the band performing is Timbuk Three; and several exteriors along Sixth Street. The extreme heat everyone keeps talking about at Christmas time would be quite unusual in Austin, although temperatures in the seventies are not unheard of in December. But don't look for any tar pits around Austin, and don't expect a Christmas carnival involving costumes like Meg Ryan's; in Texas, that would be Halloween.

Blood Simple (1984)
John Getz, Frances McDormand, Dan Hedaya,
and M. Emmet Walsh
Written and directed by Joel and Ethan Coen

The now almost legendary Coen brothers chose Austin for the location to shoot their very first movie, a film-noirish crime story focusing on the characters' darkest and most perverse qualities. *Blood Simple* is a fitting title for this film, suggesting both the violence and the lack of intelligence which leads to misunderstandings of facts known all too well by the viewer but not at all by the self-absorbed characters.

As in *D.O.A.*, the slow-paced, heavily ironic crime story could take place almost anywhere, but the Coens infused some Texas flavor beyond the locations. The male characters wear cowboy boots and hats, and they swagger in a would-be-cowboy kind of way as they focus on issues of machismo, such as punishing wayward wives and hustling strange women. Several high-profile Austin-area sites show up nicely. Mount Bonnell Park, where Hedaya's character orders a murder, takes on a much less jovial atmosphere than it conveyed at the end of *Slacker*, but its vistas are still spectacular. None of the scenes in *Blood Simple* are exactly cheerful, including the ones shot at the Heart of Texas Motel on Highway 290, or on Sixth Street—where the apartment setting for the final, bloody climax is located—or, most especially, in the plowed field near the little town of Hutto, where a not-quite-dead body is laboriously buried.

Secondhand Lions (2003)
Michael Caine, Robert Duvall, Haley Joel Osment,
and Kyra Sedgwick
Written and directed by Tim McCanlies

The pairing of Duvall and Caine as a pair of wildly eccentric elderly uncles who reluctantly take an adolescent nephew under their colorful wings sounds like a great premise for a movie, and it generally delivers if you enjoy watching these grand old performers have a grand old time growling and squinting and finally revealing their loving hearts. However, despite the fact that the movie was written and directed by a Texan and filmed entirely in Texas, nothing much would have been different if it had been set in, say, Alabama or Iowa. The setting of 1960s rural Texas is only incidental to dramatizing the general idea that bonds of love can be forged through the miracles of imagination. Writer/director McCanlies created a much more Texas-specific film with his *Dancer, Texas Pop. 81*. However, for those interested in the landscape around Austin, the *Secondhand Lions* DVD includes a lengthy piece that identifies the actual filming locations and demonstrates how the filmmakers changed a perfectly nice modern house belonging to a perfectly nice family named Littlefield into a dilapidated farmhouse and then changed it back again.

HILL COUNTRY TRAVELOGUES
Scouting the Locations

Driving around the Hill Country can be a glorious experience—especially if you time your visit to coincide with wildflower season. The riot of colors during a good year will take your breath away. Bluebonnets, Indian paintbrushes, winecups, coreopsis, and multitudes of others in almost all hues imaginable put on a spectacular display, usually peaking in April. But if you like winding country roads and laid-back towns, you'll enjoy exploring this region any time of year. The following itineraries are designed to take you to locations associated with the movies mentioned in this chapter, but they are merely a few possibilities for seeing some of the Hill Country. If you have time to hang out for a while in the Austin area, you will discover a huge number of interesting places to visit in the immediate vicinity. You will definitely want to check out the official Travel Information Center to make sure you are aware of all the attractions. The Center is located in oldest state office building, the General Land Office, at 112 East 11th Street, beside the lovely grounds of the Capitol itself.

Austin, Downtown

The city of Austin is a vibrant combination of capital city, university town, and high-tech center; but it is not the vast, busy metropolis you might expect. Despite the horrors of its ever-increasing traffic jams, which rapidly constructed expressways with flyaways in all directions are seeking to alleviate, Austin has maintained a small-town atmosphere along with its influx of urbane sophisticates. Since the mid-1800s its downtown life has centered on Congress Avenue, the broad street that leads to the capitol, and on East Sixth Street, formerly called East Pecan Street. Both are lined with buildings dating back mostly to the nineteenth century and are worth visiting just to view the architecture and to learn something about their history. While you stroll, you might recognize the Starbucks at 600 Congress, where Sandra Bullock makes her emergency latte run in *Miss Congeniality*. You also might want to slip over to 300 Colorado Street for a look at Sullivan's Steakhouse, which played a 1920s nightclub in *The Newton Boys*. And at 11th and Guadalupe you may recognize the impressive 1930s Travis County Courthouse from its role as a police station in the opening scenes of *D.O.A.*

Sixth Street is known as the entertainment district of Austin, sometimes even compared to Bourbon Street in New Orleans. Its live-music clubs and trendy restaurants draw a youthful and boisterous crowd, and you catch glimpses of the area in movies such as *Michael* and *The Life of David Gale*, with revelers walking along the sidewalks, spilling into and out of the various establishments. The Paradise Café, at 401 E. Sixth, is one of the places where Meg Ryan and Dennis Quaid emote in *D.O.A.*, and the Old Pecan Street Café, at 310 E. Sixth, provided the upstairs apartment for the final confrontations in *Blood Simple*.

Walking northward on Congress Avenue will reward you with a rather awesome view of the capitol, which—this is Texas, after all—is the largest state capitol building in the United States and is even taller than the Capitol in Washington, DC. The beautiful pink granite exterior and the surrounding live oaks show up in the protest scenes of *David Gale* as well as in *A Perfect World*, when Clint Eastwood is preparing to set off with the governor's campaign trailer in pursuit of Kevin Costner. Its interior pretends to be an incredibly opulent college classroom building in *D.O.A.*, and the magnificent rotunda is the setting for Charles Durning's merry song and dance as governor in *The Best Little Whorehouse in Texas*.

The University of Texas at Austin

The University of Texas at Austin campus sprawls north of the capitol with lovely landscaping and old buildings gracing its 350-plus acres. Much of the money that has created this excellent institution, which is headquarters for the UT system of campuses all over the state, is provided by its huge public endowment. And that endowment goes back to the Santa Rita #1, the oil well featured in the dreamlike opening of *The Rookie*. That oil well happened to be located on land the state legislature had given to the university in the late 1800s. The lawmakers probably were as surprised as anyone when their gift of barren West Texas desert acreage began to produce black gold in 1921.

One of the most eye-catching structures in Austin is the centerpiece of the UT campus: the Tower, which reaches over three hundred feet into the air and can be seen in the background as Kevin Spacey strolls along in *The Life of David Gale*. The Spanish colonial structure, built in the 1930s, has many exquisite architectural touches, such as gold-plated clocks; and its carillon occasionally pours music over the campus. But it has also been noted for tragedy. Not only has the tower's observation deck attracted suicidal visitors over the years, but in 1966 it served as the perch for a killer. The story of Charles Whitman's murderous rampage has been the subject of at least one TV movie, *The Deadly Tower* (1975), starring Kurt Russell in the title role of the sniper who shot people at random before he was killed. This movie turns up once in a while on late-night television, but if you happen upon it, do not mistake the location for Austin. It was filmed in Baton Rouge, Louisiana.

Approximately seven blocks of Guadalupe Street running along the western edge of the campus is known as the "Drag." Although it has become slightly more mainstream since it starred in *Slacker*, it is still plenty colorful, with funky eateries, eclectic shops, and tattoo parlors. The commercial businesses are found mostly along the west side of the street, with university buildings lining the east side. However, one of the best bars for live music, the Cactus Café, is located in a campus building, at 2247 Guadalupe. On the other side of the campus, Bass Concert Hall is located on the corner of 23rd Street and Robert Dedman Drive. That's where the pageant in *Miss Congeniality* was staged.

North Austin

North Austin seems to move farther and farther north as the city spreads out, and its name now suggests shiny new malls and residential developments and computer-tech companies all the way to Round Rock. Before you get to that new stuff, though, from the UT Campus, you'll pass the venerable Austin State Hospital at 4110 Guadalupe with its beautiful grounds and well-preserved main building that dates back to 1857. Its interior was used for the hospital scenes in *Secondhand Lions*. The Perry Mansion, at 4100 Red River, was also featured in that movie's fantasy scenes of exotic places. For a down-to-earth meal, you might want to enjoy a burger at the Top Notch, 7525 Burnet, which is where the *Dazed and Confused* bunch enjoyed theirs.

East Austin

Just across I-35 from downtown and the capitol is the Texas State Cemetery, the Lone Star version of Arlington National Cemetery. Here are buried many notable Texans, from Stephen F. Austin himself to Governor John Connolly, and here is where Denzel Washington was filmed honoring fallen soldiers in *Courage Under Fire*. A little farther north and east you'll find Walter E. Long Lake Municipal Park, at 6614 Blue Bluff Road, comprising more than 3,800 acres of large shaded areas and open picnic spaces, which was the setting for the beer bust in *Dazed and Confused*. The Moonlight Tower featured at that event was constructed just for the movie and is no longer there. But real Austin Moonlight Towers still dot the city after more than a century. The "moonlight" they produce was originally created by carbon arc lamps; today it comes from mercury vapor bulbs. Of the original thirty-one towers, only seventeen remain, but they have been restored and provide automated illumination to areas of central Austin.

South Austin

South Austin is proudly different from the rest of Austin. As a popular bumper sticker asserts, "78704 is more than a zip code. It's a way of life." Located just south of downtown across the Colorado River and between South Fifth Street and South Congress Avenue, the area exudes a small-town atmosphere with a strong Mexican influence. Compared to the rest of Austin, it has more pickups and bicycles and fewer SUVs. Its houses may lack central air conditioning. The easygoing small businesses and artistic community combine to create a pace of life much slower that that of the downtown or university areas. The Continental Club, featured in *Slacker* and in *D.O.A.*, is located at 1315 S. Congress Avenue and epitomizes the laid-back lifestyle as a live music venue. The Old Alligator Grill, at 3003 South Lamar, demonstrated its acting ability when it dropped its South Austin demeanor to take on the frantic "flair" of Chotchkie's, where Jennifer Aniston's character unhappily toiled in Mike Judge's *Office Space*. Judge, the creator of *Beavis and Butthead* and *King of the Hill*, is also a denizen of Austin and a buddy of fellow movie mavericks Richard Linklater and Robert Rodriguez, the latter of whom utilized South Austin's Texas School for the Deaf, at 1102 S. Congress Avenue, to portray Herrington High School in *The Faculty*. Linklater used the Bedichek Middle School at 6800 Bill Hughes Road to play the *Dazed and Confused* high school; and in *A Perfect World* Kevin Costner stopped to feed his young hostage a Sandy's hamburger at 603 Barton Springs Road.

Austin ➤ Pflugerville ➤ Hutto ➤ Taylor ➤ Georgetown ➤ Round Rock ➤ Leander ➤ Liberty Hill ➤ Kingsland ➤ Dripping Springs ➤ Austin (205 miles)

This excursion is designed as a day trip out of Austin, but it may be a little long for one day. If you want to spend much time at all in any of these towns, you'll need to break it up into two days or more. Popular filming locations, only a few of which can be mentioned here, abound in the Austin area, whatever direction you drive.

As you head north on I-35, the exit to Pflugerville is hard to resist just because the name sounds so intriguing; and the picturesque little town, settled by Germans in 1849, will look familiar to viewers of such disparate films as *The Newton Boys*, *The Best Little Whorehouse in Texas*, *Secondhand Lions*, and *The Return of the Texas Chainsaw Massacre*, featuring then unknowns Matthew McConaughey and Renée Zellweger.

Take FM 685 out of Pflugerville north, and before you turn east on US 79 into Hutto, you should see the two-story farmhouse featured in *Flesh and Bone*. But you may not recognize it since it was dirtied up for the film and then restored to its pristine former self. In *Blood Simple*, Dan Hedaya's character refused to stay buried in one of the fields outside Hutto.

Continuing east on 79, you will come to Taylor, where the offices of DeathWatch in *The Life of David Gale* were filmed and which has provided backdrops for other movies such as *The Rookie* and *Where the Heart Is*. Highway 95 out of Taylor leads north to Highway 29, which runs east to Georgetown. This lovely old city is home to three National Register Historic Districts and to Southwestern University, founded in 1840. Georgetown's more modern aspects, however, seem to show up most often in movies. The Williams Elementary School on University Avenue played the junior high school in *Dazed and Confused*; upstairs apartments on Eighth Street were featured in *Michael*, along with exterior shots of the courthouse; and the high school football stadium was redecorated for a role in *Varsity Blues*.

You might as well brave I-35 again to drop back south to Round Rock, which is a kind of Mecca for *Texas Chainsaw Massacre* fans. Most of that cult fave was shot on Quick Hill, which may have completely disappeared to development before you can get there. A large hotel already overlooks the former site of the house, which has been moved to Kingsland; and State Highway 45 has been extended to run parallel to the property. The site of a much cheerier scene is Dell Diamond, the baseball park that played the Durham, North Carolina, stadium in *The Rookie*.

You can continue your retracing of grim *Chainsaw* sites by heading east to Highway 183 and going north to Leander, where at the northeast corner of FM 2243 and North Bagdad Road, you will encounter the cemetery that is so gruesomely featured in the movie. Continue north on 183 to Highway 29, which will take you west to Liberty Hill. Near this small town, one of the stops for the Hill Country *Flyer*, the train robbery in *The Newton Boys* was staged. But if your mind is still on Leatherface, continue west on 29 past Burnet to FM 1431, which leads south to Kingsland. There, on the grounds of the historic Antlers Hotel, you will find the Four Bears Restaurant, formerly the home of Leatherface and his kin.

A leisurely drive back to Austin via 1431 will take you through Marble Falls, a town near the middle of the chain of Highland Lakes extending along the Colorado River into Austin. The chain starts with Lake Buchanan at the north end, followed by Lake Inks, Lake Lyndon B. Johnson, Lake Marble Falls, Lake Travis, Lake Austin, and Town Lake. These scenic lakes are worth a tour all to themselves if you have the time, and they have provided scenery for movies such as *Outlaw Blues* and *Spy Kids*, the latter of which also showcased the Trois Estate, a kind of castle near Lake Austin at 3612 Pearce Road. At Lake Buchanan, the Lake Point Cottages provided locations for the 1995 remake of *Lolita*.

If, instead of following the shorelines of these lakes, you would rather see some of the Hill Country associated with President Lyndon Johnson, take 281 south out of Marble Falls to Johnson City. From there you can take 290 west to Stonewall and the LBJ ranch, adding at least another thirty miles to this itinerary, or you can jog down to take 290 east back into Austin by way of Dripping Springs, where you might be lucky enough to catch a glimpse of the enormous set built for the 2004 version of *The Alamo*. So many choices exist here that you will have to let your energy be your guide as you decide which winding roads to follow among the lovely hills just west of Austin. But for sure don't miss Mount Bonnell, seen in the final shots of *Slacker* and in *Blood Simple*. This two-hundred-foot limestone escarpment, with its 103 steps to the summit, offers great views of the surrounding Hill Country and the city. It can be reached via RR2222 or by following W. 35th Street out of the city.

Austin ➤ San Marcos ➤ Martindale ➤ Wimberley ➤ Fischer ➤ New Braunfels (90 miles)

The open countryside between Austin and San Marcos along I-35 is disappearing rapidly as development booms along the highway. The site of the wooden oil derrick used in *The Newton*

Boys and *The Rookie*, just east of the interstate near the Nieder-wald exit, has already been obliterated by construction.

But the charming city of San Marcos still conveys a sense of the predevelopment slower pace, at least for the time being. It is also growing, but mainly as a result of the burgeoning enrollment of Texas State University. The amazingly clear waters of the San Marcos River run though the middle of town, and in many spots its banks look just as lush as they appear in the dream river sequence at the end of *Still Breathing*. On the university campus, you can admire the buildings seen in *D.O.A.*, and on the square, at Hopkins and Guadalupe, you'll find that the "First Bank of Beacon City," robbed by Steve McQueen in *The Getaway* is now a restaurant. This same grand old bank building was robbed in real life by the Newton Gang in the 1920s.

While in San Marcos, a movie lover will want to visit the Film and Television Archives of the Southwestern Writers Collection, housed in the Albert B. Alkek Library at Texas State University. The collection includes hundreds of movie scripts and behind-the-scenes memorabilia associated with Texas films such as *Apollo 13*, *The Last Picture Show*, *Raggedy Man*, and *The Good Old Boys*. The *Lonesome Dove* archives are especially extensive and document the filmmakers' efforts to make the production as historically accurate as possible in terms of costumes, locations, and buildings.

Just a few miles south and east on Highway 80 you'll find Martindale, where the main street will look familiar to those who have seen *A Perfect World*. Or head west on RR 12 to Wimberley, near which the huge set was constructed for *American Outlaws*. The construction of that set, by the way, is documented on the DVD version of the movie. South of Wimberley, follow RR 32 along the scenic "Devil's Backbone," which winds along a ridge and was the site of automotive mayhem in 1975, when *Race with the Devil's* climactic chase scenes were filmed there. You'll also encounter tiny Fischer on RR 32, with its historic dance hall featured in *Honeysuckle Rose*. When you reach US 281, turn left and head south to Highway 46, which will take you into New Braunfels. This friendly German town includes the village of Gruene, where you will find another grand old dance hall. When John Travolta performed his heavenly line-dance moves in *Michael*, he was on the well-scuffed boards of Gruene Hall, a place to enjoy live music most any day or night of the week.

New Braunfels ➤ Hondo ➤ Uvalde ➤ Brackettville (150 miles)

You can make this trip via major highways only, I-35 to US 90, but there's more scenery along Highway 46 to Bandera, then down 173 to Hondo, home of the 777 Ranch, where much of *Ace Ventura: When Nature Calls* was filmed and where the African village con-structed for that movie still stands. Just about thirty-five miles far-ther west on 90 lies Uvalde, home of the real-life Newton boys; and another forty miles will bring you to Brackettville, where Alamo Village continues to welcome visitors to the well-used movie set constructed originally for the John Wayne version of *The Alamo*. Those who have savored such films as *Lonesome Dove*, *The Good Old Boys*, and *Barbarosa* will recognize some of the locations here; and in addition to the familiar movie sets, Alamo Village offers family-oriented entertainment in a theme-park atmosphere.

New Braunfels ➤ Boerne ➤ Comfort ➤ Junction ➤ Sonora ➤ Ozona ➤ Big Lake (300 miles)

Fans of *The Rookie* may want to make a pilgrimage to Big Lake, the location of the real high school where Jim Morris coached his baseball team, a great many miles from any of the other sites in the Hill Country. This route leaves New Braunfels on Highway 46 and hooks up with I-10 at Boerne, where scenes for *Father Hood* were shot at Cascade Caverns. From there, I-10 will carry you through some of the loveliest spots in the heart of the Hill Country, be-tween Comfort and Junction. By the time you reach Sonora, how-ever, you will know you are beginning to reach into somewhat less

Part of large movie set built for John Wayne's filming of *The Alamo*, and still an active filming location and tourist attraction known as Alamo Village, near Brackettville. Courtesy of Michael Amador/TxDOT

green territory, and the dust will increase as you take 163 north from Ozona for about thirty miles to Barnhart, from which you can follow 67 west to Big Lake.

HILL COUNTRY CAST AND CREDITS

Some notable movie folk who were born or grew up in the Hill Country:

Dabney Coleman, actor, born in Austin
Dale Evans, actress, born in Uvalde
Ethan Hawke, actor, born in Austin
Tobe Hooper, director, born in Austin
Tommy Lee Jones, actor, born in San Saba
Guich Koock, actor, born in Austin
Matthew McConaughey, actor, born in Uvalde
Zachary Scott, actor, born in Austin

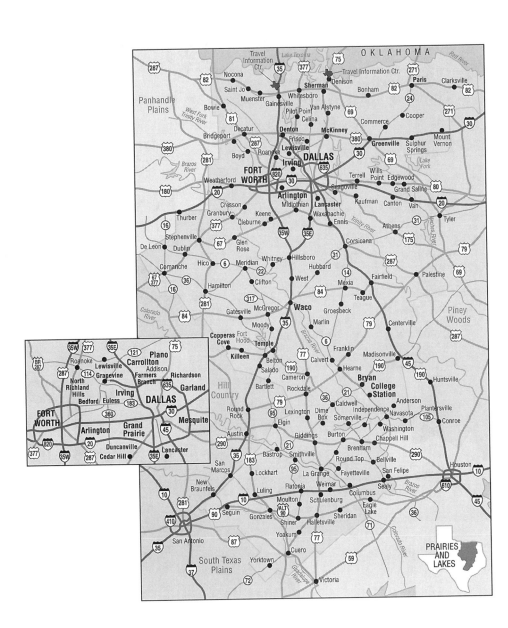

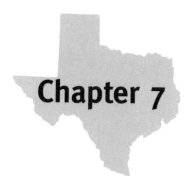

Chapter 7

Prairies and Lakes

And this old porch is the Palace walk-in
On the main street of Texas
That's never seen the day / Of G and R and X's
With that '62 poster / That's almost faded down
And a screen without a picture / Since Giant *came to town.*
Lyle Lovett and Robert Earl Keen, "The Front Porch Song"

ESTABLISHING SHOTS

The Region on the Map

THE IRREGULAR CHUNK of the map that the Texas tourism folks have designated Prairies and Lakes is defined by the Red River on the north; then it stretches way down to a point south and east of San Antonio. It comprises what most Texans refer to as North Central Texas as well as plain old Central Texas; for most, it is what is left over after identifying West Texas, East Texas, and South Texas. But the Prairies and Lakes region does not lack personality. At its edges, it shares many of the characteristics of its neighboring regions: pines to the east, desert to the west, brush country to the south, and even hints of the humid Gulf to the southeast. But you will also find unique cities and towns that reflect a blending of the Old South and the Old West.

The Dallas–Fort Worth Metroplex dominates the northern half of Prairies and Lakes, while the southern half is dotted with small cities and towns that proudly express their individuality and historical roots. The prairies often reach as far as the eye can see, with some of the richest farmland in the country; but the region also boasts some fifty lakes and reservoirs that provide recreational centers for fishing and boating activities.

Visitors entering the state from the north, by way of Oklahoma, may choose between two TxDOT Travel Information Centers, one on I-35 at Gainesville and the other on US 75 at Denison.

The Region Onscreen and Off

The moviemaking industry has generally focused on the far north and the far south of the Prairies and Lakes region. The southern section's prominence as a filming site may be attributed to its proximity to Austin and San Antonio, both major centers for film production. But Dallas, in the north, has had its own ties to the movie industry, going back at least to the 1936 Gene Autry film *The Big Show*, which was set on the grounds of the newly built Fair Park. Dallas enjoyed a kind of heyday as a film location in the 1960s with a number of low-budget horror flicks churned out for both the big screen and TV. Some are actually available on DVD, such as *The Killer Shrews* (1959) and *Mars Needs Women* (1967). Needless to say, however, these films hardly reflect the day-to-day reality of North Texas, although *Mars Needs Women* does offer great shots of Dallas as it appeared in the 1960s.

Except for the glittering big business center of Dallas, the Prairies and Lakes region has been populated mostly by people whose living depended on the land's suitability for farming or ranching on a fairly modest scale, people depicted in such films as *The Southerner* and *The Return of the Texan*. The legendary vast cattle ranches were established farther south and west, but the fact that the Chisholm Trail ran right through the middle of the region makes the Prairies and Lakes a part of the history of the great cattle drives, as portrayed in movies such as *Red River* and *Lonesome Dove*. Modern inhabitants of this region include the superwealthy wheeler-dealers in the TV series *Dallas*, but the majority are down-to-earth folks, whether inhabiting city or country. And today a good many of them are not native Texans. Since the 1970s, Texas has welcomed a great influx of people from other states, particularly into the Dallas–Fort Worth area. At least through the 1950s, non-Texans were a small minority of the people you would encounter in a casual visit to Dallas. Nowadays, you may well find yourself in a large gathering where every single person is not only from another part of the world, but has had little if any contact with native Texans. Like the rest of the country, Texas is undergoing rapid changes in its culture and the nature of its citizenry, but through certain movies you can experience some of the historical roots and some of the more recent manifestations of characteristics that make Texas unique—more specifically, characteristics that make North or Central Texas unique.

REEL-LIFE AND REAL-LIFE TOURS

Feature Presentations: Prairies and Lakes in a Starring Role

True Women (1997)
Dana Delany, Annabeth Gish, Angelina Jolie,
Powers Boothe, and Michael York
Directed by Karen Arthur

Reel-Life Tour

Originally a TV miniseries, *True Women* is a marathon of a movie, almost three hours long, and the built-in breaks for commercials are a bit distracting; but the film offers substantial amounts of exciting Texas history from the female point of view. The best-selling book on which it is based was written by Janice Woods-Windle about her own ancestors' experiences, which mirrored the experiences of many early Anglo Texans, including migration from the Deep South in the early nineteenth century, racial tensions with both Native Americans and African Americans, recurring wartime violence, and the daily struggle simply to survive.

Annabeth Gish plays Euphemia Ashby, who is orphaned in Georgia and goes to Texas to live with her sister Sarah (Dana Delany), the wife of a Texas Ranger homesteading near Seguin. The year is 1835, so the family is right in the middle of the Texas battle for independence from Mexico. The terrors of that enterprise are followed by Indian battles, then by the Civil War and Reconstruction. The quantity of disasters visited upon the characters would seem unbelievable if *True Women* weren't based on historical facts. Shot on location near where the events took place, the film creates a satisfying sense of place and time. One small jarring detail, however, must be noted, and that is the blatantly fake bluebonnets and Indian paintbrushes stuck into the ground in an early scene. You must not mistake those stiff and garish travesties for the glorious blooms that cover the rolling Central Texas hills and plains in springtime.

Real-Life Tour: McDade, Seguin, Gonzales

The tiny town of McDade was chosen as the filming location for much of *True Women* since its single row of buildings could be transformed with hand-lettering on the windows to look like a downtown of more than a century and a half ago. But most of the historical events portrayed in *True Women* took place a bit farther south and east, in the vicinity of Gonzales, Seguin, and San Marcos. The popularity of Janice Woods-Windle's book about her family's history has resulted in a surge of tourism, in Seguin particularly. You can even take a virtual *True Women* tour of the Seguin locations online at www.seguin.net/truwomen.html.

An actual trip to this historic part of the state is highly recommended, though, if only for all the significant landmarks you can visit. Near Gonzales, for instance, stands the Sam Houston Oak, which was the starting point for the Runaway Scrape, the flight of Texas pioneers, including Sarah and Euphemia, to escape Santa Anna's approaching army. You can also visit graves, homes, and other sites associated with the saga of frontier Texas recounted in *True Women*.

The Ballad of Gregorio Cortez (1982)
Edward James Olmos, James Gammon, Tom Bower,
Bruce McGill, William Sanderson, and Barry Corbin
Directed by Robert M. Young

Reel-Life Tour

Like *True Women*, *The Ballad of Gregorio Cortez* is a TV film based on actual events, and like the documentary *Border Bandits*, it offers an alternative to the traditional belief that Texas Rangers were always the flawless heroes of the Old West. The title character is a Mexican American folk hero who eluded an enormous posse for several days. Although the events took place in 1901, the story involves timely issues of racism, misunderstandings based on faulty translation between English and Spanish, and the news media's manipulation of public opinion. The legend of Gregorio Cortez began when he was questioned by a sheriff who suspected him of stealing a horse. The inadequate skills of the deputy who was serving as interpreter for the non-Spanish-speaking sheriff resulted in a misunderstanding so serious that the encounter ended with gunfire on both sides. Gregorio fled after killing the sheriff, and he soon killed another sheriff in a gun battle with a pursuing posse of Rangers.

Newspapers all over Texas portrayed Cortez as a vicious leader of bandits. In the film, Bruce McGill plays a reporter embedded with the posse, whose stories reflect the Rangers' point of view; but multitudes of Mexican Americans admired Cortez for standing up to the lawmen. Captured just ten days after the chase began, he stood numerous trials and was supported by a network of people working for his defense, one of whom is played by Barry Corbin.

Cortez ended up serving twelve years before receiving a pardon in 1913. By that time he had already been long celebrated in *corridos*, or "border ballads," for his courage in resisting the cruelty and prejudice of the despised Rangers. The film tells the story from various viewpoints, demonstrating that the initial killing, the resulting chase, and the subsequent deaths were all caused by an Anglo's misinterpretation of Cortez's answer in Spanish to a question in English. For viewers who do not understand Spanish, the movie emphasizes the confusion created in this situation by having Olmos, portraying Cortez, speak his lines in Spanish with no English subtitles.

Real-Life Tour: Gonzales

The actual pursuit of Gregorio Cortez covered hundreds of miles, but the Texas filming location selected for the movie was the historic town of Gonzales, where the first of Cortez's many trials was held. Much of the film was shot in the Old Jail Museum, an 1887 building that housed many wanted men besides Cortez, including John Wesley Hardin. Touring this museum, with its displays of historical artifacts, is a good way to start your exploration of the town where, it is said, the first shot for Texas independence was fired in 1835.

Bonnie and Clyde (1967)
Warren Beatty, Faye Dunaway, Michael J. Pollard,
Gene Hackman, and Estelle Parsons
Directed by Arthur Penn

Reel-Life Tour

Having a star like Warren Beatty on hand to film a major movie was a very big deal in 1960s North Central Texas. *Bonnie and Clyde* not only foreshadowed the boom of filmmaking in this part of the state but also was the precursor of later films, such as *The Wild Bunch*, which depict the grisly details of violence, often in slow motion. The movie was controversial upon its release, with some critics deploring a perceived glorification of criminals, but it has since been generally hailed as a classic.

Beatty and Dunaway portray the 1930s bank-robbing pair with much style and verve, so it's understandable that some people saw the presentation as inappropriately creating folk heroes out of killers. In fact, Larry Buchanan, the *Mars Needs Women* director, quickly produced a docudrama to counter the Hollywood version of the story. Entitled *The Other Side of Bonnie and Clyde* (1968), it features actual witnesses to Bonnie and Clyde's depredations, including Texas Ranger Frank Hamer, who led the ambush that ended their career. Both the Hollywood version and the documentary use footage of places that Bonnie and Clyde visited; and both convey many of the characteristics of most Texans living in this region in the 1930s, members of an agrarian society dealing with hard economic times.

Real-Life Tour: Ponder, Pilot Point, Venus, Red Oak

The cinematography of Beatty's film won an Oscar for Burnett Guffey, who captured the landscape beautifully and recreated the Depression-era atmosphere of old houses and buildings. Scenes of the first bank robbery were shot in Ponder, a small town near Denton, and the bank building still looks much the same as it does in the film. Halfway down the block from it is a restaurant that features on its walls newspaper clippings and photos of Beatty and other luminaries who dined there during the filming. The town square of Pilot Point, also near Denton, formed the backdrop for another robbery, as did the even smaller towns of Venus and Red Oak, south of Dallas. The Parker family gathering was filmed near Red Oak, where a local woman watching the filming was invited into the scene to play Bonnie's mother. The gently rolling countryside shows up nicely in many shots, with old barns squatting here and there, giving the viewer a good look at the landscape between Denton and Ellis Counties.

Places in the Heart (1984)
Sally Field, Lindsay Crouse, Ed Harris, Amy Madigan,
John Malkovich, and Danny Glover
Written and directed by Robert Benton

Reel-Life Tour

Like *Bonnie and Clyde*, *Places in the Heart* is set in Depression-era North Central Texas. It was filmed in Waxahachie, where writer/director Robert Benton grew up. Even though he has lived in New York since college, his roots run deep in this region of Texas; and with *Places in the Heart* he pays moving tribute to the community he knew as a child. The movie's realism will be appreciated by anyone who has known the challenge of making a living on a farm. Particular details of cotton farming in north Texas are vividly presented.

Sally Field won her second Oscar for playing Edna Spaulding, occasioning her infamous, but heartfelt, outburst, "You like me—you really like me!" in her acceptance speech. The fact is, you *do* really like her in this movie. After Edna's husband is killed, she is faced with trying to save the family farm and support two young children, which she proceeds to do in the pluckiest of fashions. The countryside in Ellis County and the town of Waxahachie are lovingly photographed, and the characters and their relationships are realistic; those folks on the screen could really have lived in this region of Texas in the 1930s. You even see them performing the cotton-eyed Joe, a dance that is still popular today in Texas dance halls. There is also a spectacular, and realistic, depiction of a tornado's terrifying approach, unfortunately a fairly common occurrence in North Texas.

Real-Life Tour: Waxahachie

The seat of Ellis County, Waxahachie is home to a magnificent courthouse, which you see in the opening shots of *Places in the Heart*, along with many other historic structures that have been seen in a variety of movies. In fact, Waxahachie bills itself as the most popular movie set in Texas. Located about thirty miles south of Dallas, the town blossomed when cotton was king and was growing as far as the eye could see in the fertile blackland prairie. The growers prospered and built magnificent Victorian homes, dozens of which have survived in a "Gingerbread City" that combines with the downtown historic district to provide a perfect backdrop for period movies. The Chamber of Commerce has published a map that can guide you to many locations that appear not only in *Places in the Heart* but also in other movies such as *Tender Mercies* and *The Trip to Bountiful*. A good place to pick up a copy of that map is the Ellis County Museum, located at the southeast corner of the courthouse square on College Street.

"Our State Fair Is a Great State Fair"—a Double Feature:
The Big Show (1936)
Gene Autry, Smiley Burnette, Kay Hughes, and Sally Payne
Directed by Mark V. Wright

State Fair (1962)
Pat Boone, Bobby Darin, Ann-Margret, Tom Ewell,
and Alice Faye
Directed by José Ferrer

Reel-Life Tour

Someone needs to make a popular movie showing what the colorful Texas State Fair grounds look like today, but until then these two historical records will have to do. Of course, Texas really does have the biggest state fair anywhere, and generations of kids have looked forward each fall to visiting the magical place of corny dogs, stomach-churning carnival rides, and animal exhibits both domestic and wild. In 1936 the Gene Autry movie *The Big Show* coincided with the inauguration of the fairgrounds, built to celebrate the Texas Centennial, and the film provides a great visual record of that gala event, including shots of newly built, massive Art Deco buildings still being used today. The centerpiece of the centennial, a pageant called the Cavalcade of Texas, is featured extensively, along with that year's SMU marching band and the Light Crust Doughboys, a singing group still performing today. A native Texan, Autry plays a Hollywood stuntman who stands in for a popular actor who has reneged on his commitment to appear at the centennial. The stuntman becomes an honorary Texas Ranger, gets to collar some bad guys, and because of his singing ability, ends up replacing the star in the next movie.

Somewhat less satisfying than this B-western, in its plot at least, is *State Fair*, the third remake of a story originally set in Iowa and moved to Texas presumably to take advantage of the "biggest and best." This squeaky-clean tale of a wholesome family traveling from the farm to compete in various events at the fair supports a view of Dallas as home to what are today called traditional family values. A highly publicized fact upon the film's release was that Pat Boone's religion would not permit him to kiss any woman other than his wife, so a scene with Ann-Margret had to be cut just before their lips touched. The critic Leonard Maltin has labeled this movie "third-rate Americana," but some of the Rodgers and Hammerstein songs are enjoyable. And the movie provides some great shots of the early 1960s Dallas skyline and freeways as well as the spiffy state fairgrounds.

Real-Life Tour: Fair Park, Dallas

Every September the Dallas fairgrounds come alive with the huge State Fair of Texas, visited by millions during the course of its

Art Deco Hall of State Building at Fair Park, Dallas, and its Tejas Warrior sculpture, brand new for *The Big Show* in 1936 and still grandly impressive today. Courtesy of Michael Amador/TxDOT

three-week extravaganza; obviously, if you can time a visit for this event, you should do so. However, at any time of the year Fair Park is a treasure trove of attractions. Designated a National Historic Landmark in recognition of its magnificent Art Deco architecture, it is also the home of the Cotton Bowl Stadium, which hosts major collegiate football games; and a splendid variety of museums and scientific exhibits, including the Dallas Aquarium, the Museum of Natural History, Texas Discovery Gardens, and the Women's Museum. Big Tex, the fifty-two-foot symbol of the fair, still greets visitors as he did in *State Fair*, but the modest Ferris wheel the young stars rode in 1962 has been superseded by the gigantic Texas Star, rising a breathtaking 212 feet above the midway.

An Assassination Film Retrospective:
The Trial of Lee Harvey Oswald (1964)
George Russell, George Edgley, Arthur Nations,
and Charles Mazyrack
Directed by Larry Buchanan

JFK (1991)
Kevin Costner, Kevin Bacon, Tommy Lee Jones,
Laurie Metcalf, and Gary Oldman
Directed by Oliver Stone

Ruby (1992)
Frank Orsatti, Sherilyn Fenn, Jeffrey Nordling,
and Danny Aiello
Directed by John Mackenzie

Reel-Life Tour

As much as Texans would wish it otherwise, Dallas will always be known as the site of one of the most traumatic events in the nation's history. And decades later, conspiracy theories about the murder of John F. Kennedy continue to circulate. The three films in this retrospective suggest the wide range of treatments that have been offered on film to suggest various scenarios. *The Trial of Lee Harvey Oswald* was a quickie production, coming out only months after the assassination. It was co-written and directed by none other than Larry Buchanan, who apparently was an intrepid seeker of truth, whether it involved exposing Martians' need for Earth's women, debunking the glamorization of Bonnie and Clyde, or questioning the identity of the president's killer. Buchanan's film, billed as having been "Filmed Secretly in Dallas," is set in a courtroom and presents dramatized testimony drawn from published news sources. The actors address the camera as if speaking to the jury, and leave the verdict up to the audience.

Oliver Stone's *JFK* is, of course, in a totally different class of movie making, a blockbuster considered a great film by many critics. The artistry is mostly undisputed. Stone insisted on authentic details as he filmed in Dallas, right down to repainting the window frames of the School Book Depository Building the color they were in 1963, and he pulled riveting performances from his actors. The problem that many who were around for the actual events have with this film is that it presents as facts a number of patently untrue, or at the very least, unprovable assertions. Its very effectiveness as a dramatic presentation, some have argued, makes it a real disservice to history, since viewers are invited to believe that everything they are seeing is based on documentable evidence. Admirers of the film, however, argue that viewers should be able to recognize that *JFK* is not a documentary and appreciate its merits as a work of art. Roger Ebert has written, for example, that Stone was not dealing with facts but with feelings, and that his movie is "a brilliant reflection of [the American people's] unease and paranoia, our restless dissatisfaction" with the official versions of events.

More conspiracy theories are presented in *Ruby*, this time from the perspective of the man who shot Lee Harvey Oswald. Although he's physically a much larger man than Ruby was, Danny Aiello projects an amazingly accurate physical likeness of the title character. This account of Jack Ruby's involvement in those traumatic days is almost as fanciful as Stone's, but without the redeeming production qualities that inspire critics to defend it. The basic story retold in these three films, minus the hypothesizing, is the one familiar to almost everyone: President Kennedy was fatally shot as his motorcade passed in front of the School Book Depository Building in Dallas on November 22, 1963. Oswald was arrested a few hours later and charged with the murder, only to be shot to death himself on national TV two days later, a crime for which Jack Ruby was subsequently tried and convicted.

Real-Life Tour: Dallas

The aftermath of the assassination was very difficult for the city of Dallas, which was portrayed in the media as a hotbed of extremists and hatred for anyone of the liberal persuasion. Gradually, however, Dallas began to move beyond that stereotype; although others invariably took its place, of course, thanks in part to the popularity of the TV series *Dallas* and the huge success of the Dallas Cowboys football team. But part of Dallas's own way of diffusing the lingering shadow of those dark days in 1963 was to acknowledge the tragedy openly and create a dignified memorial site. Instead of razing the notorious Texas School Book Depository Building as some residents desired, the city decided that a museum would be appropriate in that location. The Sixth Floor Museum at Dealey Plaza features a permanent multimedia exhibition on the life, death, and legacy of the slain president. This popular and educational tourist attraction is near the Memorial Park at Main and Market Street with its cenotaph and landscaped monument dedicated to the memory of John F. Kennedy. If you are interested in visiting other sites relevant to the assassination, there are various tours and tour guides available that will lead you to the residences of Oswald and Ruby; to the Texas Theatre in Oak Cliff, where Oswald was apprehended; and to the former city jail, where he was shot. Those too young to remember may not realize that the Kennedy assassination created a national trauma of shock and grief. According to the manager of the Paramount Theatre in Abilene, Texas, the tragedy occasioned the only time he ever edited a film that was running at his theater. The movie, *Take Her, She's Mine*, included a scene with a young man who looked so much like Kennedy that the studio asked theater managers to edit out the shots of him, fearing audiences would be upset by the likeness.

Tender Mercies (1983)
Robert Duvall, Tess Harper, Betty Buckley, Wilford Brimley, and
Ellen Barkin
Directed by Bruce Beresford

Reel-Life Tour

Horton Foote won an Oscar for his *Tender Mercies* script, which, like *Baby, the Rain Must Fall*, was adapted from one of his Texas plays. Robert Duvall also won an Oscar for his spot-on portrayal of country singer Mac Sledge, whose career has been derailed by alcohol and who finds himself at the end of his rope in a motel run by Rosa Lee, a Vietnam War widow. She allows Mac to work off the bill he cannot pay on the condition that he will not drink on the premises, and thus begins his difficult return to self-respect. He falls in love with Rosa along the way, and they marry, but the movie avoids the simplistic saved-by-the-love-of-a-good-woman conclusion. Instead, it depicts the rocky road Sledge must travel in fighting temptations to return to the bottle.

The honesty of the film extends to its portrayal of everyday life in a small Texas town. The pace is slow, probably too slow for many of today's hyped-up audiences, but it accurately reflects the character of its location, semirural areas around Waxahachie. In keeping with the story of hard-won personal redemption, the landscape's more desolate qualities are emphasized rather than the elegant Victorian neighborhoods seen in other films. The characters are authentically presented; especially noteworthy are the church members, who are exactly like those you will meet in many of the small churches in Texas. Duvall's accent is perfect for a native of East Texas, and his singing is entirely convincing as that of a talented country singer/songwriter.

Real-Life Tour: Waxahachie, Grapevine

The map published by the Waxahachie Chamber of Commerce lists locations that appear in *Tender Mercies*, and you can pick up a copy at the Ellis County Museum, located at the southeast corner of the courthouse square on College Street. Musical performances were filmed at the Grapevine Opry, formerly the Palace Theatre, which was built to show movies in 1940. Closed down for a time in the 1960s, it reopened in 1975 as a showcase for country music talent and provided a venue for many big names, including Willie Nelson, Leann Rimes, and Ray Wylie Hubbard. Grapevine is located about forty-five miles northeast of Waxahachie, near DFW airport.

Lighter Side of Country Music—a Double Feature:
Baja Oklahoma (1988)
Lesley Ann Warren, Swoosie Kurtz, Peter Coyote,
and Julia Roberts
Directed by Bobby Roth

Pure Country (1992)
George Strait, Lesley Ann Warren, Isabel Glasser,
and Rory Calhoun
Directed by Christopher Cain

Reel-Life Tour

Infinitely lighter weight in terms of both story and production values than the award-winning *Tender Mercies*, these two cheerful movies offer glimpses of Fort Worth that can be contrasted with the Dallas depicted in movies such as *Dr. T and the Women*. Although they are close neighbors and are lumped together both in the airport's designation as DFW and in the ubiquitous term "Dallas–Fort Worth Metroplex," these cities project quite different personalities.

One highly touted aspect of Fort Worth is the honky-tonk scene, most famously represented by Billy Bob's, the enormous dance hall similar to Gilley's of *Urban Cowboy* fame. *Baja Oklahoma* captures that scene beautifully in telling the story of Juanita Hutchison, a goodhearted woman eking out a living as a barmaid while dreaming of a career as a singer/songwriter. Written by Texan Dan Jenkins, the script based on his hilarious novel of the same name includes many allusions to Fort Worth's culture, expressed in dialogue full of idioms that are authentic if somewhat exaggerated for humorous effect. Juanita, played by Lesley Ann Warren, believably struggles with her own record of bad relationships while trying to handle an eighteen-year-old daughter bent on running away with a dope-dealing boyfriend. The return of her high school sweetheart signals a turnaround in her life, and Juanita eventually performs one of her compositions in a duet with none other than Willie Nelson himself.

In *Pure Country*, Warren plays a much different sort of character. Here, she is Lula Rogers, the hard-as-nails manager of Dusty Wyatt Chandler, a successful country singer—played by Strait—who is dissatisfied with the way his performances are being turned into spectacles that overshadow the songs and the singing. This film is a George Strait vehicle all the way, and for his many fans, that is enough. For a movie lover's tour of Texas, it offers shots of downtown Fort Worth, Texas Stadium, and the surrounding countryside along with some of Texan Strait's unpretentious singing. As Dusty, he walks away from his touring performances to try to regain his roots in rural North Texas near Terrell, where he meets a woman whose attraction to him is not based on his public persona. Her ranching family's eccentricity is a bit over the top, even for stereotypical Texans, but one unexpected pleasure is seeing veteran actor Rory Calhoun in his final role as the father. He still had those great eyebrows, and according to at least one extra in the *Pure Country* cast, he enjoyed recounting stories about his Hollywood glory days.

Real-Life Tour: Fort Worth, Terrell

No visit to Fort Worth is complete without a stop at the Stock-yards National Historic District, where renovated Old West stores and eateries line traditional boardwalks and brick-paved streets. The live country music scene that forms the backdrop for both *Baja Oklahoma* and *Pure Country* also graces this part of the city in venues small, like the White Elephant Saloon, and huge, like Billy Bob's. The Sundance Square Downtown Entertainment District, not far away from the Stockyards, also provides an exciting night life among its twenty blocks of theaters, art galleries, museums, and restaurants. Fort Worth's shiny skyscrapers, with twinkling lights outlining their shapes against the prairie night skies, gaze benignly down on the throngs of people enjoying the urban hospitality of a city known fondly as Cowtown.

Fort Worth is the only setting for *Baja Oklahoma*, but *Pure Country*'s scenes range out into the surrounding countryside. The big concert at the beginning takes place in Texas Stadium, over in the Dallas suburb of Irving; and the family ranch scenes were shot near Terrell, east of Dallas.

Hope Floats (1998)
Sandra Bullock, Gena Rowlands, Mae Whitman,
and Harry Connick Jr.
Directed by Forest Whitaker

Reel-Life Tour

She's not a native Texan, but Sandra Bullock has become a high-profile resident of Austin. She seems to feel right at home there and apparently enjoys showcasing her adopted state in her movies. *Hope Floats* begins in Chicago, but when Bullock's character, Birdee, finds out in just about the cruelest possible way that her husband has dumped her for another woman, she heads back home to Texas with her little girl. She moves back in with her mother in the town of Smithville, where she was the high school beauty and reigned as the Corn Queen on parade floats, which helps explain the movie's otherwise dopey-sounding title. Filmed in and around Smithville, about forty miles east of Austin, the movie shows off the surrounding countryside as well as the town itself.

Bullock's accent isn't bad, and her interactions with her former high school classmates ring true as she painfully encounters those to whom she'd always felt superior, such as the "fat girl," who is now an attractive, successful businesswoman. The other characters' reactions to the humiliation of the former beauty queen are typical of most small-town residents; they initially express a certain amount of satisfaction at her comeuppance, but in the end, they are kind, sympathetic folks. Harry Connick Jr. believably plays a fellow who is comfortable in his little Texas town, where he is building a house of nineteenth-century Texas pine. Like George Strait's character in *Pure Country*, he has returned to his Texas roots, to what he loves; and he courts Birdee, hoping that in her heart she shares his love of the laid-back life.

Real-Life Tour: Smithville

Smithville obviously welcomed the filming of *Hope Floats* to its picturesque streets, for the Chamber of Commerce has been kind enough to list filming locations on its Web site. Main Street was used for the parade; the baseball park on Pleasant Hill Road for the outdoor movie theater; the "red brick building," at 901 NE Sixth Street, for the schoolroom scenes; the Towers Nursing Home at 907 Garwood for the touching scene with Birdee's father; Heubel's at W. 2nd and Cleveland Street for the bar scene. Outside of Smithville, scenes were shot at the Waterson Dance Hall near Rosanky; at the Catholic Church in Kovar, about eight miles south of Smithville; and at Buescher State Park just north of Smithville.

A Football Film Festival:
Varsity Blues (1999)
James Van Der Beek, Amy Smart, Jon Voight,
Paul Walker, and Scott Caan
Directed by Brian Robbins

Necessary Roughness (1991)
Scott Bakula, Hector Elizondo, Robert Loggia,
Larry Miller, Sinbad, and Kathy Ireland
Directed by Stan Dragoti

North Dallas Forty (1979)
Nick Nolte, Mac Davis, Charles Durning,
G. D. Spradlin, and Dabney Coleman
Directed by Ted Kotcheff

Reel-Life Tour

Football is a big deal in Texas, whether it's played by high school students, college students, or professionals. *Varsity Blues* captures the ambience of small-town football mania in its depiction of the fictional West Canaan High School's Coyotes and their stereotypical coach, played by Jon Voight, whose only goal is winning. In his thirty-fifth year of coaching the Coyotes, he wields great influence in the town; the fathers of his current players were also coached and are still awed by him. James Van Der Beek plays the main character, John Moxon, a sympathetic young man who is suddenly called on to be the starting quarterback when another player is injured. Used to being second-string and not especially interested in football, Moxon has to deal with the stress and the rewards of the responsibility that has landed on him. Although the story is mostly told humorously and with the required scenes of adolescent grossness, some serious issues do come up: the football players' being allowed to break the law with impunity, the fathers' potentially dangerous obsession with their sons' performance, the racism of the coach. But these issues are balanced with comic interludes. And while high school coaches in Texas tend to be very strict disciplinarians, thankfully most are no more like the heartless character Voight plays here than they are like the alien-possessed coach in *The Faculty*.

The intensity of high school football is captured in the footage of the games in *Varsity Blues*. The filmmakers recruited some of the best young players in Texas to surround the actors on the field and to make the football plays as realistic as possible. The atmosphere was deftly created as well. The night skies, the screaming crowds in the stands, the players taking real hits under the signature water towers are all familiar to followers of high school football in Texas. The general landscape shows up well. The location towns of Elgin and Coupland, situated just a few miles east of the Hill Country, open out into vast flat lands and big Texas skies, both of which are effectively presented in *Varsity Blues*.

College football is the next step for successful high school players. The team depicted in *Necessary Roughness* is several rungs down the ladder from well-known teams such as those from UT–Austin and Texas A&M, but the movie deals with the issues of college football that one reads about in the newspapers. The fictional team here, known as the Texas State Fightin' Armadillos, has won a national championship in the Cotton Bowl. But that triumph has been followed by imposition of the "death penalty" from the NCAA because of violations involving drugs, illegal payments to players, recruiting activities, and grade tampering. A new coach is hired who is determined to build a new, law-abiding team with a thirty-four-year-old quarterback and a female kicker. The story is played for laughs, not always successfully, but the movie offers light entertainment with likeable actors along with great shots of the University of North Texas campus in Denton as it looked in the early nineties. Much has changed since then, but Fouts Field is still recognizable, as are the exteriors and interiors of the Administration Building. Fort Worth's giant honky-tonk, Billy Bob's, is also featured in several scenes.

Besides filming recognizable landscapes and landmarks of North Texas, the producers of *Necessary Roughness* included authentic details to convey a sense of place. Bakula's character seems at home on a tractor when he is working the family farm, listening to George Strait's music on his radio. The extras in the scenes at Billy Bob's look like regular customers. The characters of the academic dean and of the professor who becomes Bakula's love interest are not particularly believable as academic types, but at least they are not depicted as stereotypical Texans. One inside joke for professional football fans: The members of the "Texas Penitentiary Convict Team" bused in to scrimmage with the Armadillos are played by various pros, including former Texas stars Tony Dorsett, Ed "Too Tall" Jones, Randy White, and Earl Campbell.

Another film often classified as a comedy is *North Dallas Forty*, but its take on professional football in Texas could appropriately be called only very dark comedy. Written by Peter Gent, this movie is a fictionalized but recognizable account of the Dallas Cowboys of the early 1970s, the days of Don Meredith and Tom Landry. People who know football and who knew it back then have vouched for its authenticity. The professional football stars may be idolized by the public, but to the coaches and owners, they are simply commodities. As long as they win, they can get away with almost anything; but once past their prime or seriously injured, they are casually discarded. The Cowboys, of course, are as much a part of the Dallas mystique as is J. R. Ewing's clan; and some observers have suggested that the ascendancy of "America's team" was what finally lifted the dark clouds of JFK's assassination from the city.

Real-Life Tour: Elgin, Coupland, Denton, Irving

The cities of Coupland and Elgin served as the main locations for *Varsity Blues*. Several of Coupland's farmhouses were adapted to play the residential sections of the fictional West Canaan, complete with the gaudy billboards picturing the football stars outside the players' homes. Main Street in nearby Elgin, with its interesting storefronts, played West Canaan's town center. Elgin's middle school provided the interiors for the movie's high school, and its

Wildcat Stadium provided a home field for the Coyotes. In *Necessary Roughness*, the Texas State Armadillos play their hearts out in Denton, the home of the University of North Texas, some thirty miles north of Dallas/Fort Worth. "Mean" Joe Greene played football for UNT; other famous alums include Roy Orbison, Peter Weller, and Larry McMurtry. *North Dallas Forty* fans will probably want to visit Texas Stadium, located in the Dallas suburb of Irving.

Dr. T and the Women (2000)
Richard Gere, Helen Hunt, Farrah Fawcett, Laura Dern,
and Shelley Long
Directed by Robert Altman

Reel-Life Tour

Robert Altman includes so much detail about Dallas in *Dr. T and the Women* that the city almost becomes a character in the film. The story about an immensely popular Dallas gynecologist, played by Gere, whose devotion to the women in his life finally backfires on him was filmed on location, and Altman appears to have been determined to include in the movie everything anyone associates with Dallas. In fact, some of the more esoteric references—to previous mayors, for example—while appreciated by Dallasites, may have simply mystified other viewers and contributed to the movie's less-than-enthusiastic reception.

Gere's office is opulent, but not unbelievably so for one of Dallas's more successful physicians—except perhaps for the mink coverings on the stirrups of his examining table. His home is actually rather modest compared to others you will see if you drive through some of the more affluent areas of Dallas. One of his daughters, played by Kate Hudson, is an SMU student and a Dallas Cowboy Cheerleader. The other daughter works at the JFK Conspiracy Museum and leads tours of Dealey Plaza. They, along with mother Farrah Fawcett and aunt Laura Dern, go shopping at the ritzy NorthPark mall; and the Hudson character's wedding takes place at the Dallas Arboretum. Other female characters are agitating to have a freeway named for a woman, and they speak out in the chamber of the Dallas City Council, where council members unrealistically wear cowboy hats but where names of actual prominent Dallas women are suggested for nomination: Annette Strauss, Mary Kay Ash, and—by one of the cowboy-hat-wearers, of course—Jayne Mansfield.

Although *Dr. T's* view of Dallas is limited and full of the usual clichés, including the unpredictability and potential violence of the weather, it offers a glimpse of one Dallas reality—that of wealthy women who manage to contain their lives within the bubble their money affords them. The Stonebriar Country Club, where several scenes were shot in the pro shop and on the elegant golf course, epitomizes this glossy side of Dallas. Helen Hunt's character offers the only suggestion of a slightly lower-rent lifestyle. As an employee of the golf course, she drives an Isuzu with a Texas Tech bumper sticker and lives in an apartment that she says costs only $750 a month. That figure, by the way, is one of the less-believable details in the movie. The musical score is a real Texas plus. It was written and performed by Lyle Lovett, one of the best Texas singer/songwriters around and an Altman favorite as an actor in such films as *The Player*, *Short Cuts*, and *Cookie's Fortune*.

Altman has said he was "trying to capture a particular culture, a certain strata . . . a slice of Dallas life," and he piled up the details to do so, including references to pimiento cheese sandwiches, a Texas dietary staple. And if you visit NorthPark's high-end stores or attend a lavish wedding at the Arboretum, you will see a variety of dissimilar folks who call Dallas home; but you will also see perfect examples of Dr. T's women.

Real-Life Tour: Dallas, Frisco

Other films set in Dallas, such as *State Fair* and *JFK*, provide views of the city as it used to be. *Dr. T and the Women* brings some of the views up to date as of the beginning of the twenty-first century.

Since the 1960s, for example, the skyline has exploded with sky-scrapers and looks entirely different from the way it did back when the neon Flying Red Horse, rotating atop the twenty-nine-story Magnolia Building, loomed over all of downtown and was visible from miles away. Preservationists have labored to maintain that fig-ure of Pegasus as a symbol of Dallas, and consequently you will see representations of it frequently associated with the city. But *Dr. T* is not concerned with the old Dallas. It zeroes in on the shiny new of-fice buildings, the ritzy suburban mansions, and the upscale malls, although the mall where the women of Gere's family go shopping at Tiffany's and where Farrah Fawcett strips to dance in the fountain is actually rather historic. It is NorthPark, which was built in the 1960s but has been renovated regularly since then and still stands at the higher end of the shoppers' food chain despite its age. The ele-gant Stonebriar Country Club is located in booming Frisco, a town just north of Dallas that up until a few years ago was a tiny farming community. The Dallas Arboretum, scene of the climactic wedding, is near White Rock Lake; and Dealey Plaza and the nearby Conspir-acy Museum, where Tara Reid's character works, are in downtown Dallas. Kate Hudson's character performs dismally as a Dallas Cow-boys Cheerleader in the huge dance studio in the affluent Valley Ranch area of suburban Irving, where the real cheerleaders practice and where the football team's headquarters are located.

Short Takes: Prairies and Lakes in a Supporting Role

The Great Waldo Pepper (1975)
Robert Redford, Bo Svenson, Susan Sarandon,
Edward Herrmann, and Margot Kidder
Directed by George Roy Hill

Reportedly, director Hill was hoping to achieve another Redford/Newman hit like *Butch Cassidy and the Sundance Kid* with this tale of post–World War I daredevil barnstorming pilots, but Paul New-man ultimately took a pass. Maybe *The Great Waldo Pepper* would have been a bigger success if the duo had stayed intact, but it is still an exciting movie to watch if you like stunt flying in antique airplanes. It also provides great views of the Central Texas landscape, which stands in for the American Midwest. The town of Elgin was chosen for much of the shooting, partly because its main street was wide enough to fly a plane down between the vintage buildings that line each side. Seguin, a few miles south of Elgin, was the site of Herrmann's character's plane crash, at a real World War II training field. Seguin's historic Texas Theatre served as the set for the movie theatre scene.

Fantastic, Futuristic Dallas—a Triple Feature:
Phantom of the Paradise (1974)
Paul Williams, William Finley, Jessica Harper,
and Gerrit Graham
Directed by Brian De Palma

Logan's Run (1976)
Michael York, Richard Jordan, Jenny Agutter,
Roscoe Lee Browne, and Peter Ustinov
Directed by Michael Anderson

RoboCop (1987)
Peter Weller, Nancy Allen, Dan O'Herlihy,
Ronny Cox, and Miguel Ferrer
Directed by Paul Verhoeven

In the late 1960s Dallas started sprouting glass-walled buildings and immense structures, some with a decidedly futuristic look to them. Moviemakers took notice. *Phantom of the Paradise* featured one towering bauble then known as the Zale Building; but the filming also took advantage of one of the historic downtown buildings, the spectacular Majestic Theater. Brian De Palma's excursion into a 1970s rock musical mixes together Faust, Hitchcock, Dorian Gray, Rod Serling, and, of course, *The Phantom of the Opera*. This musical excess is sometimes compared to *The Rocky Horror Picture Show*—which, by the way, was set in Denton, Ohio, and not Denton, Texas—but *Phantom of the Paradise* has its own charms, not the least of which is the Majestic's portrayal of the Paradise rock palace.

Logan's Run also features the former Zale Building, located off I-35E just south of the Mockingbird Lane exit; but it made greater use of other buildings along I-35E, aka Stemmons Freeway, including the massive buildings of the Dallas Market Center, the Apparel Mart, and the Bruton Park Building, now called Park Stemmons. The movie is set in a distant future when citizens inhabit a domed city and are not allowed to live beyond the age of thirty. The title character, played by Michael York, goes on the run to try to find Sanctuary, a place where the overage can be safe. Most scenes make use of Dallas landmarks, but the conclusion was filmed at the Water Gardens near Fort Worth's Convention Center.

Roughly ten years after *Phantom* and *Logan* showcased the Dallas skyline and some of its awesome interiors, *RoboCop* came along to offer an update, with Dallas playing the city of Detroit in a not-too-distant but horribly bleak future. Some of the cityscapes had to be redecorated so they would appear to have been trashed by all the violence, but you can still recognize City Hall and the Dallas Public Library, which are practically across the street from each other downtown. You may have to look twice at the City Hall, however, since matte artists added seventy stories for its portrayal of Omnicorp Headquarters. Other buildings were similarly disguised. A great automobile chase scene along I-35E affords good views of the skyline, including Reunion Tower. The Detroit Police Station is played by the Sons of Hermann Hall, a wonderful old two-story wooden structure built in 1911 to house a German fraternal organization. Today it offers a venue for live music performances, and *RoboCop* fans who visit can have the extra pleasure of entering the ballroom through enormous doors that were built specifically for that movie.

Benji (1974)
Patsy Garrett, Allen Fiuzat, Cynthia Smith,
Frances Bavier, and Edgar Buchanan
Written and directed by Joe Camp

A sweet little stray dog charms the inhabitants of McKinney, a town of lovely old Victorian homes north of Dallas, and then saves two children who have been kidnapped by bad guys. A quintessential family film with a story told from the dog's perspective, *Benji* made a movie star of Higgins, the dog from the 1960s TV sitcom *Petticoat Junction*. The movie also trades on the familiarity of other benevolent mid-century TV faces, including those of Edgar Buchanan, of *Green Acres*, and Frances Bavier, of *The Andy Griffith Show*. Both McKinney and the nearby city of Denton are featured prominently in several scenes. You'll see the elegant courthouse that graces Denton's downtown square in several shots. The courthouse itself looks pretty much the same today as it did in 1974, but the stores surrounding it have been spiffed up considerably. Scenes also take place in Denton's Civic Center Park and inside its municipal building, designed by architect O'Neil Ford.

What's Eating Gilbert Grape? (1993)
Johnny Depp, Leonardo DiCaprio, Juliette Lewis,
Mary Steenburgen, and Darlene Cates
Directed by Lasse Hallstrom

Set in a fictitious town called Endora, Iowa, this quiet tale of domestic drama was filmed mostly in Manor, not far from Austin; but the town square it features is that of Lockhart. Johnny Depp plays the title character, who is burdened with responsibilities for his mentally challenged brother and his reclusive, grossly overweight mother. His total dedication to family responsibilities is challenged when he meets Juliette Lewis's character, a free-spirited young woman passing through town. The Grape family home was played by a house outside of Pflugerville; but it no longer stands there on Hodde Lane, for its destruction by fire in the climactic scene of the movie was the real thing.

Waiting for Guffman (1996)
Christopher Guest, Eugene Levy, Fred Willard,
Catherine O'Hara, and Parker Posey
Directed by Christopher Guest

Not long after pretending to be Endora, Iowa, for *Gilbert Grape,* the versatile town of Lockhart convincingly played Blaine, Missouri, in *Waiting for Guffman.* This funny send-up of a small town's amateur theatrical pageant celebrating the town's 150th anniversary opens with sweeping views of the outskirts of Lockhart and then moves on to the square and courthouse. A scale model of the downtown square is used by the celebration's planners to decide such matters as the placement of portable toilets and trash cans for the upcoming sesquicentennial. Various storefronts and buildings in Lockhart are easy to recognize, but the storyline uses them as an Any Town, USA, setting and not as representative of any Lone Star State heritage.

True Stories (1986)
David Byrne, John Goodman, Spalding Gray,
Swoosie Kurtz, and Annie McEnroe
Directed by David Byrne

The real Texas state sesquicentennial is the occasion for another city's "Celebration of Specialness" in *True Stories.* David Byrne, of the Talking Heads musical group, narrates this film and introduces us to a number of inhabitants of the fictional Virgil, a small town on the north Texas prairie. Exceedingly whimsical, and sometimes poignant as well, these characters are ripe for satire, but Byrne approaches their weird lives with a sunny objectivity and sweetness. Their stories are not particularly Texan; apparently Byrne and his co-writers, Beth Henley and Stephen

Caldwell County Courthouse, in versatile Lockhart, Texas, which played Blaine, Missouri, in *Waiting for Guffman* and Endora, Iowa, in *What's Eating Gilbert Grape?* Courtesy of Kevin Stillman/TxDOT

Tobolowsky, who both attended SMU, based their characters on universal types seasoned with tabloid-worthy eccentricities. For example, Swoosie Kurtz plays The World's Laziest Woman, who has not left her bed in years. However, the Texas location itself is a big part of the story. The opening scene shows a dirt road stretching across a flat North Texas landscape, and Byrne launches into what purports to be the history of Texas in this anniversary year. Appropriately for this particular region of the state, he emphasizes the economic development that moved from cotton, to cattle, to oil, and finally, to the microchip. Filmed mostly around the suburbs of Dallas, *True Stories* includes scenes of electronics assembly lines and office interiors that could be those of any number of local corporations, such as Texas Instruments. The freeways snaking around Dallas are featured; but you should be aware that even though there were fewer of them in the 1980s, they were not as clogged with traffic as they are now. The sense of space is captured along with the vast skies over North Texas, but the film also shows how suburbia has sprawled into the countryside. When Byrne, his convertible stopped beside a deserted roadway with no buildings in sight, observes, "I think I see Fort Worth from here," he could have been on I-35W, where indeed the skyline of Fort Worth is visible from many miles away. Today, however, the undeveloped spaces along that interstate have almost disappeared.

PRAIRIES AND LAKES TRAVELOGUES
Scouting the Locations

Denton ➤ Ponder ➤ Pilot Point ➤ Tioga ➤ Sherman/Denison ➤ McKinney ➤ Dallas (160 miles)

Located at the "Top of the Golden Triangle," just about equidistant from Fort Worth to the southwest and Dallas to the southeast, Denton has sometimes been called "Little D," in reference to its larger neighbor. *Bonnie and Clyde* first put Denton on the movie lover's map when much of the film was shot in surrounding towns, and its gala premiere was held at Denton's Campus Theatre. Later, *Benji* showcased the downtown square, with its elegant courthouse; and still later, *Necessary Roughness* offered a visual tour of the University of North Texas campus. Moviemakers have continued to be drawn to Denton for films such as *Slap Her, She's French* and *Finding North*.

Nearby Ponder, a quiet little town on FM 156, is the site of the first attempted bank robbery in *Bonnie and Clyde*; the robbery fails because the teller informs the pair that there is no longer any money in the bank. You will have no trouble recognizing the bank building. From Denton take US 380 west to FM 156, and go south about four miles.

To visit another of the bank robbery locations, take FM 156 back north to US 380, and travel east to US 377, which leads north to Pilot Point. The turn-of-the-century Farmers and Merchants Bank Building, on the town square, served as the site for the movie's dramatic robbery in which Bonnie and Clyde are joined by the boastful Buck Barrow.

The next town north on US 377 is Tioga, the birthplace of Gene Autry. The townspeople host a Gene Autry Festival every September to honor their favorite son. If you are in the mood for a pleasant country drive, continue north to US 82 and then head east to Sherman and Denison, historic cities near the Oklahoma border. One of the excellent Texas State Travel Information Centers is located on US 75 just north of Denison. On Main Street in Denison is the restored Rialto Theater, built in 1920, site of the 1948 world premiere of *Red River*. Take US 75 south to McKinney to see some of the lovely old houses seen in *Benji*, and then go on to Dallas, where the next itinerary begins.

Dallas ➤ Frisco ➤ Irving ➤ Arlington ➤ Fort Worth (85 miles)

Inside the Loop　For the purposes of this itinerary, "Dallas" refers to that part of the city enclosed by Loop 12, a major roadway that encircles the city completely and goes by various names, such as Northwest Highway and Walton Walker, as it winds around. The name changes can be confusing, but the "Loop 12" sign usually pops up often enough to reassure the motorist seeking to follow this particular route. Even with such a spatial limitation, there is no way to include here all the movie-related sites you might want to visit in Dallas; but below is a list of some you probably don't want to miss. You can obtain maps and other information from the helpful staff at the Dallas Convention and Visitors Bureau, located downtown at 1201 Elm Street, Suite 2000, or at one of the other visitors information centers at NorthPark Center and West End Marketplace, to help you navigate around the city to these sites:

- Fair Park, where *The Big Show* and *State Fair* were filmed.
- Dealey Plaza, the School Book Depository Building (now The Sixth Floor Museum), Parkland Hospital, and Love Field, all featured in *JFK* and other films about the assassination. A related site, The Conspiracy Museum, is where one of the characters works in *Dr. T and the Women*.
- NorthPark Center Mall and the Arboretum, both of which epitomize the lifestyles portrayed in *Dr. T and the Women*.
- Dallas Market Center, which served as much of the domed city in *Logan's Run*.
- The former Zale Building and the Majestic Theatre, which were utilized to create futuristic and spooky settings for *Phantom of the Paradise* and *Logan's Run*.
- Dallas City Hall, the J. Erik Jonsson Central Library, and the Sons of Hermann Hall, which portray Detroit locations in *RoboCop*; and Reunion Tower, which stands out in that movie's freeway chase scene that skirts the downtown skyline.

Outside the Loop   Venturing north from Dallas via Highway 289, Preston Road, or via the Dallas North Tollway, you will arrive at Frisco after twenty miles or so. The Westin Stonebriar Resort is located in this burgeoning suburb. Its championship golf course graces many scenes in *Dr. T and the Women*. Upscale shopping malls and ritzy corporate headquarters on acres of rolling, beautifully landscaped "campuses" surround this formerly sleepy little farming center.

If you head west out of Dallas, you'll be on the way to an even more high-profile suburb, the city of Irving, which is currently the home of the Dallas Cowboys. Texas Stadium, seen in many movies such as *Pure Country* and *Any Given Sunday*, is located here, as are the team's headquarters at Valley Ranch, where Kate Hudson suffers embarrassment as a cheerleader in *Dr. T and the Women*. Irving's greatest gift to the movie lover, however, is the facility known as The Movie Studios at Las Colinas, which offers moviemakers the largest sound-stage complex between Florida and California. Movies such as *Leap of Faith*, *Silkwood*, and *JFK* have been produced here, along with countless TV shows, commercials, and music videos. The best news is that you can take a tour of the studios, see how special effects are created, and discover what a Foley artist does. Actual sets, such as the Oval Office from *JFK*, and a collection of famous costumes and props are also on display.

From Irving, you can take Highway 183 to FM 157, go south to Arlington, and visit Ameriquest Field, formerly the Ballpark at Arlington, where Dennis Quaid played his first big-league game in *The Rookie* and where you will find numerous attractions besides baseball games. From Arlington, Fort Worth is a short distance north and the starting point for the next itinerary.

Fort Worth ➤ Grapevine ➤ Red Oak ➤ Waxahachie ➤ Maypearl ➤ Venus ➤ Waco (155 miles)

Fort Worth and Dallas may have been forced to meld into the singular urban sprawl of the "Metroplex" in the parlance of local newscasts and weather reports, but happily, the two cities enjoy amazingly distinct personalities. Dallas is the Big City, business-and-consumer-oriented, tending to stress its more sophisticated qualities. Fort Worth still has a small-town feel about it and is happy to be "Where the West Begins." It glories in its historic stock-yards and its past as a stopping point on the Chisholm Trail. It has created halls of fame dedicated to cowboys and cowgirls. And yet its Cultural District boasts the exquisite Kimbell Art Museum and the architectural treasure that is the Modern Art Museum.

Fort Worth claims fewer movie locations than Dallas does, but its historical connections to western movies even the score somewhat. The Stockyards National Historic District captures the atmosphere of the Old West and is home to the world's biggest honky-tonk, Billy Bob's, where the Armadillos of *Necessary Rough-ness* get into a brawl with opposing team players. Billy Bob's is also a major showcase for country singers, such as the characters fea-tured in *Baja Oklahoma* and *Pure Country*.

Less than twenty miles northeast of Billy Bob's is another mu-sic venue in the small city of Grapevine, which is also home to DFW International Airport. Grapevine Opry is housed in the old Palace Theatre, and scenes for *Tender Mercies* were shot there.

From Grapevine, you can head on over to I-35E via Highway 114, passing Texas Stadium along the way, and travel south to Red Oak, where one of the bank robberies in *Bonnie and Clyde* was filmed—the one during which Clyde shoots a bank employee through the getaway car's window. Travel about ten more miles south on I-35, and you'll come to Waxahachie, a mother lode of movie locations for blockbusters like *Places in the Heart*, *Tender Mercies*, *The Trip to Bountiful*, and *Bonnie and Clyde*.

About a fifteen-minute drive southwest from Waxahachie on FM 66 will bring you to the tiny town of Maypearl, nestled in a lovely rolling countryside that is breathtaking when dressed in spring wildflowers. Even here the open spaces are beginning to fill, though, with developments that look much like those David Byrne displayed in *True Stories*—raw, treeless expanses dotted with tract houses. If you travel north on FM 157 from Maypearl, you will find equally tiny Venus about ten miles away, another location you might recognize from *Bonnie and Clyde*.

From Venus, this itinerary takes you east to I-35W, by way of Highway 67, and carries you on southward to the Central Texas town of Waco, a beginning point for itineraries in the southern part of the Prairies and Lakes Region.

Waco ➤ Bartlett ➤ Thorndale ➤ Thrall ➤ Manor ➤ Elgin ➤ Coupland ➤ McDade ➤ Bastrop (145 miles)

Waco was important to cattle drivers on the Chisholm Trail as a major crossing of the Brazos River. The Waco Suspension Bridge was constructed in 1870 and provided the cowboys with the only bridge across the Brazos. Like Fort Worth, Waco is of interest to the movie lover primarily for the historical locations prominent in western films, rather than as a site for moviemaking. However, if you have time to take in the Texas Ranger Hall of Fame and the Dr Pepper Museum, you will enjoy a true taste of pure Texana.

Head south from Waco on I-35; but at the northern edge of Temple, take Highway 95 south for a ramble through the central Texas countryside and its picturesque little towns so attractive to filmmakers. When you reach Bartlett, you may feel as though you have stepped back in time, for it was transformed in the 1990s to create sets for *The Newton Boys* and *The Stars Fell on Henrietta*. The spruced-up storefronts and antique signs remained after the filming was done, and they may also look familiar to you if you saw *The Whole Wide World*.

At the intersection of Highways 95 and 79, you'll encounter Taylor, which has provided locations for a number of movies, including *The Life of David Gale, Home Fries, Varsity Blues*, and *Where the Heart Is*. Travel east on Highway 79 to reach Thrall and Thorndale, both of which provided backgrounds for Disney's *The Rookie*. Or take FM 973 south to Manor, where much of *What's Eating Gilbert Grape?* was filmed.

East of Manor on US 290 lies Elgin, where the flight down Main Street was shot for *The Great Waldo Pepper*. Popular with filmmakers because of its Any Town, USA quality, Elgin also provided the downtown set for *Varsity Blues*, while Coupland, located just north of Elgin on Highway 95, provided the residential locations for that film. The Coupland Dance Hall has been seen in movies such as *Lonesome Dove*, *A Perfect World*, *Cadillac Ranch*, and *Flesh and Bone*.

Following US 290 east out of Elgin will bring you to McDade, which bills itself as an "Old West Town Where the Prairie Meets the Piney Woods" and which provided many locations for *True Women*. Taking Highway 95 south out of Elgin will lead you to Bastrop, whose historic buildings and beautiful surrounding countryside have served as backdrops for numerous films, including *The Whole Wide World*, *True Women*, *Courage Under Fire*, *The Great Waldo Pepper*, and the 2004 version of *The Alamo*. Drop by the Visitor Center at 927 Main Street for more information.

Bastrop ➤ Smithville ➤ La Grange ➤ Hallettsville ➤ Gonzales ➤ Seguin ➤ Lockhart (165 miles)

Friendly Highway 95 continues south from Bastrop to Smithville, and there you can visit most of the locations where Sandra Bullock emoted in *Hope Floats*. From Smithville, if you fancy a scenic country drive, continue southward on 95 to La Grange, whose Fayette County Courthouse appeared with John Travolta in *Michael*. And if you've come this far, you might as well follow US 77 for about thirty-five miles south to another historic courthouse. The Lavaca County Courthouse at Hallettsville had a rollicking good time in *The Best Little Whorehouse in Texas*.

Follow US ALT 90 east from Hallettsville to Gonzales and you can focus on more somber movies, exploring locations related to *The Ballad of Gregorio Cortez* and *True Women*. Continuing in the same direction to Seguin will bring you to the treasure trove of actual historical sites depicted in *True Women*. From Seguin, take the back road FM 20 toward Lockhart and savor the landscape that saw an amazing amount of early Texas history. At Lockhart, you'll find a town that, like Bastrop, has welcomed more than its share of moviemakers over the years. The downtown scenes for

What's Eating Gilbert Grape? were shot here, and the town has been featured in other movies, such as *Secondhand Lions, The Faculty,* and *The Great Waldo Pepper.* After all is said and done, however, Lockhart's picturesque square and courthouse probably never shone brighter than when the town portrayed Blaine, Missouri, in *Waiting for Guffman.*

PRAIRIES AND LAKES CAST AND CREDITS

Some notable movie folk who were born or grew up in the Prairies and Lakes region:

John Alonzo, cinematographer, born in Dallas
Gene Autry, actor, born in Tioga
Joe Don Baker, actor, born in Groesbeck
Etta Moten Barnett, actress, born in Weimar
Robby Benson, actor/director, born in Dallas
Robert Benton, director/writer, born in Waxahachie
Larry Buchanan, director/writer, born in Mexia
K Callan, actress, born in Dallas
Kate Capshaw, actress, born in Fort Worth
L. M. Kit Carson, actor/director, born in Dallas
Morgan Fairchild, actress, born in Dallas
Frederic Forrest, actor, born in Waxahachie
Jamie Foxx, actor, born in Terrell
Larry Hagman, actor, born in Fort Worth
Linda Hart, actress, born in Dallas
Angie Harmon, actress, born in Dallas
Meat Loaf, actor, born in Dallas
Terence Malick, director, born in Waco
Steve Martin, actor, born in Waco
Peter MacNichol, actor, born in Dallas
George "Spanky" McFarland, actor, born in Dallas
Fess Parker, actor, born in Fort Worth
Bill Paxton, actor, born in Fort Worth

Robin Wright Penn, actress, born in Dallas
Steve Railsback, actor, born in Dallas
Rip Torn, actor, born in Temple
Luke Wilson, actor/director, born in Dallas
Owen Wilson, actor/writer, born in Dallas

Index of Movie Titles

Index of Places

231

About the Author

VEVA VONLER, PH.D., is a native Texan and lifelong movie fan. Her love of movies was possibly instilled before she was born when her mother saw almost every movie shown in the Arcadia Theater in little Ranger, Texas, while pregnant and waiting for her husband to return from World War II. Love of the movies was a family affair. Her great Aunt Myrtle played the piano for the silents shown in the Thurber, Texas, Opera House. At age twelve, Vonler won the local newspaper's contest for predicting that year's Oscar winners, earning a three-month free pass to the Campus Theater in Denton, Texas. Her professional life has included teaching writing and literature, international consulting on education, and university administration. She has written for a number of academic and popular publications such as *The New Rambler* and *Westward Magazine* and has coauthored a composition/literature text published by Harcourt Brace.